D1237166

THE IRWIN SERIES IN ECONOMICS

CONSULTING EDITOR

LLOYD G. REYNOLDS
YALE UNIVERSITY

BOOKS IN THE IRWIN SERIES IN ECONOMICS

THE INVESTMENT, FINANCING, AND VALUATION
OF THE CORPORATION

THE INVESTMENT, FINANCING, AND
VALUATION OF THE CORPORATION

by MYRON J. GORDON, Ph.D.

Associate Professor of Industrial Management

Massachusetts Institute of Technology

1962

RICHARD D. IRWIN, INC.

HOMEWOOD, ILLINOIS

To My Mother and Father

PREFACE

During the last twenty-five years the gap between economic theory and business practice has been narrowed to the benefit of both in a number of fields. Investment or capital formation is among the fields where the greatest progress has taken place, both in public policy and in business policy.

The depression of the thirties, Keynesian theory of income determination, and evidence on the rate of growth in Soviet output have dramatized the importance of capital formation as a determinant of both the current level of output and the rate of growth in output. In neoclassical theory, economists had an instrument to explain and predict the level of investment by a firm and an economy. However, the assumptions on which the theory rested and its level of abstraction made its usefulness for investigating problems of stability and growth extremely limited. Their confidence in the received theory shaken and interested in finding answers to important questions of public policy, economists turned to business practice in investment and financing for new insights. Moreover, they were less quick to reconcile what they observed with neoclassical theory and reject what could not be reconciled. The result was new theories of investment, theories that were comparatively simple, could be related to observed data and tested, and were employed to explain our experience and provide advice for public policy.

Therefore, positive theory on the level of the firm, theory that is concerned with what firms actually do, turned to business practice for information. At the same time normative theory on the firm level, the theory that is concerned with what firms should do, has turned to neoclassical theory for guidance. The normative literature on finance and investment had for the most part been a reflection of business practice, which consisted largely of top management's judgment and a variety of rules of thumb. Dissatisfaction with this practice, due to a combination of postwar developments—the increased level of capital expenditures, the growth in the size of firms, and the movement toward decentralization—stimulated interest in the rationalization of capital budgeting. A rational system of capital budgeting requires first the establishment of a decision criterion for the firm, and a logical candidate for the criterion is the maximization of the firm's value. Since this is the firm's objective in neoclassical theory, it was quite natural for the emerging normative literature to draw on neoclassical theory. In this literature, the firm's capital budget decision has been treated as a two-stage process: (1) arrive at the rate of profit on each investment opportunity; and (2) decide on the level of the capital budget. On the first stage there has been a considerable amount of work, and this work has had a significant impact on business practice. The second stage, commonly referred to as the cost of capital problem, has long been recognized in the literature, but only recently has there been any serious attempt to deal with the subject.

In a sense the cost of capital is the subject of this book. I say *in a sense* because stated exactly, my purpose is to create a model for explaining the valuation of a corporation that may be used to find the investment and financing by the corporation that maximize its value. With respect to investor behavior, the purpose is descriptive, while in the domain of corporate behavior, the objective is normative. The major elements of the theory (of stock valuation) are to be found in Chapters 4, 6, 8, and 9. The evidence on the theory appears in Chapter 12, and the normative use of the model by a corporation is discussed in Chapter 14. The other chapters provide background, elaboration, and by-product information that grew out of the study. Chapter 15 may be of special interest in that it presents the descriptive information on corporate investment and financing obtained from the data.

For those, including myself, to whom writing does not come easily, a sense of discovery is needed to keep the weary mind and hand at the task. All too often a writer gives this sense of discovery artificial support by indulging in critical observations on the work of others. I hope that I have not erred too much in this direction. My references to the literature, particularly the recent literature, should provide adequate evidence of the great extent to which I have drawn upon it.

Financial support from the Sloan Research Fund of the School of Industrial Management, Massachusetts Institute of Technology, provided me with time and other assistance for carrying out this work. Through the Computation Center, M.I.T., I learned what a large scale computer could contribute to empirical research, and I profited greatly from this knowledge.

My colleagues, Albert Ando, Gregory Chow, David Durand, Edwin Kuh, Eli Shapiro, Gordon Shillinglaw, Bob Solow, and Zenon Zannetos were kind enough to take time from their own research interests to discuss the substantive and statistical problems I raised with them. On the latter problems, any lack of sophistication in my use of data is no reflection on the competence of my advisers on the methods of econometrics.

Miss Joanne Bowler deserves more than passing recognition. Her ability to convert illegible, poorly organized script into attractive, orderly typed drafts was remarkable. The patience and good cheer with which she then typed final draft after final draft of each chapter, kept track of the latest final draft, and attended to a multitude of details, contributed materially to the progress of the work.

Those yeomen of academic research, the graduate assistants, served nobly in this cause. Ray Philip, Tsvi Ophir, Sydney Levine, and in particular, Harvey Kriss, Otto Poensgen, and Henry Wan, collected data, programmed the computation work, edited the manuscript, solved problems, and did numerous other things beyond the time and competence prescribed for their positions.

The support I have received from my wife has been too pervasive and personal for public acknowledgement. I will only note that she joined Joe and David in refusing to be persuaded that the importance of my research justified forgetting my family. With infinite patience, unfailing good cheer, and unflagging determination, they overcame my persistent rebuffs and took me away from my work. I thank them for the pleasures they forced on me and confess their having done so improved the quality and sped the completion of this book.

MYRON J. GORDON

Cambridge, Mass.
January, 1962

TABLE OF CONTENTS

Chapter 1 INTRODUCTION

Given the profitability of the investment opportunities available to a corporation, its capital budget decision involves the determination of (1) the size and (2) the financing of its investment outlay. It is the purpose of this book to present a solution to this problem which recognizes both uncertainty as to the future and aversion to risk and which assumes the corporation's objective to be maximization of its market value.

1.1 Framework of the Study

With one important qualification, our problem is the same as the fundamental problem posed and solved by the neoclassical theory of the capital of a firm. In neoclassical theory the objective of the firm is to maximize its value: the value of a firm is a function of its future income, and its future income is a function of its investment. With knowledge of these two functions, the value of a firm may be predicted given its investment; and given the value maximization behavior rule, its investment may be predicted. One may say that the task of the theory is to obtain information on these two functions so as to allow empirical statements on the value and investment of a firm.

However, under the neoclassical theory of capital, it is assumed that the future is known with certainty. This is such a drastic simplification of the real world that its decision rules for the firm and its descriptive statements about the firm are of extremely limited value. There have been attempts, of course, to enlarge the theory so as to recognize the consequences of uncertainty and aversion to risk, but these attempts have met with very little success. Consequently, the attempts to deal with uncertainty within the framework of neoclassical theory have given rise to models without empirical content

1

—models that could not test or enrich the development of the theory through use of the considerable body of published data that exists on publicly owned corporations. As a result, there is a large, unresolved gap between the neoclassical theory of capital and the literature of corporation finance—a literature that is concerned with the investment and financing behavior of real corporations.

In stating earlier that a corporation's capital budget decision involves the size and financing of its investment outlay, we assumed as given the profitability of each available investment opportunity. Obviously, this information must first be established. The considerable literature on capital budgeting in the postwar period has been concerned primarily with the solution of this problem, and much progress has been made in the area. Insofar as possible we will take the profitability of a firm's investment opportunities as known and not deal with problems of establishing this information.

We shall also not be concerned with whether or not the maximization of its value is the sole criterion of the firm in making its investment and financing decisions. In other words, it is not our objective to predict the investment and financing that corporations actually undertake. Our purpose is to arrive at the investment and financing a corporation should undertake if its objective is to maximize its value. The realization of this purpose requires the construction of a model that provides the value of a corporation as a function of its investment and financing. The test of our model's validity is its accuracy in predicting the variation in a corporation's value with these variables. The usefulness of the model to a corporation in its investment and financing decisions depends on the importance it attaches to the value at which its stock sells. We shall consider the correspondence between the "optimum" and the actual values of the investment and financing of corporations, but the extent of the correspondence is not relevant to the validity of the model.

Chapter 2 surveys the neoclassical theory of a firm's capital and the major attempts that have been made to modify the theory to deal with uncertainty. Since neoclassical theory provides a statement of our problem and its solution under certainty, and since reformulating the theory to deal with uncertainty is our task, the survey presented in Chapter 2 is a useful starting point for the present investigation.

The inadequacy of the neoclassical theory of capital as a basis for empirical research on the behavior of the firm has had a significant impact on the direction of both theoretical and empirical re-search in the field. The result has been a form of empiricism under which theories of investment seek to explain and predict the invest-ment of a corporation without reference to its value, and theories of value seek to explain and predict the market value of a corpora-tion without reference to its investment. Since the theory advanced in this book is concerned with both the investment and the value of a corporation, surveying both these *branches* of "applied" capital theory will provide useful background. A survey of this literature which will include the "finance," as well as the "economics," litera-ture is the subject of Chapter 3.

1.2 Outline of the Basic Theory

Chapter 4 presents the foundation on which our theory is built. The fundamental proposition of capital theory is that the value of an asset is the future payments it provides discounted at the appropri-ate rate. In this initial statement of the theory, the stream of future dividends the share is expected to provide is taken as the future pay-ments investors consider in arriving at the value of a share in a cor-poration. Further, it is assumed that the corporation engages in no outside financing, in which case, it is shown, the dividend expecta-tion is determined by the corporation's current income, its invest-ment or retention rate (the two are the same with no outside financ-ing), and its rate of return on investment. The product of the return and retention rates turns out to be the expected rate of growth in the dividend.

The result is a model that predicts the value of a share on the basis of four variables—current income, retention or investment rate, rate of return on investment, and the rate of profit investors require on the share. The decision variable a corporation may use to influ-ence the price of its stock is its retention rate, and given the values of the other three variables, the price of a share for any retention rate may be determined.

Current income and the rate of return on investment (which may be a function of the investment rate) can be estimated by a corporation from internally available data. However, the rate of profit that investors require is not obtainable from data of the cor-poration. Alternative hypotheses with respect to the required rate of profit are explored, and the hypothesis that the variable is an increasing function of the expected rate of growth in the dividend is found to be attractive for a number of reasons. For one, the stock price model is made empirically operational in that share price is made a function of observable variables, and the parameters of the function which determines the required rate of profit may be estimated from sample data. Given the parameters and the values of the variables for a corporation, the model may be used to find the optimum investment (retention) rate for the corporation.

The model developed in Chapter 4 has one provocative implication. It implies that the retention rate per se (i.e., apart from the profitability of the investment undertaken) influences share price. The validity of this proposition is the subject of Chapter 5. The chapter begins on the question whether an investor buys a share's future earnings or its future dividends. The analysis reveals that between the two, the dividend must be what the investor buys. All that the earnings advocates may logically maintain is that the distribution of earnings between dividends and retention is irrelevant to the price of a share. However, for this to be true it is necessary that the rate at which the dividend expectation is discounted be independent of the expected rate of growth in the dividend.

Examination of the question reveals, however, that the required rate of profit may rise, fall, or remain unchanged as the rate of growth in the dividend expectation rises. What the required rate of profit does depends on how rapidly the uncertainty of a dividend increases with its time in the future and on investor aversion to risk. The conclusion reached therefore is that the relation between the required rate of profit on a share and the expected rate of growth in the dividend is a question of fact. The question cannot be resolved by deductive argument, from which it follows that there is no a priori basis for rejecting the model developed in Chapter 4. On the contrary, the analysis suggests that we should be most surprised to find the value of a share independent of a corporation's dividend rate.

1.3 Extensions of the Theory

The model established in Chapter 4 explains the variation in price among common stocks on the assumptions that all the corporations engage in no outside financing and that they all have the same degree of risk apart from the rate of growth in the dividend. Chapter 6 is devoted to allowing the withdrawal of the last assumption. Consideration of the finance literature suggests that the factors which influence the uncertainty of a dividend expectation, apart from its rate of growth, are (1) the instability of the corporation's leverage-free earnings, (2) its debt-equity ratio, (3) the liquidity of its operating assets, and (4) the maturity structure of its debt. Problems of measurement for each of these variables are investigated and resolved as well as possible. Questions with respect to interrelations among them in influencing the valuation of a share are similarly examined and resolved. Finally, the model established in Chapter 4 is enlarged to include these variables and thereby recognize the influence of the variation in risk among corporations on the rate of profit investors require.

In our stock price model a future dividend expectation is what an investor buys. However, *he is not considered so naive as to assume that every future dividend is equal to the current dividend*. He is interested in both the current dividend and its rate of growth. The latter depends on the corporation's current income and return on investment as well as the current dividend. Chapter 7 is concerned with the measurement of these quantities.

For a world where the future is known with certainty, economic theory has laid down clear and exact definitions of income, capital, and return on investment that cannot be questioned. It is not uncommon for investigators to use these definitions in constructing theories and then to undertake empirical work on the basis of accounting definitions that are materially different and that are considered unsatisfactory. The belief that the correct definitions of the variables for a world of certainty are also true where the future is uncertain may well be due to the inadequate attention given to the implications of their use in an uncertain world. Consideration of this neglected question reveals that the extension of the definitions to deal with uncertainty is beset with formidable difficulties. The resultant definitions are not merely nonobservable: they do not provide a basis for the theoretical analysis of the problems for which they are to be employed. The remainder of Chapter 7 is devoted to accounting rules for the measurement of income, wealth, and return on investment. The definitions employed in accounting theory prove to be satisfactory for the purposes of our problem, i.e., the estimation of a corporation's future dividends. However, the rules of measurement by which accounting theory are implemented in accounting practice must be objective. In obtaining the data of our variables for a corporation for the purpose of testing the theory, we also must use objective measurement rules. The consequence is that the rules we adopt for observing the variables result in data that contain some error as representations of investor expectations. Examination of this question reveals that the measurement of a corporation's current income and its return on investment are particularly subject to error and are a weak spot in our theory.

Chapters 8 and 9 withdraw the assumption that corporations engage in no outside financing. The first of the two chapters deals with debt financing. On the assumption that a corporation is expected to maintain its existing debt-equity ratio, the model is readily extended to provide (1) the value of a share given the corporation's retention rate, debt-equity ratio, and other variables; and (2) the retention rate, debt-equity ratio, and investment that maximize the value of a share. At this point the Modigliani-Miller theorem that a corporation's cost of capital is independent of its debt-equity ratio is reviewed. Their theorem suggests a superior relation between leverage and the required rate of profit than the one established in Chapter 6. However, their theorem assumes among other things that the corporation pays out all of its earnings in dividends. An attempt is made to extend their theorem to the case where a corporation is expected to retain some fraction of its income, and a modification of our stock price model to incorporate the findings is established.

Chapter 9 begins with a review of earlier work on the influence of outside equity financing on share price. This we see has barely scratched the surface of the problem. Largely in order to indicate the nature of the problem, a solution is obtained for a corporation that undertakes a stock issue and is not expected to engage in further financing. The model of Chapter 8 is then extended to find the value of a share when the corporation is expected to engage in outside equity financing at some rate more or less continuously over time. A theoretical solution to the problem is obtained that appears quite satisfactory. However, an examination of the question reveals that the empirical implementation of the theory is beset with serious difficulties, among which are the validity of the statistical methods that must be employed to incorporate outside equity financing in the valuation model.

The model arrived at by the end of Chapter 9 is in its fundamentals the same as that presented in Chapter 4. The value of a share is given by its dividend expectation and the required rate of profit on the expectation. The dividend expectation is represented by the current dividend and its rate of growth. Now, however, the current dividend depends on the corporation's retention and leverage rates, and the rate of growth depends on these variables plus the outside financing rate. The required rate of profit is now a function of these variables and of other variables that influence risk such as earnings instability. The form of the model, however, still allows estimation of its parameters from sample data by conventional statistical methods.

If the theory supporting the model is correct, it provides the value of a share in a corporation under its existing investment and financing policies and it may be used to estimate what the share price would be under alternative values for the financing and investment rate variables. A distinctive characteristic of the model is that it is not concerned with the consequences of a single- or *one-period* investment and financing decision. The investment and financing variables are expressed as rates because they reflect what the corporation is expected to do for the indefinite future. This approach is necessary because the value of a share is determined by the dividend expectation for the indefinite future and not just one period.

Up to this point the analysis has proceeded on the assumption that income taxes, corporate and personal, do not exist. Chapter 10 examines the validity of this assumption. The corporate income tax proves to be no problem. With one minor qualification that has interesting implications for the influence of leverage on share price, the model may be employed on the basis of the after corporate income tax values of the variables.

The personal income tax poses a more difficult problem than the corporate tax. Ordinary income is taxed at different rates depending on the level of income, and capital gains are taxed at a flat, generally lower, rate. In view of this it can be argued that investors buy capital gains rather than an indefinite stream of dividends, and a different model is appropriate to the valuation of this expectation. A model is constructed which assumes that investors buy the dividend for one period and the price of the stock at the end of the period. Analysis of the theory leads to the following conclusions: (1) under the assumptions of the model which seem plausible, the variables which determine the price of a share are the same as those employed in the dividend expectation model; and (2) the two hypotheses with respect to what an investor is buying result in somewhat different functional relations among the variables, but the general qualitative characteristics of the relations are the same.

The model in which share value is determined by the one-period dividend and end-of-period price is not operational, and it is employed only to obtain the qualitative findings described above. However, further research may overcome the problem of making it operational, and it appears that the solution of these problems will enrich the theory of stock valuation by taking account of considerations that we have been forced to ignore.

1.4 Summary of the Empirical Findings

The remainder of the book is devoted to testing the theory developed in Chapters 4 through 9 and to the empirical statements on the valuation, investment, and financing of a corporation that may be made on the basis of the theory. Chapter 11 reviews the prior statistical work which reflects the evolution from simple dividend and earnings stock value models to that contained in Chapter 4. A major purpose in this review is to demonstrate the importance of rules for measuring the variables and of correct functional relation among them for the performance of a stock price model. For instance, it is shown that exponential smoothing greatly improves the accuracy of historical data for variables such as income when these variables are used to represent what investors expect will happen. It is also shown that the model of Chapter 4 is a striking improvement over the previous efforts at explaining the variation in price among shares. The parameter estimates for the two main variables, current dividend and expected rate of growth, prove to be highly significant and quite stable among samples.

Chapter 12 presents the empirical findings obtained from testing the models described in Chapters 8 and 9. In these tests two samples were employed, one consisting of 48 food and the other of 48 machinery corporations, and for each sample parameter estimates were obtained for each of the years 1954–58. In the first model tested, the two major variables are current dividend and rate of growth in the dividend. The secondary variables, included to account for the influence on price of differences in risk among corporations, are earnings instability, leverage, corporate size, and asset liquidity. In the food sample the primary variables are not only highly significant from a statistical point of view but also their parameter estimates vary little over time. The parameter estimates for the secondary variables all have the right sign and are statistically significant, often at the 1 per cent level. However, some vary enough from one year to the next to make the accuracy of an estimate obtained from one sample year open to question.

The machinery samples did not perform as well, probably because of the greater error in our rules for measuring the variables when applied to the type of firm in this sample. The coefficients of the primary variables are highly significant, but the growth coefficient is generally lower than in the food samples, and it appears abnormally low in some years. The machinery sample parameter estimates for the risk variables at best are significant at a lower level than the food sample's, and for two of the variables, leverage and asset liquidity, it cannot even be said that the data yield the correlation with price predicted by theory.

The second model tested differs from the first in that the simple leverage variable is replaced by the definition of the variable suggested by the Modigliani-Miller theory. The result is a remarkable increase in the statistical significance and stability of the estimates of the leverage parameter for the food sample. Further, they come surprisingly close to the numerical values suggested by the Modigliani-Miller theory. By contrast the coefficients of the leverage variable in the machinery sample are not materially improved.

The third model tested takes account of outside equity financing. This involves two things: (1) the rate of growth in the dividend is increased to reflect the benefit to the existing shareholders from the expected new equity financing; and (2) the change in the required rate of profit due to the outside equity financing is recognized by means of a new variable, the outside equity financing rate. In most of the sample years the correlation between the new variable and price has the right sign, but other considerations make the finding highly suspect. The inconclusive nature of the results may be due to the fact that measurement of the variables involved is very difficult and the rules we employed were not exact enough for the job.

The conclusions one may draw from these tests of the theory are mixed. On the one hand, the models do a better job of explaining stock prices than previous efforts. The high statistical significance and the modest variation among sample years for many of the coefficients is impressive. For the variables that did not perform so well, the risk variables, common experience with other models has been failure to even obtain significant correlation. By contrast, our findings convincingly demonstrate that other things the same, the greater the evidence that a corporation's dividend expectation is uncertain, the lower the price that investors are willing to pay for the expectation.

On the other hand, the accuracy of the parameter estimates is open to question. Since our objective in the theory was to include all the variables investors consider in pricing a share, the estimates of a coefficient should not differ materially between samples drawn from two industries. There also is no obvious good reason for large year-to-year fluctuations in the parameters. Finally, we failed to obtain satisfactory estimates of the influence on share price of the corporation's expected new equity financing. The conclusion to be drawn is that room exists for further progress in the measurement of the variables and possibly also in the theory on the relations among the variables.

1.5 Information on the Valuation and Financing of Corporations

The parameter estimates reported in Chapter 12 were obtained by means of least-squares regressions on sample data. These estimates are the best estimates of the parameters when the sample data and the problem satisfy certain conditions. These conditions are not satisfied, and the method of estimation causes bias and variability among samples in the parameter estimates. In Chapter 13 these problems are discussed, and on the basis of this discussion parameter values are established that are considered more accurate. The variation in share price with each independent variable, dividend, growth, leverage, etc., is then examined. That is, each independent variable is varied over its relevant range with representative values assigned to the other independent variables. Examination of the resultant data serves a number of purposes. First, a feel for what the model says with respect to share price, dividend yield, and required rate of profit is provided. Second, the materiality of each variable's influence on share price may be assessed. Third, in some cases the data are used to test the validity of controversial propositions on which theory is based.

Chapter 14 undertakes the normative statements on corporate investment and financing policy that may be made on the basis of the theory. We put ourselves in the position of a corporate financial officer and the methods by which he might use the model to find the investment and financing that maximize the value of the corporation's stock are presented. In view of the unsatisfactory empirical results obtained with the model that recognized outside financing, the model that excludes it is used. The corporation is assumed to use only leverage and retention to finance investment.

When the theory is used to arrive at the value of a share, the corporation's investment, financing, and rate of return are taken as given. When the objective is to find the investment, leverage, and retention that maximize share price, these quantities are no longer given, and certain problems arise. The rate of return on investment may be a function of the investment rate. The investment rate in turn is a function of the retention and leverage rates. The specification of these functions and the treatment of related questions involved in the use of the model are examined.

Partly to illustrate the above use of the model and partly for other reasons, share prices are presented and discussed for a large combination of values of the independent variables. That is, high, average, and low values are assigned to a corporation's rate of return on investment and to its leverage-free required rate of profit, and under each combination of values for these variables, the variation in share price with leverage and retention is presented over a considerable range of values for these decision variables. Analysis of the data provides further information on the sensitivity of share price to each variable and new information on the influence of co-variation in the independent variables on share price. For instance, it appears that the influence of leverage and retention on share price and the optimum values of each increase with the value of the other.

Since we have been so bold as to provide the "simple" directions by which a corporation may use our model to find the investment and financing that maximize a share's price, it seems fitting that some recognition be given to the unresolved problems, the dangers in so using the model. The observations made on this subject clearly indicate that much can be done to improve the operational value of the model.

In contrast with most writers we do not in our model use the cost of capital concept in finding the optional investment and financing for a corporation. Chapter 14 closes with a comparative analysis of the two approaches to capital budgeting.

The final chapter is devoted to certain topics that are of interest, but could be left aside in the development and testing of our theory. In constructing our theory, it was assumed that investors expect a corporation's leverage, retention, and return on investment rates to be the same in every future period. An analysis of the past data of these variables is undertaken for the purpose of testing these assumptions. The tests employed are not very efficient: the variation in each variable over time within a corporation is compared with the variation in the variable among corporations. Low intrafirm variation in relation to interfirm variation is found for all three variables. This behavior on the part of a variable may be considered to indicate it is relatively stable over time, which in turn makes reasonable the assumption that investors do not expect it to change over time. Although the data indicate the assumptions are reasonable, they are not optimal. The refinements in the model and the establishment of the information necessary to withdrawing the assumptions that investors expect a corporation's leverage, retention, and return on investment rates to be the same in every future period are acknowledged to be highly desirable.

The major concern of Chapter 15 is the analysis of the relations among the independent variables for the information they provide on the financial structure and the financing policies actually followed by corporations. In many respects the data indicate corporations behave as theory has suggested they do. Leverage has a strong inverse correlation with earnings instability and a strong positive correlation with corporate size. Another such finding is a positive correlation between earnings instability and rate of return on investment, meaning that high rates of profit are required and are realized by corporations in businesses which have a high risk. On the other hand, certain of the findings are somewhat surprising. Correlation between retention rate and return on investment is negative, and after allowing for correlation with earnings instability and size there is also negative correlation between leverage and rate of return on investment. In other words, the data do not suggest that corporations with high rates of return retain and borrow more than those with low rates of return. However, for the machinery sample at least there is correlation between change in leverage and rate of return on investment. Investment refers of course to existing investment, and the validity of the findings are limited by the confidence that can be placed in this measure of rate of return on investment.

The construction of a theory for the discovery of over- and underpriced shares is not a purpose of this investigation. However, interest in this subject is so widespread that failure to mention it might cause some surprise, possibly even suspicion. Chapter 15, therefore, closes with some observations on the possible use of the model by investors in security analysis.

Chapter 2

NEOCLASSICAL THEORY OF THE INVESTMENT AND VALUATION OF A FIRM

On a very general level the structure of the neoclassical theory of a firm's investment and valuation is quite simple. It may be summarized as follows: the objective of the firm is assumed to be the maximization of its present value; its present value is a function of its future income; and its future income is a function of its present investment. Hence, given these two functions, we may find the investment that maximizes the value of the firm, and given the behavior assumption, we may expect it to undertake this investment. Hence, the theory provides the investment and value of a firm to the extent it is able to establish information on the two functions stated above.

On this level of generality the structure of the theory to be presented in this work is the same as that of neoclassical theory. Nonetheless, the differences between the two theories are quite substantial. First, neoclassical theory proceeds to a solution to the problem under two assumptions: (1) the future is known with certainty; and (2) the firm can freely lend or borrow at a given rate of interest.[1] Second, neoclassical theory is concerned with the investment of the firm in order to arrive at theorems on industry or economy variables such as the rate of interest, the quantity of capital, output, etc. Both as a consequence of the assumptions under which the problem is investigated and the purposes in investigating the problem, the theorems on the investment and valuation of the firm provided by neoclassical theory have unique characteristics.

Under neoclassical theory the financing of the firm is no prob-

---

[1] Actually the second assumption follows from the first. Some investigators in the interest of realism have withdrawn the second assumption and allowed the interest rate to be a function of the firm's level of debt. This is not consistent with the certainty assumption, and it does not fully recognize the consequences of uncertainty.

lem and its valuation is a trivial problem. The main problem and the one on which the major theorems are established is the relation between a firm's investment, level and technoeconomic characteristics, and the terms under which investment takes place. The latter includes the interest rate, the wage price structure, and changes in the technology of production. In large measure due to the nature of the problem, the models created to arrive at the theorems are grossly simplified representations of firms and they do not provide a basis for undertaking empirical work directed to the verification and enrichment of the theory of a firm's investment.

In this work uncertainty as to the future and aversion to risk are accepted. The consequence is that the financing and valuation of the firm, as well as its investment, prove to be challenging problems. Further our objective is to obtain answers to these three interrelated questions—answers that have empirical content. Operating under this constraint we find it impossible to elaborate the theory to provide information on the technology of the firm's investment. Also, while the results obtained may be of interest for predicting the variation in a firm's investment with industry and economy variables, this application of the theory will not be considered here.

The purpose of this chapter is to review the neoclassical theory of the investment and valuation of a firm. A basis for establishing the differences between the two theories will thereby be laid. What is more important, the present theory has important roots in neoclassical theory, and the review will serve as a foundation for the argument to follow. The neoclassical literature on the investment and valuation of the firm is considerable and difficult, and an attempt at a comprehensive review would result in a diffused and meaningless survey. Therefore, we will for the most part confine our attention to the work by Lutz and Lutz, *The Theory of Investment of the Firm* [1951]. It by far is the most complete statement of neoclassical theory on the subject.

2.1 A Simple Illustration of the Theory

Let us begin with some fundamental definitions and concepts. An investment may be defined as an outlay of money at one point in time for the rights conveyed to receipts at one or more subsequent points in time. The outlay may be for a bond, a piece of machinery, a business enterprise, a share in a firm, or some other item. The subsequent receipts may be certain or uncertain in the mind of the investor. Further, there may be a statement of the future receipts at the time of the investment or the receipts may be dependent on the employment of the asset and other events subsequent to the investment.

It is evident from the above definition of an investment that its evaluation requires a basis for comparing money at different points in time, i.e., of establishing the equivalent at one point in time of an amount of money at another point in time. The basis for such comparisons is the theory of interest. If money can earn interest at a rate of i per period, an amount P will grow in one period to

$$R_1 = P(1 + i) \tag{2.1}$$

Alternatively, we can say that if a return of i is required on investment, the amount R_1 at the end of one period has a present value of P. Textbooks on the mathematics of finance such as Todhunter [1937] demonstrate how this statement can be elaborated to convert amounts at one or more points in time to their equivalent, given a rate of interest, in one or more other points in time. In particular, if an investment will provide the receipts $R_1, R_2, \ldots, R_n$, and the interest rate is i, the present value of the future receipts the investment provides is

$$P = \sum_{t=1}^{n} \frac{R_t}{(1 + i)^t} \tag{2.2}$$

Alternatively, if the receipts will be received continuously over time

$$P = \int_0^n R_t e^{-it} dt \tag{2.3}$$

For a simple illustration of the neoclassical theory of capital, assume the following. (1) A firm has a fixed sum of money W, but it can borrow freely at a given rate of interest i. (2) The firm has an investment opportunity of the point-input point-output type. That is, by making an investment K now it will obtain a receipt after an interval of exactly t periods, that is a function $f(K)$ of the investment. (3) Given K, the receipt $f(K)$ is known with certainty, and the technology of the investment opportunity is such that the marginal receipt[2] $f'(K)$ increases with K up to some value of K and then falls. (4) The objective of the firm is to maximize its value, P.

The amount the firm will borrow is $K - W$, and the value of the firm is its net worth plus the amount by which the present value of $f(K)$ exceeds K. Hence,

[2] The increase in $f(K)$ per unit increase in K.

$$P = W + f(K)e^{-it} - K \tag{2.4}$$

The investment that maximizes the value of the firm under the assumed conditions is obtained by taking the derivative of P with respect to K, and finding the value of K that satisfies $\partial P/\partial K = 0$. Taking the derivative, we find

$$\frac{\partial P}{\partial K} = f'(K)e^{-it} - 1 \tag{2.5}$$

and P is maximized by the value of K that satisfies

$$f'(K)e^{-it} = 1 \tag{2.6}$$

The rate of return on the investment, sometimes called the internal rate of return, is the rate of discount that equates the present value of the future receipts with the investment. That is, the rate of return on the investment is the value of r that satisfies

$$K = f(K)e^{-rt} \tag{2.7}$$

The marginal rate of return on investment r' is the rate of discount that equates the present value of the increment to the future receipts with a unit increment to the investment. It is the value of r' that satisfies

$$1 = f'(K)e^{-r't} \tag{2.8}$$

In other words, given $f(K)$, $f'(K)$ may be established for each value of K, and the value of r' that satisfies Eq. (2.8) is the marginal rate of return on investment at that level of investment.

Comparison of Eqs. (2.6) and (2.8) reveals a decision rule for this firm that is highly attractive for its simplicity and intuitive appeal. The firm should carry its investment to the point where the return on the last dollar invested is equal to i, the rate of interest at which it can borrow. A smaller investment involves foregoing opportunities that can earn a return greater than their cost, and the opposite is true for investing beyond this point.

Among the problems of interest to Lutz and Lutz was whether or not alternative possible decision rules resulted in the optimum investment by the firm. By assumption the optimum maximizes P, the value of the firm. We just saw that for the investment situation under consideration, the investment that equates r' with i maximizes P. An alternative possible decision rule is the maximization of r, the internal rate of return on the investment. Solving Eq. (2.7) for r we obtain

$$r = \frac{1}{t} ln[f(K)/K] \qquad (2.9)$$

Taking the derivative with respect to K, setting the result equal to zero, and simplifying somewhat we have

$$\frac{1}{t}\left[\frac{f'(K)}{f(K)} - \frac{1}{K}\right] = 0 \qquad (2.10)$$

Substituting Eq. (2.7) for K, and rearranging terms

$$f'(K) = f(K)/f(K)e^{-rt}$$

or

$$f'(K)e^{-rt} = 1 \qquad (2.11)$$

In other words, maximizing r implies that K should be carried to the point where $r = r'$. Compare Eq. (2.8).

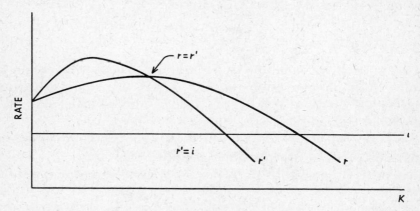

FIGURE 2.1

RELATION AMONG AVERAGE AND MARGINAL RATES OF RETURN
ON INVESTMENT AND THE RATE OF INTEREST

Comparison of the two decision rules is illustrated in Figure 2.1. The relation between r and r' requires that r be at its maximum when $r = r'$. Hence, if r exceeds i for any value of K, the investment that realizes $r = r'$ must be smaller than the investment that realizes $r' = i$, and it can be shown at this smaller investment P is smaller than at $r' = i$. The only case in which $r = r' = i$ is possible is where $r = i$ at the value of K where r is maximized, but in this event the investment is not worth undertaking. Another possible criterion for the firm is maximizing the rate of return on W, the firm's net worth.

This, Lutz and Lutz showed, results in the maximization of P, and it is a satisfactory decision criterion in the present case.

2.2 Refinements in the Theory

The classic textbook problem is the optimum age of a stock of wine. Here the investment is given but the period of the investment is variable. A problem exists because the price per gallon of wine increases by increasing amounts up to some age and then increases by decreasing amounts.[3] Let the value of a wine stock that can be purchased for K expressed as a function of the stock's age be $f(t)$. The value of a firm with a net worth of W and with a stock of wine that costs K is

$$P = W + f(t)e^{-it} - K \tag{2.12}$$

The value of the firm is a function of t, the number of periods the stock is aged, and it can be shown that the firm's value is maximized by the period of investment that satisfies

$$\frac{f'(t)}{f(t)} = i \tag{2.13}$$

That is, the stock should be aged until the percentage increase in its value falls to the rate of interest. It is evident that holding the wine one period longer will provide a smaller income than selling the stock and lending the proceeds to earn a rate of return i.

What happens in the present investment situation if the firm maximizes the rate of return on its net worth? For a stock that is aged t periods, Lutz and Lutz [p. 28] defined this rate of return as g in the formula

$$We^{gt} = f(t) - (K - W)e^{it} \tag{2.14}$$

Taking logs and solving for g, we find

$$g = \frac{1}{t} \, ln \left(\frac{f(t) - (K - W)e^{it}}{W} \right) \tag{2.15}$$

Taking the derivative with respect to t and solving for the value of t that maximizes g, we find that to maximize g, the stock should be aged until g falls to the value that satisfies

$$\frac{f'(t)}{f(t)} = g - (g - i) \left[\frac{(K - W)e^{it}}{f(t)} \right] \tag{2.16}$$

---

[3] It is more correct to say that the second derivative of the price per gallon becomes negative after some point in time.

In other words, at the value of t that maximizes g, $f'(t)/ft$ is less than g. We saw in Eq. (2.13) that P is maximized when $f'(t)/f(t) = i$. Is this also true when g is maximized? For $f'(t)/f(t) = i$, when g is maximized $g = i$ is necessary. However, if the profitability of the investment is such that the maximum rate of return on the net worth is no greater than the rate of interest, the investment is not worth undertaking. Assume $g > i$ when g is maximized. It can be shown that at this t we have $f'(t)/f(t) > i$, and P is increased by increasing t. Therefore, maximizing the rate of return on net worth is not a correct decision rule in this investment situation. It can also be shown that maximizing the investment's internal rate of return is also not a correct decision rule in the present case.

The main concern of Lutz and Lutz was to introduce refinements with respect to the characteristics of the investment situation and investigate the statements that could be made about the firm's optimum investment under these successively more realistic assumptions.

To elaborate on the various types of investment situations, Lutz and Lutz distinguished between *dependent* and *independent* investment horizons. The horizon is dependent if the firm is to be liquidated when the asset is sold or after M cycles of asset purchase and sale. It is independent if the firm is to be liquidated after n periods, n being independent of the investment period, and the horizon is infinite if an indefinite cycle of asset purchases and sales is contemplated. A firm's funds horizon may be dependent or independent of its investment horizon. If the funds horizon is independent of the investment horizon, it must of course be longer. Lutz and Lutz also distinguished between scale and technique variability. Scale variability refers to the size of the initial investment, and technique variability refers to the period of the investment.

In the wine stock case just discussed, both the investment and the funds horizons were dependent and only the technique was variable. Numerous combinations of investment and funds horizon and scale and technique variability represent possible investment situations. In each case the appropriate functional relation between the value of the firm and its investment was established, and the solution to the problem—the amount, life, and other properties of the investment that maximizes the value of the firm—was found. Then to the extent possible the findings were compared with the consequences of alternative decision rules—maximizing the return on net worth, maximizing the return on capital, and equating the marginal return on investment with the rate of interest.

The above analysis was first applied to the point-input point-output case under various assumptions with respect to horizon and variability of scale and technique. A number of chapters were then devoted to inventories that do not increase in value with age—manufacturers' inventories of raw material, work in process, and finished goods—under various assumptions with respect to the purposes in holding inventories. Finally, four chapters were devoted to the important problem of investment in durable goods—point input with output over two or more periods.

A durable goods problem is the life of a machine with a given technique. If it is not to be replaced, the machine should be employed until the quasi rent (income before depreciation) in a period falls below the interest on the scrap value. For the infinite chain "the individual machine should be discarded as soon as it ceases to earn a quasi rent which covers interest on its scrap value *plus* interest on the capitalized value of all the future goodwills" [p. 107]. For the proof, let

$Q(t)$ = quasi rent of a machine t periods after it is acquired.
C = cost of a machine.
S = scrap value of a machine which for simplicity is a constant.
T = life of a machine.

$$P = \left[\int_0^T Q(t)e^{-it}dt - C + Se^{-iT} \right]\left[1 + e^{-iT} + e^{-2iT} + \cdots \right] + W \quad (2.17)$$

$$= \frac{1}{1 - e^{-iT}} \left[\int_0^T Q(t)e^{-it}dt - C + Se^{-iT} \right] + W$$

The value of T that maximizes P, it can be shown, is the value that satisfies

$$Q(T) = iS + \frac{i}{1 - e^{-iT}} \left[\int_0^T Q(t)e^{-it}dt - C + Se^{-iT} \right] \quad (2.18)$$

The first term on the right side is the interest on the scrap value, and the second term is the interest on the present value of the goodwill on all future machines—the goodwill on a machine being the amount by which its discounted quasi rents and scrap value exceed its cost.

The economic rationale of this solution may be explained as follows. By holding the machine one additional period, the firm gains its quasi rent in the period, $Q(t)$. The firm, however, foregoes the interest on its scrap value, iS. The firm also defers for one period the quasi rents on all succeeding machines. The cost of doing this is the last term on the right side of Eq. (2.18).

Lutz and Lutz went on to consider the consequences of various complications to the model such as changes in technology, a multi-machine firm, the choice of technique (machines of different life), and the scale of investment. They did not find it possible to arrive at an exact solution in every case. However, they were usually able to carry the analysis far enough to make some generalizations about the questions for which the analysis is considered of interest to economists. That is, given the decision rule a firm follows, inferences can be drawn in some cases about how its investment and capital output ratio will react to changes in parameters such as the rate of interest, the prices of factors and products, and the cost of equipment. Of course, insofar as the assumptions are applicable, the models may also be used as decision guides by firms.

2.3 Some Observations on the Theory

The material described in the previous section occupies well over one half of Lutz and Lutz. It may be considered under two headings. One is the information on a firm's marginal efficiency of capital schedule, and the other is the information on its investment given the afore-mentioned schedule.

The great variety of models constructed would seem to provide an arsenal of equipment for arriving at a firm's marginal efficiency of capital under a variety of assumptions with respect to the technology of production and the horizon of the firm. There is some reflection of these models in the literature on capital budgeting that deals with the ranking of investment opportunities.[4] However, it does not prove possible to take much advantage of these models in our study. First, we consider only corporations with an infinite expected life. Second, at the decision level of this study there is no information to differentiate assets according to technoeconomic characteristics. Third, unlike Lutz and Lutz it is recognized that the firm's existing stock of capital is given; i.e., investment decisions are not reversible.

Accordingly, for the initial statement of the theory in Chap-

4 Cf. the papers by Lorie and Savage [1955], Solomon [1956], and Dean and Smith [1955].

ter 4, it is assumed that the corporation is expected to earn its current earnings on its existing capital stock and to have a return on investment that is a function of its investment rate. The refinement and elaboration of these assumptions with respect to return on capital and investment in Chapter 7 proceed for the most part along different lines than those followed by Lutz and Lutz. The reason is that they built models for a world of complete information, whereas I am dealing with a system in which the future is uncertain and information about it is summarized and lost as it is transmitted from corporate agents to corporate directors and to stockholders.

Given some functional relation between a firm's investment and its future income, two related assumptions are necessary for the Lutz models to yield a firm's investment and value. One is that the firm can freely lend or borrow at a given rate of interest, and the other is that the future is certain. The use of these two assumptions was explicitly recognized by the authors. The chapter following the above material was introduced with the statement, "Up to now we have been treating investment decisions as though the method of financing was irrelevant, or as though in any period there was in the economic system only a single interest rate which could be applied to all units of funds invested" [p. 169]. A later chapter began, "In the preceding chapters we have assumed that the entrepreneur had single-valued expectations, i.e. that he had perfect confidence in his forecasts of prices, costs, etc" [p. 179]. The fact that both assumptions were made is no coincidence, since "the essence of the distinction between different sources of funds, equity and loan capital, depends on the fact that expectations are not single-valued" [p. 178].

Whether or not the conclusions reached for a world in which the future is certain and money is freely available at a given interest rate apply in the real world is open to question. Lutz and Lutz did not test the theorems established by reference to the actual behavior of firms. Nor did they indicate solutions to numerous problems one would encounter in putting the propositions in a form amenable to empirical verification.

The Lutzes of course recognized the seriousness of these two assumptions: practically all of the remainder of the book is devoted to the consequences of withdrawing them. They dealt at length with the implications of allowing alternative methods of finance under uncertainty, but the lack of rigor in dealing with the subject contrasts sharply with the first part of the book. They simply could not join the two subjects, and all they succeeded in doing was to present a very able statement of the generalizations found in the unprecise literature of finance. The critical questions are those posed by the recognition of uncertainty, and the remainder of this chapter is devoted to an examination of their treatment of risk and uncertainty.

2.4 Uncertainty and Aversion to Risk

The Lutzes began their chapter on risk and uncertainty with a general review of the widely accepted alternatives for representing the valuation and choice among investments when recognition is given to the fact that the future receipts are uncertain. The problem arises, it should be noted at the outset, because investors are assumed to have an aversion to risk.[5] There are alternative possible definitions of risk, but the variance or standard deviation of an expectation seem to have the widest acceptance. Given aversion to risk and the measurement of it, one solution to the valuation problem is to assume that investors take the mean or expected value of the receipt in each period, reduce it by an amount related to its risk, and then discount the *certain equivalent* at the rate of interest on risk-free investments. An alternative means of obtaining the present value of an uncertain expectation is by discounting the expected value of the receipt in each period at a rate that varies with the risk of the receipt.

We will return to these two valuation rules later. The Lutzes found fault with both of them, but the purpose served by their objections is not clear to me. They argued it is not legitimate to have the entrepreneur estimate the receipt frequency distribution directly.[6] Instead, he should be looked on as estimating the underlying frequency distributions of prices and costs for each period. However, the Lutzes also consolidated these distributions into a receipt distribution. Further, they recognized it is incorrect to assume "that the probabilities of costs and prices are independent . . ." [p. 186],

[5] Without aversion to risk, investors would simply use the expected value of an uncertain expectation in place of the single value of a certain receipt. Knight [1921] has argued that investors may have a love of risk and/or they may be overly optimistic in their expectations. The view that all types of attitudes toward uncertainty may be true has been expressed by Friedman and Savage [1948], among others. However, the more generally accepted position is that investors look on a gamble as being inferior to the alternative of obtaining its expected value with certainty. This is brought out in the able review of the subject by Arrow [1951].

[6] They also maintained that account must be taken of the distinction drawn by Hart [1940] between expectations for which the probabilities are known and those for which even the probabilities are uncertain. However, they did not indicate what one is to make of the distinction.

which suggests that it may be best to estimate the receipt frequency distribution directly.

What Lutz and Lutz proposed is that the entire probability distribution of receipts in each future period that is provided by an investment be discounted in total to obtain an aggregate probability distribution of present values. Deducting the cost of the investment from each possible present value of future receipts results in a frequency distribution of net profits that the entrepreneur may use to evaluate an investment. After some broad generalizations on the possible influence of machine flexibility and machine life on the attractiveness of an investment, they bravely concluded as follows [p. 188]: "In similar fashion all the various choices before the entrepreneur, which were dealt with in the previous chapters in terms of single-valued expectations, could be redefined in terms of probability distributions of the present value of total net profits $(V - C)$, or in terms of certain parameters of such distributions." It would appear that nothing is lost by the recognition of uncertainty.

To elaborate on the nature of the investment decision under uncertainty, the Lutzes proposed that the probability distribution of the present value of net profits be represented by two parameters, the mean M and the standard deviation σ. The behavior of the entrepreneur is represented by the indifference map appearing in Figure 2.2, each curve of which represents the combinations of M and σ, including a risk-free M, among which the entrepreneur is indifferent.[7] The dots on the graph represent *investment plans*, i.e., alternative capital budgets, and not individual investments, entrepreneurs may undertake. The opportunity curve $0-0'$ joins the dots which provide the largest M for each σ, and the entrepreneur undertakes the capital budget that puts him on the highest attainable indifference curve, the one furthest to the right.

It is possible that the objective of the Lutzes was to put the theory of the firm's investment in the same format as that employed for the theory of consumer demand. Further, by converting a set of probability distributions in time into one probability distribution of present values, it would seem that they have converted the investment problem into an ordinary gamble. It may seem that the work in statistical decision theory and the utility analysis of choice among

[7] The curves do not rise vertically from the horizontal axis because of aversion to risk, and the curvature of the curves increases with the entrepreneur's aversion to risk. Preferred positions are obtained by moving to the right because this increases M for given σ.

uncertain alternatives could thereby be employed to deal with the problem. This representation of the firm's investment so that it may benefit from the developments in consumer demand, and utility theory does not impress me as having gone very far. It leaves too many unsolved problems.

The Lutzes recognized some of the difficulties connected with the approach they recommended. They stated, "It is important to

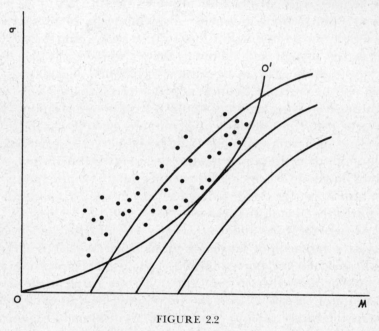

FIGURE 2.2

A REPRESENTATION OF A FIRM'S INVESTMENT DECISION

notice that the combinations between σ and M represented by various investment plans do not depend only on the investment opportunities in the narrower sense; they depend also on the terms on which outside funds are obtainable. The way in which outside funds are obtained (as well as the investment opportunities) affects, as we shall see in the next chapter, the σ and M of the probability distribution of the entrepreneur's own profits" [p. 191]. In other words, each capital budget appears as a dot on Figure 2.2 as many times as there are combinations of debt and equity capital that may be used to finance the budget, each combination having its own M and σ. This is only a practical consideration, but it is a large one.

The consideration becomes even larger when it is noted that

given a set of n investment projects, all possible combinations of them under each method of financing must be evaluated. The set of points is practically as well as theoretically infinite. To make his task manageable the entrepreneur must have a means of ranking individual projects according to their attractiveness, but it is not clear how this is to be done in the above framework.

There is a theoretical problem that may be considered even more serious, since all practical problems may be left to the entrepreneur. Note, a single frequency distribution in the present is obtained from the set of distributions in time by discounting the latter back to the present and summing them. Nowhere did the Lutzes state the discount rate to be used, which would suggest that they would use the pure rate of interest. Is this discount rate a satisfactory weighting factor for arriving at the risk of an expectation? Their statement that ". . . investment in durable goods of which the revenues (and operating expenses) tend to be heavily concentrated in the more distant future will tend to be less favored than investment in durable goods of which the revenues (and operating costs) are more heavily concentrated in the near future" [p. 188] indicates they recognized that a problem exists.

At best the Lutz and Lutz theory of valuation under uncertainty is a rationale of entrepreneurial behavior that is far more complicated and no more informative than the simpler rationales that may be derived from the valuation rules stated at the start of this section. Compare it with the proposition that an entrepreneur converts the future receipts provided by an investment opportunity to their certain equivalents, discounts the certain equivalents at the pure rate of interest, and undertakes all investments that provide a positive net profit. If the utility function that converts a probability distribution to its certain equivalent is not specified, this model is general and empty enough to be consistent with anything we observe, and it contributes as much to understanding and predicting an entrepreneur's behavior as its alternatives.

As long as theory remains on the level of abstraction pursued in the previous section, argument over alternative modes of representing entrepreneurial behavior serves no useful purpose. The alternative is to accept as the task of theory the development of propositions on the investment of the firm that have empirical content and may be tested and refuted by observation. The type of firm that should be used as the point of reference in constructing the theory is the large, publicly held corporation, because information on such corporations is publicly available and because the behavior of investors in these corporations and of their managers is rational.[8]

The valuation of a share by investors may be represented by the type of model used by neoclassical theory under the assumption of certainty. To do so, however, requires establishing how stockholders determine from the information available to them the future income on a share and how this income is expected to vary with the corporation's investment and its financing. Under uncertainty, of course, the income expectation is discounted not at the pure rate of interest but at a rate that depends on the risk attributes and possibly also the financing of the expectation. A second task therefore is to establish how the rate of discount at which a future income stream is valued varies with its risk attributes and financing. These are the tasks to which this investigation is addressed.

[8] The managers are rational in the sense that the behavior in a large bureaucracy follows an objective set of rules, not in the sense that only profit or wealth maximization is rational economic behavior. Investment in the stock of publicly held corporations is rational according to this criterion.

Chapter 3

ALTERNATIVE THEORIES OF INVESTMENT AND OF VALUATION

The neoclassical theory of capital explains the valuation of a firm and provides the investment that maximizes the value of a firm under the assumptions the future is certain and the firm can borrow freely at an interest rate that is a known function of the amount borrowed. Efforts at carrying the theory into an uncertain world have not been successful—they have yielded little if anything more than broad nontestable generalizations about what the firm does. The consequence is that modern theories of investment and of valuation directed toward providing empirical information have little or no connection with the neoclassical theory. Further, the theories of a firm's investment make no reference to its valuation, and the theories of its valuation make no reference to its investment. The purpose of this chapter is to survey these theories and the normative literature on the investment and financing of a firm. The latter we will see is closer to the neoclassical theory of investment than the theoretical literature concerned with describing what firms do.

3.1 Accelerator Principle

A simple unqualified statement of the accelerator principle is that a firm's capital is a linear function of its output, i.e., investment during a period is a multiple of the change in output during the period. In this form the principle implies a very naive understanding of business operation, and the innovator of the principle in its modern form, J. M. Clark [1917], as well as subsequent writers on the subject, has noted the severe theoretical limitations on its validity.[1] In particular, when production is falling and when it is rising but has not reached the firm's capacity, the principle does not operate. Investment may nonetheless take place to reduce production costs,

[1] Cf. Hicks [1950], Eckaus [1953], and Neisser [1954].

29

open new markets, etc. When production is at a firm's *rated* capacity, the accelerator as stated may work, but then only if production costs turn up very sharply in response to a rise in output. Also, the accelerator refers to net investment, and in practice a distinction cannot be drawn between investment for replacement and for added capacity.

Empirical work reflecting this naive formulation of the principle confirmed the theoretical objections to it. Using time series industry data, Tinbergen [1938] and Chenery [1952] either found no correlation between investment and change in sales or obtained better results with alternative independent variables. Using cross-section firm data, Meyer and Kuh [1957] obtained "mediocre and patternless results," and Eisner [1958] obtained results that could hardly be considered better.[2]

The theoretical and empirical weakness of the simple accelerator principle led to theoretical and empirical refinements. Manne [1945] and Chenery [1952] substituted the percentage of capacity utilized for the change in sales and obtained significantly better results. Meyer and Kuh [1957] did the same for cross-section firm samples and found high correlation with investment for years in which the firms were operating close to capacity. Eisner [1960] found the accelerator principle vindicated by the use of a distributed lag function of sales changes, working best in firms with rising sales and high long-term growth rates.

However, these writers did not look on the accelerator as a technological process. Rather, the firm is looked on as behaving more or less in the manner described by neoclassical theory, and the accelerator or the capacity utilization theory is looked on as being a practical empirical device for obtaining quantitative information on the consequences of their behavior. For Eisner [1960, p. 1] the acceleration principle is intended to describe "a world of risk and uncertainty in which business firms strive to maximize the mathematical expectation of some monotonic increasing function of expected future profit. . . ." Chenery [1952, p. 3] built his model of an entrepreneur's investment on the hypothesis that "the decision to increase the capacity of his plant or build a new one is based on estimates of the most profitable output to be produced in the foreseeable future."

---

[2] Meyer and Kuh [1957, pp. 23–35] provide an excellent tabular summary of the statistical findings obtained by a large number of investigators under this and other investment theories.

Stated simply, an increase in the demand for a firm's output will increase the profitability of investment, and the closer the firm's current output to its rated capacity, the greater the reaction of profitability and investment to the demand increase. The rationale for the types of models discussed, therefore, is the empirical problem involved in attempting a more faithful representation of the firm's decision process.

3.2   Profit Theories of Investment

For empirical theories of investment the major alternative to sales and sales-related variables is profit and profit-related variables. In advocating the use of profits to explain the level of investment, Tinbergen and Polak [1950, p. 166] argued that investment is motivated by profit expectations, and "to a very large extent profit expectations will be based on current facts, in particular on the current magnitude of profits." A second reason they noted for believing that investment should vary with profits is the fact that profits are a source of funds for investment, and firms are known to prefer internal financing and to face limitations on the alternatives.

Kalecki [1954, pp. 96–108] did a very nice job of developing an investment model to recognize profits in both of the roles described above. In his model, investment is a function of savings, the change in profits, and the stock of capital. The level of savings accounts for financing considerations or his "principle of increasing risk" [1937], and the change in profits and the stock of capital account for the influence of investment profitability. A very simple empirical formulation of the theory, intended more for statistical illustration than verification, did a very good job of explaining gross fixed investment in the United States over the period 1930–40. Savings and change in profits had very high partial correlation coefficients, but the stock of capital which on a priori grounds was thought to have a depressing effect on the profitability of investment did not prove to be a significant variable.

Using broadly similar type models, Tinbergen [1939], Klein [1950], and Klein and Goldberger [1952] also found profits to be a significant explanatory variable. However, none of the writers followed Kalecki in his neat distinction between the influence of profits as a source of funds and as an index of the profitability of investment. Klein and Goldberger approximated this by using a lagged function of profits.

These writers included a number of other variables in their models in order to give effect to all the variables that might influence expectations with respect to the profitability of investment. The rate of interest has a special significance, since it is the only readily observable variable in the neoclassical investment model, and the only variable easily manipulated by public policy. If all the other variables and parameters of the model are highly stable over time, investment should vary with the rate of interest. However, the above work only added to the evidence obtained from other studies that the interest rate does not have a significant influence on the level of investment.[3] The possible exceptions to this generalization are industries in which assets have very long lives and are heavily financed by borrowing.

Notwithstanding the encouraging results obtained, the above studies stimulated comparatively little interest, particularly on the level of the firm, in using profit-related variables to explain investment. One might have expected that the failure of accelerator models based on a naive mechanical view of a firm's technology would shift interest away from sales to profit-related variables. Instead, sales-related variables were refined and reinterpreted to make the models consistent with profitability as the determinant of investment. A possible explanation is the desire to support and extend the macro models of business cycles and growth based on accelerator-type investment functions. The intriguing macro models of Hicks, Domar, Harrod, et al., relate the supply and demand for output by means of accelerator investment functions.

However, the role of profits in the theory of investment was not to be denied. The accelerator is a very crude means of describing and predicting the investment of a firm motivated by profit expectations, and the empirical results provided a far from complete explanation of the variation in investment. A number of interview and similar type investigations on the level of the firm were undertaken to get fresh insights on the investment process. The researches of Merwin [1942], McHugh [1951], Heller [1951], Butters and Lintner [1945], Andrews [1940], Eisner [1956], and others provide interesting insights on the investment behavior of firms among which two points stand out. One is that firms are strongly influenced by the amount of funds provided by operations, depreciation allowances plus retained earnings, in arriving at their capital budgets. This is a self-

---

[3] Once again the reader is referred to Meyer and Kuh [1957, pp. 23-35] for a convenient summary of the findings.

imposed restriction contrary to the widely held view that the limit on borrowing, if any exists, is due to credit rationing by lenders based on conventions with respect to debt-equity ratios and similar considerations. The second point is that the interest rate appears to have little influence on the investment decisions of the firms observed.[4]

Possibly on the suggestion of the above findings, Meyer and Kuh were particularly concerned with establishing the comparative influence on investment of capacity utilization and liquidity flow. They found that in years such as 1946 and 1947 when capacity utilization and excess liquidity were extremely high, capacity utilization had the greater correlation with investment. However, with the return to more normal times and particularly in a recession period— the years 1948–50—liquidity flow variables, profits, and depreciation expense became more important. They attached particular importance to the correlation with depreciation expense on the grounds that ". . . unlike the other liquidity flow variable, net profits, it is not complicated by the fact of also being a measure of changing expectations" [1957, p. 101].[5]

Eisner, on the other hand, obtained different results. In his model, investment is a distributed lag function of sales change and profits. He found that "accelerator coefficients are all very significantly positive and generally decrease with increasing lag. Profit coefficients are both positive and negative and never differ significantly from zero" [1960, p. 19].[6] Depreciation expense, the most significant

---

[4] Eisner's attitude toward his findings that the interest rate is not important to businessmen is quite revealing. He prefaces them with a chapter devoted to illustrating the proposition "that the individual businessman does not really know, in any sense satisfactory to the economist, what determines his investment decisions" [1956, p. 7].

[5] This work by Meyer and Kuh is the most ambitious statistical investigation of a firm's investment to date. They obtained data on 22 variables for 630 corporations classified in 12 industry samples for the years 1946–50. They therefore had a total of 60 cross-section samples. Preliminary analysis of the data by various methods resulted in eliminating most of the variables and the organization of the remainder in two regression equations. Sales and change in sales were among the variables of one equation, and profits were among the variables in the other equation. The purpose in this difference was to establish and interpret the role of the two variables in the investment decision. The independent variables in each equation were used individually and collectively to test and in some cases to establish new hypotheses on the investment decision. Their findings were very interesting.

[6] The above results were obtained from sums of the moment matrics of the basic regressions over all industries for three years. Separate regressions by industry year, however, do not provide such a clear picture. The depreciation coefficient is not significant for some samples, and some of the lagged profits coefficients are highly significant. It will be seen shortly that neither the Meyer and Kuh nor the Eisner models are very efficient instruments for testing the liquidity flow hypothesis.

variable by far, with a coefficient over ten times its standard error, is interpreted by Eisner to represent replacement demand rather than internally available funds.

3.3 A Satisficing Theory of Investment

The notion that a firm's investment is related to the funds provided by operations suggests a major alternative to the neoclassical theory of investment. If profits are looked on as a measure of the profitability of investment, the difference between an appropriately designed profit model and a revised accelerator or capacity utilization model is not very serious. Underlying both models is the hypothesis that the objective of the firm is to maximize its value, and the only issue is whether profits, capacity utilization, etc., is the most effective or least ineffective instrument for predicting the investment the firm undertakes in realizing this objective.

The hypothesis that internally available funds influence the investment of a firm, however, implies a different objective than maximizing the value of the firm. The distinction between the two objectives for a sole proprietor under uncertainty is not easily made operational since the value of a proprietorship to its proprietor is a subjective quantity. Consider a proprietor who never goes into debt regardless of the investment opportunities forgone under this policy. Who can say that the value of the proprietorship to him, the only relevant person, is not maximized by this policy?

The situation for a publicly owned corporation is quite different. The valuation of a corporation is by the investors in the stock market. We may presume that these investors have a preference structure such that there is some investment policy and financing policy (debt, equity, and retention) that maximizes the value of the firm. However, this investment and financing policy may be at odds with the objectives of the management who are the immediate decision makers. The maximization of their utility may call for a different investment and financing, and conceivably we can establish whether or not this is true.

The behavior of management in maximizing its utility might appropriately be called "satisficing," a term coined by Simon [1957], and the interview empirical studies cited earlier are reasonably interpreted as evidence in support of a satisficing theory of investment. The objective of achieving or maintaining a *satisfactory* share of the market has been widely recognized as influential in numerous areas of business decision, and Kaysen [1949] has attempted to formally incorporate the concept in the theory of investment. Duesenberry [1958] in his eclectic theory of investment includes many variables which may be interpreted to reflect the objective of a satisfactory state of affairs. As we will see shortly, the business literature on investment and financing policy can for the most part be interpreted only in this way.

Notwithstanding the frequent reference in business and economic literature to rules of thumb, i.e., to the maintenance of satisfactory values for certain critical variables in investment and other decision areas, little has been done to formalize the concepts in useful theories. Haberstroh [1960] has provided a satisficing explanation of expenditure decisions on plant safety. Applications to a number of business decisions and some formalization of the concept in a model of business organization are contained in the work of Cyert and March [1959].

In the field of investment this writer [1960] has presented a satisficing theory that may be worth reviewing briefly, largely because it is in a form amenable to empirical verification and it is related to the funds flow theories mentioned earlier. The debt-equity ratio is the variable a corporation can manipulate with the greatest ease to control its risk. For instance, the management of a steel company cannot shift over to the electric power business because the latter is less risky, but it can avoid debt financing. The hypothesis suggested is that a debt-equity ratio, different for each company, is decided upon as representing a satisfactory degree of risk, and the investment of a company is given not by profitability but by the amount consistent with achieving or maintaining the target debt-equity ratio. Cross-section firm data supported the hypothesis in that corporations with high ratios tended to maintain them by borrowing and investing more in relation to equity funds than corporations with low ratios. Also, corporations in industries that are risky tend to have lower debt-equity ratios than corporations in less risky industries.

The above is a very crude satisficing theory for a number of reasons. In particular, a management also has a satisfactory dividend, share of the market, return on investment, price of its stock, etc. Quite often, given the earnings, investment opportunities available, and other independent variables, no investment is consistent with satisfactory values for all the variables, and a powerful satisficing theory must explain first how a management arrives at satisfactory values for each variable and second, adjusts their values when it is not possible to realize all of them.

3.4 Valuation Theories

Observation of investment analysts and reading the literature on security analysis, e.g., Graham and Dodd [1951], reveal a highly pragmatic and subjective method for arriving at a share's value. The analyst looks at a corporation's record of earnings, dividends, book value, debt-equity ratio, growth, instability of earnings, etc. He then looks for any information not contained in the record of the above variables—information such as a change in unfilled orders or prospects for new products—that make a change in earnings, dividends, and/or price in the near future likely. After considering all this information he arrives at a decision whether the share is fairly priced, overpriced, or underpriced.

The analyst may use bench-mark values for statistics such as the price-earnings ratio in his analysis, but by and large his conclusion is reached through an unstructured examination and interpretation of the data. One should not be quick to criticize this method of analysis. In the absence of proven methods of scientific analysis, consideration of all possible information, the use of judgment in conjunction with rules of thumb, and the heavy emphasis on any information that indicates a change in dividends, earnings, etc., seem reasonable.

Probably the earliest attempt at an objective explanation of the variation in price among common stocks is due to J. W. Meader. In a paper, "A Formula for Determining Basic Values Underlying Common Stock Prices," published in *The Annalist, Magazine of Finance, Commerce & Economics,* November 29, 1935, he reported the results of a least-squares regression of price on dividend, earnings, book value, working capital, and transaction volume during a year for 502 shares.[7] He obtained a multiple correlation coefficient of .93 and was quite pleased with the results. However, repetition of the regression with data for other years resulted in radically different coefficients for the independent variables and led him to conclude, in the June 27, 1940, issue, that the model was unsatisfactory for predicting the variation in price with a change in an independent variable. High correlation among the independent variables was the root of the trouble.

Another major use of objective statistical methods to value com-

[7] This reference was called to the writer's attention by Henry Latané.

mon stocks is represented by The Value Line Investment Survey. Up until the mid-50's, the value of a share at any point in time was obtained by use of time series data for the share. Subsequently, the model was revised to use cross-section data and to incorporate some novel features. The model is described in detail in Bernhardt [1959].

Probably the most sophisticated, in a statistical sense, attempt at explaining stock prices is the monograph on bank stock prices by Durand [1957a]. However, from an economic point of view it was an advance over Meader's work only in that the model was logarithmic, which allowed more useful and interesting statements on the relation among the variables than a linear model. Like Meader, Durand regressed price on dividends, earnings, book value, and other variables. The other variables were found to have no explanatory value and were dropped from the equation. The coefficients of the included variables fluctuated over a wide range among samples, and made reliable statements on the variation in price with the dividend payout rate, the return on investment rate, etc., extremely difficult.

Papers in *The Analyst Journal* and numerous unpublished manuscripts by students have followed the same path. A selection is made among the variables the investor is presumed to consider in valuing a share, and share price is made a linear or nonlinear function of the variables. The multiple correlation is invariably high so that the model may be a good predictor of the variation in price with a given percentage change in all the independent variables. However, the management typically cannot raise all the variables, and for the decision questions facing management, such as dividend and investment policy, the model is of little or no help. On dividend policy we have already seen that correlation among the independent variables makes the coefficients estimated highly unreliable. In addition the models reflect a superficial and untenable hypothesis with respect to how dividends enter into the determination of share price.[8] On investment policy the models are useless, since the investment of the firm is not included among the independent variables either directly or indirectly. Investment influences the value of a share by influencing expected future dividends and earnings, but these models do not recognize that future dividends and/or earnings is what the investor is buying.

Only in the area of debt financing has there been some work in

[8] For a further discussion of the limitations of these simple models see Gordon [1959].

the use of share valuation models to find the optimum debt-equity ratio. Since corporations typically can borrow at an interest rate below their return on investment, trading on the equity may be expected to increase a corporation's earnings per share. Durand [1952] has shown that there are three hypotheses with respect to the impact on the price per share: (1) The capitalization of earnings may remain unchanged with the result that price will increase proportionately with earnings. (2) The capitalization rate may rise due to increased risk so as to leave price unchanged. (3) The capitalization rate may change so that price first rises and then after reaching a maximum falls with increased trading on the equity. Few would support the first position. Modigliani and Miller [1958] have presented an impressive theoretical argument in support of the second, and Durand, along with most people in the world of finance, believes that the last is true.

There have been numerous statistical investigations of the variation in share price with the debt-equity ratio. However, these studies have been handicapped by crude definitions of debt and very imperfect elimination of the effect on price of other variables. The statistical work therefore cannot be looked on as having contributed to the solution of the problem.[9]

Before leaving the subject it should be noted that in a very sophisticated paper Kuh [1960] has arrived at a solution to the investment and outside financing, debt and equity, that maximizes the value of a share. The model, however, is on a very general level, and it can only be considered of value as a statement of the problem.

3.5 Business Practice: Capital Budgeting

We have seen that the limited progress in the theory of stock price valuation severely limits the usefulness of the theories for the comparatively easy task of security analysis. It is evident that they are

[9] This writer obtained results from earlier statistical work that are not atypical. Both the second and third theories suggest that with everything else given, share price should vary inversely with the debt-equity ratio. Most samples resulted in no or positive correlation. The explanation was that everything else, in particular the basic risk of the corporation, was not held constant due to poor measurement of risk without leverage. There will be some tendency for stable corporations to borrow and unstable ones to avoid borrowing. Hence, there will be a tendency for the debt-equity ratio to be a surrogate for the corporation's strength and be positively correlated with price. To illustrate this point, further consider a price model with earnings and debt-equity ratio the independent variables and with the sample evenly divided between machine tool and public-utility corporations. The former typically have little or no debt, and a 50 per cent debt-equity ratio or higher is ordinary for utilities.

of no value for a corporation management, considering the impact of its investment and financing policies on the price of its stock. We therefore find little explicit consideration of share price in the rules followed by corporations. In surveying business practice it is convenient to accept the division usually drawn between investment policy which is associated with the term capital budgeting and financing policy.

In capital budgeting brief mention should be made of the progress in the methods for administrating capital expenditures. Modern companies typically employ systematic procedures for establishing the information to justify a capital expenditure, for including a proposal in the capital budget, for approving the capital budget, and for comparing cost and performance on an expenditure with proposal estimates. The National Industrial Conference Board [1953], National Association of Accountants [1959], the American Management Association [1954], and numerous individuals have written on business practice in this area.[10]

A second problem faced by a firm is to arrive at a formula or method of evaluating the attractiveness or profitability of an investment proposal. For a long time the payoff period or pure judgment applied to the available data was the basis for decision.[11] However, elaborate administrative procedures for collecting and organizing information called for more sophisticated methods in using the data. Since the end of World War II the writings of Terborgh [1949], Dean [1951, 1954], and others have secured some business acceptance for improved methods of evaluation, in particular the use of discounted cash flows to arrive at a proposal's rate of return or the excess of its value over cost given a cost-of-capital figure.

The remaining problem is the rate of return a corporation should require as a condition for making an investment. The literature referred to above says little on this subject. A corporation will typically have a required rate of profit, but it is used with a great deal of flexibility, and the reasoning used in arriving at it is almost entirely judgment and tradition. The most widely recommended figure is the corporation's price-earnings ratio, and Soule [1955] presents the argument in support of it. In line with their position that

[10] Two books which summarize and extend the literature on what business practice should be in the field of capital budgeting broadly defined are Solomon [1959] and Bierman and Smidt [1960].

[11] For a discussion of the relative merits of alternative formulas see Gordon [1955].

a share's price is independent of trading on the equity by the corporation, Modigliani and Miller [1958] argue that earnings before interest divided by a corporation's total capital is the appropriate cost of capital. Some variant of earnings divided by price is widely advocated for use as a corporation's cost of capital in the belief that it is the rate of return investors require on investment in the corporation. If so, an investment that can earn a higher rate of return will raise the corporation's value, and vice versa. However, it is normal or expected earnings that should be used, and Benishay [1960] has tackled the problems of measuring a corporation's cost of capital based on normal earnings and of explaining differences in the quantity among corporations.

3.6   Business Practice: Financing

The tradition in finance has been to take the capital outlay budget as given or arrived at elsewhere in the firm and to be concerned with the methods of financing the demand for funds. More recently the concern of finance has broadened to embrace capital budgeting, the demand as well as the supply of funds. This is nicely illustrated by comparing two of the leading texts in the field. Guthman and Dougall [1948], a traditional text, is concerned with financial institutions, financial instruments, and policy with respect to reliance on different sources of funds for financing and refinancing the firm. Hunt, Williams, and Donaldson [1958] by contrast deal extensively with the topics raised in the last section, appraising investment opportunities and measuring a company's cost of capital.

It would be a false inference, however, to believe that the size of a firm's capital budget is independent of financing considerations. Management does not simply arrive at a cost-of-capital figure and undertake every investment that can be expected to yield this return or more. Policy on the method of financing, among other things, influences the final decision on the level of financing and investment. The capital budget arrived at by including all proposals that meet a given rate of return requirement is substantially modified by top management on the basis of its objectives with respect to position in the industry, growth, competitive position cost-wise, etc. The change may be made directly by changing the cutoff point or by revising the assumptions under which subordinates estimate cash flows and profitability.

The literature on the subject offers the following observations on how financial considerations enter into the determination of a firm's capital budget. The finance people estimate the funds that will be available for investment. First, as noted earlier, the underlying riskiness of the firm and the desire of the management for security result in a policy with respect to debt financing, i.e., a desired debt-equity ratio. Given the existing debt-equity ratio, the funds available from borrowing or required for debt retirement are determined.

Turning to outside equity financing, it is commonly presumed that there will be none. Some firms occasionally undertake it, but the issues involved are so numerous and complex that there has not even been a start on a theory that can predict when a corporation will undertake new equity financing, and how much it will be. All we have are a few broad observations on the conditions favorable to it, and for the most part, these conditions are difficult to observe.

Texts such as Guthman and Dougall [1948, pp. 507–29] and Hunt, Williams, and Donaldson [1958, pp. 632–55] present the arguments for and against a stable dividend, a high dividend payout rate, etc. In the light of this information—consideration of stockholder desire for dividends versus capital gains, the management objectives with respect to the price of its stock, the long-run demand rate for investment funds, and attitudes towards other sources of funds—the management arrives at a dividend policy. The expected earnings for the period less the dividend indicated by policy provides the funds available from operations in excess of depreciation allowances.

If the supply of funds differs from the demand, the two must be brought into equality. Although little is known of the process by which the management and directors of a corporation achieve this equality, we can be sure that the adjustment is not solely or even predominantly in the supply of funds. When the supply exceeds the demand, the dividend may be liberalized and the financial position strengthened, but there is also a rise in research and development expenditures, greater interest in growth by acquiring other companies, and a relaxation in the standards for accepting investment proposals. When the demand exceeds the supply, an increase in the dividend may be postponed, and the postponement may be made permanent in the form of a lower dividend payout rate. A corporation may raise its debt-equity ratio or issue stock, but such action is usually taken with considerable reluctance, it appears. The statements of business and finance people indicate that deferring the in-

vestment is the preferred alternative. Crisis situations, maintenance of position in the industry, and the like are considered more justifiable reasons for departing from established financial policies than super profits.

This description of business practice might appear to indicate that a theory to explain the investment and financing of a corporation must of necessity be a satisficing theory. However, it should be recognized that any situation where the theory needed to provide an optimal solution does not exist, the use of judgment based on a complex of considerations and data will prevail, and it will seem that the decision process is best described by a satisficing theory. However, the methodology of constructing and testing a satisficing theory to provide quantitative information on the behavior of a firm is still in the primitive stages. Further, the behavior described above may not differ materially, if at all, from that which maximizes the value of a share. The formal commitment of corporate officers and directors to act in the interest of its stockholders, the threat to those in control by a substantial difference beween the actual and potential price of the stock, and the widespread use of stock option plans all make the investment and financing that maximizes the value of a share of practical as well as theoretical interest.

Chapter 4

A VALUATION AND INVESTMENT MODEL

As shown in Chapter 2, under neoclassical theory the objective of the firm is to maximize its value, the value is a function of its future income, and the future income is a function of its investment. The task of the theory is to provide information on the nature of these two functions. If the behavior postulate is correct, the information benefits both the investment decisions of firms and the study of capital formation and its relation to other economic variables in a capitalistic economy. We saw also, however, the usefulness of the theory is severely restricted by the assumption that the future is certain and by the related assumption that funds are freely available at a given rate of interest.

The purpose of this chapter is to construct an analogous theory of the valuation and investment of a corporation with the existence of uncertainty as to the future and aversion to risk on the part of investors recognized. The statement of the theory in this chapter will be under certain restrictive assumptions with respect to financing policy and the variation in risk among firms. The succeeding chapters will be devoted to the task of withdrawing these assumptions. Throughout the development of the theory a prime consideration will be its representation in models that have empirical content. That is, it will be possible to observe the variables, estimate the parameters, test the behavior statements, and implement the decision rules contained in the theory.

4.1 Theoretical Foundation of the Model

The first problem encountered in constructing the theory is deciding what is the future income provided by a share of stock in a publicly owned corporation. The three alternatives that readily come to mind are: (1) the future earnings per share, (2) the future divi-

43

dends per share, and (3) the future dividends for a finite number of periods plus the price at the end of that time.[1] Each of these alternatives appears to have some intuitive merit. However, in the absence of differential tax treatment of capital gains the third, it would seem, reduces to the second, since the price at any future date may be expected to depend on the subsequent income.[2] The major issue is between dividends and earnings. The theory to be developed in this chapter assumes that the future dividends are what the investor buys in a share. The validity of the assumption will be examined on theoretical grounds in the following chapter, and the empirical information on the issue will be examined in the next section of the book.

The symbols to be used frequently in this chapter are defined below.

P_t = Price of a corporation's share of stock at end of period t.

D_t = Dividend per share paid by the corporation during t.

Y_t = Income per share earned by the corporation during t.

r = Return on investment the corporation is expected to earn in every future period.

b = Fraction of income the corporation is expected to retain in every future period.

k = Return on investment that stockholders require on the corporation's stock.

d = Dividend yield based on current dividend, $d = D_0/P_0$.

Under certain assumptions k may also be looked on as a corporation's cost of capital. When the time subscript refers to a period in the future, the value of a variable is the mean or expected value of a probability distribution the investor is assumed to estimate subjectively. Also, P_t, D_t, and Y_t without subscript will be used at times to refer to the current values of the variables.

Assume a corporation for which the following is true. (1) It engages in no outside equity financing. (2) It has a quick ratio of one[3] and no long-term debt; i.e., it does not use debt financing. (3) It *will* earn a return of r on investment in every future period. (4) It *will* retain the fraction b of its income in every future period.

---

[1] There are special situations in which the price of a share reflects other considerations, such as the desire of a group to gain control or the liquidation value of a corporation. These situations may be ignored, however.

[2] Throughout the analysis the existence of corporate and personal income taxes will be ignored, but in Chapter 10 the consequences of these taxes for the theory will be examined.

[3] The quick ratio is the ratio of cash, government bonds, and accounts receivable to current liabilities.

For this corporation the dividend in any future period is certain, and it will simply be

$$D_t = (1 - b)Y_t \tag{4.1}$$

If the income per share during $t = 0$ was Y_0, the income in the next period will be

$$Y_1 = Y_0 + rbY_0 = Y_0(1 + rb) \tag{4.2}$$

In words, the fraction b of Y_0 has been retained and invested during $t = 0$. Income in $t = 1$ therefore will be Y_0 plus rbY_0, the amount provided by a return of r on bY_0. From the mathematics of compound interest it follows that

$$Y_t = Y_0(1 + rb)^t$$
$$= Y_0 e^{rbt} \tag{4.3}$$

if growth takes place continuously. The product rb is the rate at which earnings will grow, and from Eq. (4.1) it is also the rate at which the dividend will grow.

The stream of receipts a stockholder in this corporation will receive on a share is the dividend. Hence, if k is the rate of return required on the dividend, $D_t, t = 1 \to \infty$, the value of the share at the end of $t = 0$ is

$$P_0 = \int_0^\infty D_t e^{-kt} dt \tag{4.4}$$

From Eqs. (4.1) and (4.3) we can rewrite Eq. (4.4) as follows:

$$P_0 = \int_0^\infty (1 - b) Y_0 e^{rbt} e^{-kt} dt$$
$$= (1 - b) Y_0 \int_0^\infty e^{-t(k-rb)} dt \tag{4.5}$$

The condition for carrying out the integration is that $k > rb$. Since this is the condition for the price of the share to be finite, we may presume it is satisfied.

Carrying out the integration we find that

$$P_0 = \frac{(1 - b)Y_0}{k - rb} \tag{4.6}$$

Eq. (4.6) is a stock valuation model.[4] It states that the price of a

---

[4] The history of this expression is of some interest. In a number of articles, Durand [1959, 1957b] has noted that Eq. (4.6) is a standard actuarial formula. However, the actuarial literature has no reference to the economic content contained in the above derivation of the formula (cf. Todhunter [1937, pp. 48–49]). To this writer's knowledge, the first approach to the valuation of a common share along the above

share is its current dividend divided by the amount that the rate of profit investors require on a share exceeds the rate of growth in the dividend. Eq. (4.6) is also an investment model on the assumption that the objective of the firm is to maximize its share price. By assumption, retention is the only source of funds to finance investment, and the value of b given Y_0, r, and k that maximizes P_0 is the optimum annual rate of investment.

4.2 The Rate of Return and Retention Rates

Of the four assumptions made in arriving at Eq. (4.6), the first two, that the firm engages in no outside debt or equity financing, will be withdrawn in later chapters. Keeping them for the present will facilitate examining the questions we must consider on the relation among dividends, earnings, and price.

The assumptions that a corporation *will* earn a return on investment of r and retain a fraction of income b in every future period are clearly untenable in building a theory the purpose of which is to deal with an uncertain world. An investor cannot know r and b. However, if future dividends are what he is buying in a share, he cannot make an intelligent investment decision without estimating r and b, or estimating data that can be represented by Y_0, r, and b. Therefore, r and b are estimates of what the corporation will earn and retain in each future period. The usefulness of the theory will depend in large measure on the accuracy with which we can arrive at the numerical values of r and b investors obtain from historical data.

It should be noted that r and b are not dated, which reflects the assumption that investors estimate the same value of each for every future period. This is a simplifying assumption supported by a number of considerations. First, the model would become unmanageable empirically if different values in each future period were allowed for r and for b. Second, investors rarely have clear if any kind of notions as to how r and b will change over time. Third, positive support for assuming that b is expected to remain the same indefinitely is the fact

lines is due to J. B. Williams [1938]. However, he could not accept the expectation of constant values for b and particularly r, and he did not get as far as Eq. (4.6). His model became unmanageably involved, and it was abandoned in his empirical work on the valuation of a share of stock. The first statement of Eq. (4.6) as a stock value model and the first examination of its theoretical implications was contained in Gordon and Shapiro [1956], and empirical uses of the model were first explored in Gordon [1959].

that corporations quite commonly follow a policy of paying a stable fraction of their normal earnings in dividends.[5] Fourth, in the absence of information to the contrary, the assumption that r is expected to be the same in every future period seems to be reasonable and free of bias. Information to the contrary may at times exist, but investors will only have a broad idea as to the extent and timing of the change in r, and it is not clear how such expectations may be represented. Chapter 7 will go into the theoretical basis for estimating r and the modification of the model to recognize the possibility that investors expect r to change. For the present, we will proceed on the assumption that investors expect r and b to be the same in every future period.

Of course, the assumption that at any point in time investor estimates of r and b are constants does not prevent a corporation from changing b, and it does not preclude the possibility that r changes over time. Furthermore, the value of r estimated by investors may be a function of a corporation's investment. It should also be noted that the use of Eq. (4.6) does not require that investors go through the thought process implied in its development or even make the calculation indicated. Eq. (4.6) reduces to the statement that the price investors put on a share is the current dividend divided by the dividend yield, $d = k - br$, they require on the share. Investors may arrive at d by any consideration of the share's quality and the expected rate of growth in the dividend, requiring a smaller yield the more favorable the values of these two variables. All the model requires is correspondence between k and br as we observe them and what investors consider in reaching judgments on the quality of a share and the growth of its dividend.

4.3 The Optimum Investment and Retention Rate

To review the argument leading up to Eq. (4.6), we began with the plausible assumption that the value of a share is its expected future dividends discounted at the rate of profit required on the expectation. We then showed that under the assumptions (1) the corporation engages in no outside financing, and (2) it is expected to earn r on investment and retain the fraction b of its income, the entire dividend expectation may be represented by $Y_0(1 - b)$, its cur-

[5] Most textbooks on corporation finance contain a chapter on dividend policy which provides normative statements on dividend policy that support this view. E.g., see Guthman and Dougall [1948, pp. 507–29]. Some empirical findings on the subject are contained in Lintner's work [1956].

rent value, and rb, its rate of growth. We saw further that the value of a share is equal to

$$P_0 = \frac{(1 - b)Y_0}{k - rb} \tag{4.6}$$

It would seem possible to estimate the values of Y_0, r, and b from the history of a corporation, and alternative measurement rules for doing this will be examined in the empirical part of this book. However, how one finds k, the rate of profit investors require on the share, is not immediately evident. This question will be taken up in the next section.

Given k as well as the other variables, Eq. (4.6) may be used not only to find the value of a share but also to find the investment (equal retention) rate that maximizes the value. Assuming that r and k as well as Y_0 are independent of b, we take the derivative of P_0 with respect to b and obtain

$$\frac{\partial P}{\partial b} = \frac{Y_0}{(k - rb)^2} (r - k) \tag{4.7}$$

The first conclusion to note, one that will be recalled in the next chapter, is that price is independent of the retention rate when $r = k$. If $r > k$, price increases with the investment rate, and if $r < k$, price falls as the retention rate increases.

No one would find any disagreement between these conclusions and the neoclassical theory on the subject as stated for instance by Modigliani and Miller [1958]. A point worth noting is that the question they considered was whether or not a particular investment has a rate of profit above k. Their argument was that share price will rise, fall, or remain unchanged, depending on whether the investment's rate of profit is above, below, or equal to k. Considering only a single investment, they could only state what the change in price would be. To predict the current level of a share's price, the profitability of all future investments must be considered, since future dividends depend on future investments. Every stock price model contains—by design or default—a prediction of future investment and its profitability.

A moment's reflection on the conclusion just reached with respect to the variation in share price with b, reveals that a corporation should retain all of its income or liquidate, depending on whether $r \gtrless k$. There is of course an easy way out of this implausible conclusion. It may be argued that the assumption, r is independent of b, conflicts with highly plausible economic laws, and that we should consider r a function of b. Specifically, r is the average rate of return on net investment in a period when the investment is the fraction b of income in the period. The terms $\partial r/\partial b$ and r' will refer respec-

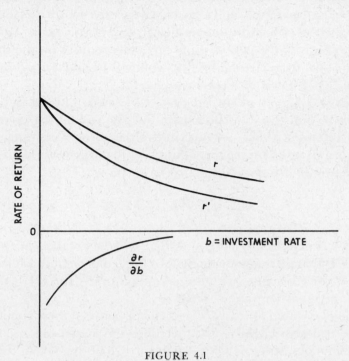

FIGURE 4.1

tively to the change in the average return with b and the return on the incremental investment. Under the assumption that investment opportunities are perfectly divisible, r' falls continuously, and r, which is an average of the r' up to b, falls less rapidly. $\partial r/\partial b$ is, of course, always negative since r is falling. The relation among r, $\partial r/\partial b$, and r' is illustrated in Figure 4.1.[6]

Keeping the assumption that k is independent of b, the variation in price with retention rate with r, a function of b, is

[6] The curves r' and r asymptotically approach a limit on the assumption that a corporation at the worst can buy securities in other corporations to earn some positive rate of return.

$$\frac{dP}{db} = \frac{Y}{(k-rb)^2}\left[-k + rb - (1-b)\left(-r - b\frac{\partial r}{\partial b}\right)\right]$$

$$= \frac{Y}{(k-rb)^2}\left[r - k + b(1-b)\frac{\partial r}{\partial b}\right] \tag{4.8}$$

There is some finite b at which P is maximized in this model. If $r > k$ when $b = 0$, dP/db is positive at $b = 0$. However, as b rises, r falls and the absolute value of b $(1 - b)$ $\partial r/\partial b$, which is negative, rises. Hence, there is some finite b at which $dP/db = 0$ and P is maximized.[7] If $r < k$ at $b = 0$, P is maximized by a negative net but possibly positive gross investment.

All this is very good if k is known and independent of b. The function r is of b may presumably be obtained by a corporation from internally available data. However, not only do we have the problem of observing k, but it may possibly vary with b, in which case the function must also be established.

4.4 An Empirical Adaptation of the Model

For the theory of valuation and investment developed in the preceding pages to be of any practical use, some means for establishing k, a corporation's cost of capital, must be found. Solving Eq. (4.6) for k, we obtain

$$k = \frac{(1-b)Y_0}{P_0} + br = d + br \tag{4.9}$$

where d is the dividend yield at which a share is selling. In other words, the rate of profit investors require on a share is equal to the dividend yield at which it is selling plus the rate of growth in the dividend.

This tells us nothing directly since we want k to predict P_0, and d assumes P_0 is known. However, it is evident from Eq. (4.9) that the assumption k is independent of b, and r implies that as b changes, d must fall in a one-to-one ratio with the increase in br. If the assumption that k is independent of both b and r is true, we may estimate it as follows. Obtain a sample of corporations all of which have the same k, e.g., they all come from the same industry and have the same degree of risk, and compute d and br for each corporation. The value

---

[7] Bodenhorn [1959, p. 487] has noted that when P is maximized, the return on the incremental investment is less than k. Gordon and Shapiro [1956] speculated, incorrectly it turns out, that when P is maximized, $r' = k$.

of k computed from Eq. (4.9) for each corporation should be the same.

They will not be the same, but it can be argued that the firms in an industry may differ in risk. To test the proposition allowing for differences in risk among the corporations, consider the expression

$$d = \alpha_0 - \alpha_2 \, br + \alpha_i u \qquad (4.10)$$

where u refers to whatever risk variables might appropriately be included in the model. Reflection on Eqs. (4.9) and (4.10) reveals that if k is independent of b and r, $\alpha_0 + \alpha_i u$ is an estimate of k for a corporation with uncertainty u, *and we would expect to find* $\alpha_2 = 1$.[8] However, we can be sure that if this investigation were undertaken, α_2 would prove to be significantly less than one. The more we consider Eqs. (4.6) and (4.10), the more suspect is the estimate of k provided by the latter and the more suspect is the assumption that k is independent of br. For instance, it implies that for a corporation with a sufficiently high growth rate d would be negative, and the price of its stock would go through infinity.

It may be argued that $br > k$ is a condition for a finite stock price due to the restrictive financing assumptions underlying our model. An extraordinarily high value of r is necessary for $br > k$, but contrary to our assumption, investors are unlikely to expect a corporation to have a very high r indefinitely. Further, if r is very high, the corporation should at least bring its marginal value down by undertaking outside financing. On the other hand, there are corporations that are expected to earn a high return on investment for a very long time (forever is not necessary since the future is discounted); many of them do not engage in outside financing; and their shares still sell at finite prices.

An alternative explanation for why shares sell at finite prices that is very attractive on empirical grounds is the hypothesis that the required rate of profit is an increasing function of the rate of growth in the dividend. Common sense, as well as the mathematics of our model, suggests that as br increases, the required dividend yield on a share should fall—not in a one-to-one ratio, but by decreasing amounts, so that d asymptotically approaches zero. In other words, d

[8] The coefficient of br is identified as α_2 and not α_1, because α_1 is reserved for another variable in the regression equation finally adopted. The coefficients of variables will not be consecutively numbered in each equation in order to have the same coefficient number associated with a variable throughout the book.

should fall with br as illustrated by the curve in Figure 4–2 and not the straight line.

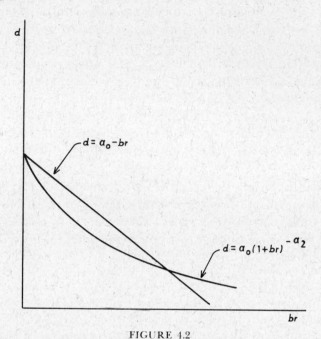

FIGURE 4.2

VARIATION IN DIVIDEND YIELD WITH RATE
OF GROWTH IN DIVIDEND

An expression that satisfies this requirement is

$$d = \alpha_0(1 + br)^{-\alpha_2} \tag{4.11}$$

In this expression the fall in d as br increases is not equal to the increase in br but to the percentage $\alpha_2/(1 + br)$ of the dividend yield. The only restriction on α_2 is that it is positive.

With the dividend yield the function of br just established,

$$k = \alpha_0(1 + br)^{-\alpha_2} + br \tag{4.12}$$

Substituting this expression for k in Eq. (4.6) we have

$$P_0 = \frac{Y_0(1 - b)}{\alpha_0(1 + br)^{-\alpha_2} + br - br}$$

$$= \alpha_0^{-1}Y_0(1 - b)(1 + br)^{\alpha_2} \tag{4.13}$$

The interpretation of this expression is quite straightforward. When $b = 0$, $br = 0$ also, and α_0 is the rate of profit investors require. Y_0 is the current dividend, no growth is expected, and price is the multiple α_0^{-1} of Y_0.[9] The value of α_0 may be expected to vary among corporations with their growth-free risk. As b increases, the current dividend falls to $Y_0(1 - b)$, and the factor by which it is multiplied rises to $\alpha_0^{-1}(1 + br)^{\alpha_2}$.

The quantity $(1 + br)^{\alpha_2}$ plays a dual role. It represents the increase in the value of the share due to the fact that the dividend is expected to grow at the rate br, and it represents the influence of the variation in k with br on the valuation of the growth. More simply, just as α_0 may be looked on as the investor valuation of a share without growth, α_2 may be looked on as the value the market places on growth.[10]

Notwithstanding the empirical attractiveness of Eq. (4.12), its theoretical justification is not obvious and its implications are contrary to widely accepted doctrines in the area. It implies that the variation in a corporation's cost of capital with the rate of growth in its dividend is

$$\frac{\partial k}{\partial br} = 1 - \frac{\alpha_2 \alpha_0}{(1 + br)^{\alpha_2 + 1}} \qquad (4.14)$$

The variation in k with br depends on the values of α_2 and α_0. Possible values are $\alpha_2 = 12$ and $\alpha_0 = .08$. Hence at $br = 0$ the second term on the right side of Eq. (4.14) may be greater than one, and for a short interval after $b = 0$ it is possible to have k falling; but as br rises, $\partial k / \partial br$ becomes positive and remains so. It also may be seen that the larger α_2, the price investors are willing to pay for growth, the smaller the increase in k with br.

Although Eq. (4.14) implies that a corporation's cost of capital is an increasing function of the rate of growth in its dividend, it does not imply that price varies inversely with the rate of growth. It is evident from Eq. (4.13) that share price increases with br and that it increases with r given b. The statement does imply that P may rise or fall with b. That is, with r given, the price of a share varies, depending on the corporation's dividend rate.

The theoretical rationale of the hypothesis that k is an increasing function of br will be discussed in the next chapter. If the hy-

[9] If, for example, $a_0 = .06$, then $a_0^{-1} = 16.67$.

[10] If investors who value current dividends highly dominate the market, a_2 will be small; and if investors who are looking for price appreciation, i.e., dividend growth, dominate the market, a_2 will be large.

pothesis is true, it yields in Eq. (4.13) a very nice combined valuation and investment model. The equation may be differentiated with respect to b to find the investment rate that maximizes the price of a share. If r is independent of b, we have

$$\frac{\partial P}{\partial b} = -\alpha_0 Y_0 (1 + br)^{\alpha_2} + \alpha_0 Y_0 (1 - b)\alpha_2 r(1 + br)^{\alpha_2-1} \quad (4.15)$$

The value of b that satisfies $\partial P/\partial b = 0$ is

$$b = \frac{\alpha_2}{\alpha_2 + 1} - \frac{1}{r(\alpha_2 + 1)} \quad (4.16)$$

The plausible result is that the optimum investment rate increases both with r and with α_2. If r is a function of b, substituting the function for r yields a solution with similar economic characteristics.

To summarize, we began with the assumption that investors buy a share for its dividend expectation, and the valuation of this expectation depends on the rate of profit required on it. On the assumption that a corporation relies only on internal financing, we saw that its dividend expectation may be represented by its current dividend and its rate of growth. In fact, the price of a share is given by the functional relation among the four variables Y_0, b, r, and k described in Eq. (4.6).

The only variable that cannot be estimated directly from the history of a corporation is k. However, the hypothesis that k is a function of br seemed plausible, and the parameters of the function may be estimated from sample data on the assumption that all corporations have the same degree of growth-free risk.

The resultant model, Eq. (4.13), yields the price of a share given the corporate variables Y_0, b, and r and given the market valuation parameters α_0 and α_2. The model may also be used to find the investment rate that maximizes the value of a share.

The following chapter deals with the interrelated (it will be seen) questions: (1) Does the investor buy dividends or earnings? (2) Does the rate of profit he requires increase with the rate of growth in the dividend? Subsequent chapters will withdraw the assumptions that corporations engage only in internal financing and that they all have the same degree of growth-free risk.

Chapter 5

DIVIDENDS, EARNINGS, AND SHARE PRICES

A question that has been of considerable interest to security analysts, whose task it is to establish the price at which a stock should sell, is the relative importance of dividends and earnings in the valuation of a share by the market. A number of economists, however, have argued that the issue between dividends and earnings is a nonsense question. They maintain that a rational investor should only consider a corporation's earnings in valuing a share. If they are right, the model developed in the preceding chapter, particularly in the form of Eq. (4.13), has no theoretical basis, since it is based on the assumption that the dividend is what investors buy.

5.1 Statement of the Question

Before undertaking a theoretical examination of the issue, it should be noted that there is considerable agreement between our model and the thinking of security analysts. The dividend hypothesis implies that investors are interested in both the dividend and earnings. The latter may be looked on as an index of the rate of growth in the dividend, since the retention rate varies with earnings given the dividend. It may also be surmised that the expected return on investment varies with earnings, everything else being the same. Therefore, the dividend hypothesis provides a theoretical rationale for the practice of looking at dividends and earnings in valuing a share. We saw further that the relative importance of dividends and earnings is a question of the relative magnitude of the dividend and growth coefficients, α_0 and α_2, in Eq. (4.13). If investors value growth highly, α_2 will be large and the price of a share will be sensitive to the variation in earnings given the dividend. A low valuation of growth im-

55

plies that the variation in price among shares will be accounted for predominantly by variation in the dividend among them.[1]

One of the most difficult tasks in resolving the issue between dividends and earnings is a meaningful statement of the issue, and this will be our first concern. It will be shown that advocates of the earnings hypothesis cannot correctly maintain that the valuation of a share on the basis of its dividend expectation is incorrect. All they can argue is that doing so is unnecessary and it may lead to incorrect inferences. The issue between the two hypotheses reduces to a question of whether k, the rate of profit investors use in valuing a dividend expectation, is a constant or is an increasing function of br, the expected rate of growth in the dividend.

The task in proving the validity of Eq. (4.13) on a theoretical level is the demonstration that k is an increasing function of br. The argument to be employed may be outlined as follows. First, it will be shown that the uncertainty of a dividend in a dividend expectation over the indefinite future increases with the time of the dividend in the future. Second, it will be shown that if the first proposition is true, the rate at which each dividend in the expectation is discounted *may* increase with its time in the future. Note that the second proposition does not automatically follow from the first; its correctness is a question of fact. Finally, if the first two propositions are true, it will be shown to follow automatically that k is an average of the rates at which the elements of a dividend expectation are discounted, and this average increases with the rate of growth in the series.

If this last proposition is correct, Eq. (4.13) is ideally suited for the task of explaining the variation in price among shares. If the proposition is not true, Eq. (4.13) is at best a useful empirical device that must be used with care to avoid misleading theoretical implications.

5.2 The Earnings Hypothesis

A crude formulation of the earnings hypothesis is that the price of a share at any point in time, say the end of $t = 0$, is $P_0 = Y_0/k$. Y_0 is the current earnings per share, and k is given by the risk at-

---

[1] In explaining their pragmatic approach to share valuation, security analysts frequently associate the earnings coefficient with interest in growth and the dividend coefficient with interest in the current dividend. E.g., see Graham and Dodd [1951, pp. 454–63].

tributes of the share. The theoretical rationale of the model is that Y_0 is the amount the share is expected to earn in perpetuity and k is the rate of profit investors require on the share. Numerous statistical investigations, including one by this writer [1959], have demonstrated that this theory is incorrect in the sense that k will vary among shares, depending on the fraction of Y_0 paid in dividends. In the paper that presented their theory of the valuation and investment of a corporation, Modigliani and Miller set aside this evidence with the statement, ". . . There is no simple way of disentangling the true effect of dividend payments on stock prices from their apparent effect . . ." [1958, p. 173]. They had no doubts as to the true effect, because in their model, "based as it is on rational behavior by investors, dividends per se play no role" [1958, p. 173].

Nonetheless, Modigliani and Miller did not long remain satisfied with Eq. (5.1) as a stock price valuation model. It requires the assumption that the corporation will not invest in subsequent periods or every investment it is expected to make will earn a rate of return exactly equal to k. If the corporation is expected to invest at a return in excess of k, the quasi rents provided by each investment add to the future income per share for the present shareholder without additional investment on his part, and the additional future income raises the present value of a share.

In a reply to Durand's comment on their paper, Modigliani and Miller [1959] presented a stock price model that recognized growth in the earning stream in the valuation of a share based on future earnings. A paper by Bodenhorn [1959] made the same point somewhat more simply, and the following will take advantage of his argument. Let k, the rate at which a corporation's expected earnings are discounted to arrive at their present value, also be the rate of profit at which new capital may be obtained by the sale of stock. That is, if I_t dollars are obtained from the issue of stock during t, the number of shares issued will be such that the new stockholders can expect to earn or receive earnings per share equivalent to $I_t k$ per period in perpetuity.[2] Let r_t be the return the corporation is expected to earn on the investment of I_t, and Y_0 be the earnings per share the corporation is expected to earn indefinitely if the firm's assets at the end of $t = 0$ are not increased by investment. The value of the share is

---

[2] We will not question here the assumption that the rate of profit at which new shares can be issued is independent of the volume of issues.

$$P_0 = \frac{Y_0}{k} + \frac{I_0(r_0 - k)/k}{(1 + k)^1} + \frac{I_1(r_1 - k)/k}{(1 + k)^2} + \frac{I_2(r_2 - k)/k}{(1 + k)^3}$$

$$+ \cdots + \frac{I_n(r_n - k)/k}{(1 + k)^{n+1}} + \cdots \quad (5.1)$$

The first term on the right-hand side is the value of the share if the corporation is not expected to grow. Each succeeding term is the value of the quasi rent on the investment during the indicated period discounted back to the end of $t = 0$.[3]

To elaborate on the meaning of these terms, at the end of $t = n$ the corporation is expected to invest I_n, and I_n will provide an income of $I_n r_n$ per period for every subsequent period. In order to obtain the money for I_n, the new shareholders must be given the right to $I_n k$ per period. Therefore, $I_n (r_n - k)/k$ is the capitalized value at the end of $t = n$ of the net increase in earnings per share for the existing shareholders. Dividing by $(1 + k)^n$ discounts the capitalized value of $I_n (r_n - k)$ per period starting at the end of $t = n$ to its value at the end of $t = 0$. The firm will set I_t in each period so as to maximize the discounted value of the quasi rents. This, it may be shown, will be the value of I_t that equates r'_t, the return on the marginal investment, with k, assuming that k is a constant.

Each term in Eq. (5.1), Y_0/k and the $I_n(r_n - k)/k$, may be expanded into its series. In the case of Y_0/k, it is

$$\frac{Y_0}{k} = \frac{Y_0}{1 + k} + \frac{Y_0}{(1 + k)^2} + \cdots + \frac{Y_0}{(1 + k)^n} + \cdots$$

and in the case of $I_n (r_n - k)/k$ we have

$$\frac{I_n(r_n - k)/k}{(1 + k)^n} = \frac{I_n(r_n - k)}{(1 + k)^{n+1}} + \frac{I_n(r_n - k)}{(1 + k)^{n+2}} + \cdots$$

$$+ \frac{I_n(r_n - k)}{(1 + k)^{n+x}} + \cdots \quad (5.2)$$

Doing so and collecting terms, Eq. (5.1)

$$P = \frac{Y_0 + I_0(r_0 - k)}{(1 + k)^1} + \frac{Y_0 + I_0(r_0 - k) + I_1(r_1 - k)}{(1 + k)^2} + \cdots$$

$$+ \frac{Y_0 + \sum_{t=0}^{n-1} I_t(r_t - k)}{(1 + k)^n} + \cdots \quad (5.3)$$

[3] $I_t (r_t - k)$ is called a quasi rent since it arises from the organization ability, consumer goodwill, and other assets of the corporation that create the expectation it will be able to invest to earn a higher return than the going rate of profit required on its stock.

The numerator of each term on the right-hand side is the income expected in the period indicated by the power of the denominator. It is evident from inspection of Eq. (5.3) that a corporation's cost of capital may differ from Y_0/P_0. Y_0/P_0 will be below k by an amount that depends on the amount by which the r_t exceeds k and on the expected investment of the corporation in the future.

5.3   Equivalence of the Two Theories

The important point with respect to Eq. (5.3) for our purposes is that since all investment is financed by stock issues, all income is paid in dividends, and each term is also the dividend in the period. What now if the investment in every period is financed internally?[4] The income in $t = 1$ is Y_1, and the dividend is $Y_1 - I_1$. In $t = 2$ the income is Y_1 plus the return on I_1, or r_1I_1. The dividend is $Y_1 + r_1I_1 - I_2$. In general, the dividend during $t = n$ is

$$Y_n = Y_0 + \sum_{t=0}^{n-1} r_t I_t - I_n \tag{5.4}$$

and the income is this quantity without deducting I_n.

As Bodenhorn observed, to take the corporation's income per share as the investor's income is an obvious case of double counting. He cannot receive both the retained earnings of a period and the subsequent profits on the investment of the earnings. Hence, the investor's valuation of the share is

$$P_0 = \frac{Y_0 + r_0I_0 - I_1}{1 + k} + \frac{Y_0 + r_0I_0 - I_1 + r_1I_1 - I_2}{(1 + k)^2} + \cdots$$

$$+ \frac{Y_0 + \sum_{t=0}^{n-1} r_t I_t - I_n}{(1 + k)^n} + \cdots \tag{5.5}$$

Here as in Eq. (5.3) the numerator of each term on the right side is the dividend expected in the period.

It is readily seen that if k is the same in Eqs. (5.3) and (5.5), P_0 has the same value in both.[5] That is, P_0 is independent of the method

[4] Internal financing in practice limits I_t to Y_t, but for the theoretical problem under consideration, we can allow $I_t > Y_t$ with the difference assessed on the stockholders.

[5] Actually, Eq. (5.5) is greater than Eq. (5.3) by I_0, the earnings during $t = 0$ invested at the end of the period. If we had looked at the two shares before the dividend declaration at the end of $t = 0$, the dividend expectation provided by the two shares would be identical.

of financing the investment. By external financing, the stockholder gets $I_n(r_n - k)$ in each subsequent period as a consequence of I_n and gives up nothing to obtain the $I_n(r_n - k)$. By internal financing, he gives up I_n at the end of n and gets $I_n r_n$ in each subsequent period. $I_n r_n = I_n(r_n - k) + I_n k$. $I_n k$ per period in perpetuity has a present value of I_n. Hence, under both methods of financing, the net gain to the stockholder is $I_n(r_n - k)$, and value of the share is increased by the present value of $I_n(r_n - k)$ in perpetuity.

One further observation. If the optimum investment in every period is the fraction b of Y_t, and if the return r_t on this level of investment is equal to r, Eq. (5.5) becomes

$$P_0 = \frac{Y_0(1 + br)(1 - b)}{1 + k} + \frac{Y_0(1 + br)^2(1 - b)}{(1 + k)^2} + \cdots$$
$$+ \frac{Y_0(1 + br)^n(1 - b)}{(1 + k)^n} + \cdots \quad (5.6)$$

If the reinvestment takes place continuously,

$$P_0 = \int_0^\infty (1 - b)Y_0 e^{brt} e^{-kt} dt \quad (4.5)$$

Therefore, under the same assumptions with respect to return on investment and its level, Eq. (5.5) is identical with the stock valuation model derived from the dividend hypothesis in the preceding chapter.[6]

What are the conclusions to be drawn from the above analysis? First, regardless of whether we start from the earnings or dividend hypothesis, the model we get can be meaningfully interpreted only if the investor's expected future income per share is taken as the dividend. The earnings may be discounted to arrive at the share's present value only in the special case when it is equal to the dividend. Second, it would appear that although the investor buys the dividend, he is indifferent to the time distribution of the dividend, i.e., the dividend rate. To elaborate, assume a given dividend rate and a given expected investment in each future period, the difference between investment and retention being financed by stock sales. The dividend in each

[6] It was noted on page 50 that the optimum retention rate in each period is beyond the investment where $r_t = k$. It now can be seen that the optimum is at $r_t = k$ if r_t is independent of the investment in prior periods. The investment should be carried beyond the point $r_t = k$, if the optimum r_t is a function of the investment rate and not simply the current investment. The economic interpretation of this conclusion is that investment now generates investment opportunities in the future, and investment now should be undertaken in part to create these future opportunities. Cf. Bodenhorn [1959].

period may be changed by any amount desired without changing the price of the stock, as long as the investment is kept unchanged in each period by compensating changes in the firm's stock financing.

The earnings hypothesis would seem to have carried the day on the important question of the existence of an optimum dividend rate. We can speak of an optimum dividend rate only when retention is synonymous with investment, but this is misleading since the variation in price is with the investment and not the dividend. This is evident in the special case when $r = k$. In this event, price is independent of investment, and it is also independent of the dividend. Reducing the dividend by I_n in period n denies the stockholder I_n but adds rI_n to his dividend in every subsequent period. Since

$$I_n = \int_n^\infty rI_n e^{-kt} dt \qquad (5.7)$$

when $r = k$, the investor is indifferent to this change in the time structure of his dividend.[7]

All of the above is true if, and only if, one assumption on which the analysis proceeded is true, i.e., k is independent of the time pattern of the dividend. Bodenhorn, Modigliani and Miller, and others have constructed elaborate models for the purpose of demonstrating that a share's price is independent of the expected future dividend without appearing to recognize that they are assuming away the fundamental problem. To prove the hypothesis, it must be shown theoretically and/or empirically that the rate at which the dividend expectation is discounted remains unchanged when, for example, a near dividend is reduced and future dividends are increased by reinvestment. Without this assumption the operations performed earlier are impossible. Conversely, to prove the dividend hypothesis, it must be shown that k is an increasing function of br.

The issue is further illustrated in Figure 5.1. Given a corporation's current earnings per share and a return on investment of r at all investment rates, the alternative possible dividend expectations provided by a share on the assumption of no outside financing appear in Figure 5.1. If the retention rate is zero, the expectation is Y_0 in every period. As b rises, the initial dividend falls and the rate of growth in the dividend rises. Let k be the discount rate when $b = 0$, and let $r = k$ for all values of b. This simply neutralizes the

---

[7] This is the same conclusion that we reached on page 48. When $r = k$, price is independent of b.

rate of profit on investment. If investors value each alternative on the basis of the same discount rate, $k = r$, the dividend hypothesis is incorrect. P_0 is independent of b. On the other hand, if k is an increasing function of the rate of growth in the dividend, the alternatives represented in Figure 5.1 have different values. Eq. (4.13) is then a theoretically correct and useful model for explaining the variation in price among internally financed companies. Further,

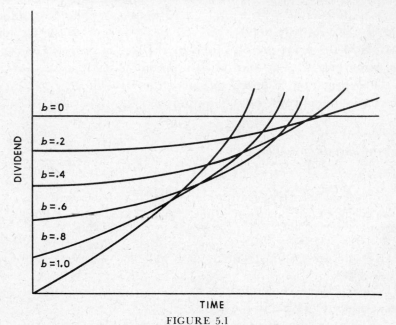

FIGURE 5.1

VARIATION IN DIVIDEND EXPECTATION WITH RETENTION RATE

the optimum investment is not independent of its financing for a company that has more than one source of funds.

5.4 The Uncertainty of a Dividend

We have seen that under all circumstances the only income stream that the investor can meaningfully use in valuing a share is the dividend expectation. At the same time, we saw that if the discount rate is given, the valuation of a share is independent of the dividend in the sense that the optimum investment and the price of a share is independent of the distribution of its financing between retention and new stock issues. We cannot be sure, however, that k is a constant for a corporation regardless of the time pattern of its dividend.

The single k at which a dividend expectation D_t, $t = 1 \rightarrow \infty$ is discounted may be looked on as an average of the k_t, $t = 1 \rightarrow \infty$, the value of k_t depending on the uncertainty of D_t. What can we say about the uncertainty of D_t as t goes from one to infinity?

Let the dividend during n be a random variable D_n with an expected value of $\overline{D}_n$. A plausible pair of assumptions is that: (1) $\overline{D}_n = D_{n-1}(1 + g_{n-1})$; and (2) the variance of $D_n - D_{n-1}(1 + g_{n-1})$ is independent of n and equal to σ^2, say. The first assumption is that the dividend expected for a period is the dividend realized in the prior period raised by the rate of growth realized in the prior period. The second assumption states that the variance of the expectation is independent of the level of D_{n-1}. It can be shown that under these two assumptions

$$\overline{D}_n = D_0(1 + g_0)^n \tag{5.8}$$

and the variance of D_n is

$$\sigma_n^2 = \sigma^2 n (1 + g_0)^{2n} \tag{5.9}$$

A measure of the risk of a dividend that is independent of its scale is the coefficient of variation. The coefficient of variation of D_n is

$$u_n = \frac{\sigma_n}{\overline{D}_n} = \frac{\sigma \sqrt{n}(1 + g_0)^n}{D_0(1 + g_0)^n} = \frac{\sigma \sqrt{n}}{D_0} \tag{5.10}$$

Therefore, under the conditions stated, the uncertainty of a dividend increases with its time in the future.

There are other plausible assumptions with respect to how investors form expectations of future dividends under which $\overline{D}_n$ and σ_n would differ from the above values. In particular, the entire prior history of the dividend rather than D_0 and g_0 alone may be used to arrive at $\overline{D}_n$ and σ_n^2. However, these assumptions are most unlikely to yield results that differ materially from the one just obtained, that the uncertainty of a dividend increases with its time in the future. What implication does the proposition that $u_t > u_{t-1}$ for all t have for the rate at which a dividend is discounted?

5.5 The Rate at Which a Dividend Is Discounted

The process by which an investor arrives at the present value of an expected future payment may be represented by one of two methods. Under the "certain equivalent" method, he takes the expected value of the dividend, converts it to its certain equivalent, and discounts it at the pure rate of interest. If the certain equivalent of an uncertain payment is a function of the dispersion of its distribution, the present value of $\overline{D}_n$ is

$$PV_n = \overline{D}_n f(u_n)(1 + i)^{-n} \tag{5.11}$$

In the above, multiplication by $f(u_n)$ converts $\overline{D}_n$ to its certain equivalent and i is the pure rate of interest.

Under the other method for representing the investor's valuation of $\overline{D}_n$, call it the "cost-of-capital method," the investor simply discounts $\overline{D}_n$ at a rate k_n that reflects its risk. That is, k_n is some function of u_n. It is evident there is some value for k_n such that

$$PV_n = \overline{D}_n(1 + k_n)^{-n} \tag{5.12}$$

There is no a priori basis for saying that one method is superior to the other. Statements obtained by one method may be obtained by the other. We may only find that in a particular problem one is more convenient to use than the other. For instance, it would have been extremely difficult to develop the argument of Chapter 4 under the certain equivalent method.

We now examine the relation between k_n and k_{n+1} for a dividend expectation with $\overline{D}_n = D_0 (1 + g_0)^n$. Let

$$PV_n = \frac{D_0(1 + g_0)^n f(u_n)}{(1 + i)^n} = \frac{D_0(1 + g_0)^n}{(1 + k_n)^n} \tag{5.13}$$

and let

$$PV_{n+1} = \frac{D_0(1 + g_0)^{n+1} f(u_{n+1})}{(1 + i)^{n+1}} = \frac{D_0(1 + g_0)^{n+1}}{(1 + k_{n+1})^{n+1}}$$

Dividing PV_n by PV_{n+1} and simplifying, we obtain

$$\frac{f(u_n)(1 + i)}{f(u_{n+1})} = \frac{(1 + k_{n+1})^{n+1}}{(1 + k_n)^n} \tag{5.14}$$

Since investors are presumed to have an aversion to risk, the more uncertain the payment the smaller a percentage of it is its certain equivalent. Hence, with $u_n < u_{n+1}$, we have $f(u_n) > f(u_{n+1})$ and we can say that

$$1 < \frac{f(u_n)}{f(u_{n+1})} = \frac{(1 + k_{n+1})^{n+1}}{(1 + k_n)^n(1 + i)} \tag{5.15}$$

The above expression is very interesting.

Let $f(u_n)$, $f(u_{n+1})$, k_n, and i have given values subject to the economic conditions that $f(u_n) > f(u_{n+1})$ and $k_n > i$. It can be seen that k_{n+1} may be less than, equal to, or greater than k_n. We cannot deductively prove anything with respect to the relation between k_{n+1} and k_n. However, it is most unlikely that they should turn out to be equal, and the proposition $k_{n+1} < k_n$ is more suspect than its opposite.

The variation in k_t with t is a question of empirical fact. It depends on how rapidly u increases with t and on the investor's aversion to risk function. If the uncertainty of a dividend increases slowly with its time in the future and if the certain equivalence function is

$$f(u_t) = \frac{1}{\lambda_0 u_t^{\lambda_1}} \tag{5.16}$$

with λ_1 small, k_t will fall as t rises. On the other hand, if u_t rises rapidly with t and λ_1 is large, then k_t will rise with t.

5.6 The Cost of Capital and the Rate of Growth in the Dividend

It will now be shown that if k_t is an increasing function of t, the single rate commonly used to discount an entire dividend series is an increasing function of the rate of growth in the series. As long as there is no growth expected in a dividend and it is an infinite series, nothing is lost by being oblivious of the fact that the single k at which the whole series is discounted is an average of the k_t. However, this is not true if the dividend is expected to grow, and the problem is to value a share under alternative assumptions with respect to its growth rate or the distribution of D_t over time.

Let x designate a share for which the dividend is expected to grow at the rate g_x. At the end of $t = 0$ the expected value of the dividend in $t = n$ is $\overline{D} = D_0(1 + g_x)^n$, and the value of the share at $t = 0$ is

$$P_x = D_0 \left[\frac{1 + g_x}{1 + k_1} + \frac{(1 + g_x)^2}{(1 + k_2)^2} + \cdots + \frac{(1 + g_x)^n}{(1 + k_n)^n} + \cdots \right] \tag{5.17}$$

There is some average of the k_t, $\overline{k}_x$ such that

$$P_x = D_0 \sum_{t=1}^{\infty} \frac{(1 + g_x)^t}{(1 + \overline{k}_x)^t} \tag{5.18}$$

Let y designate another share, a share with the same initial dividend as x, but the dividend on y is expected to grow at the rate g_y with $g_y > g_x$. The two shares have the same degree of risk or relative dispersion in that $\overline{D}_{n,x}$ and $\overline{D}_{n,y}$ are both discounted at the same rate k_n. Let discounting the series $\overline{D}_{t,y}$, $t = 1 \rightarrow \infty$ at the same rates k_t, $t = 1 \rightarrow \infty$ used to discount $\overline{D}_{t,x}$ result in a value P_y. There is some average of the k_t, $\overline{k}_y$ that satisfies

$$P_y = D_0 \sum_{t=1}^{\infty} \frac{(1 + g_y)^t}{(1 + \overline{k}_y)^t} \tag{5.19}$$

It is evident that $P_y > P_x$, but it is also true that $\overline{k}_y > \overline{k}_x$. Both $\overline{k}_y$ and $\overline{k}_x$ are weighted averages of the same set of k_t, but with $g_y > g_x$, the weights of $\overline{k}_y$ are relatively greater for the more distant larger k_t than those of $\overline{k}_x$. The consequence is that for any firm with a given degree of risk for its operations, i.e., a given set of k_t, the rate at which its dividend expectation is discounted will increase with the rate of growth in its dividend. A mathematically more rigorous proof of this statement has been presented by R. Gangolli and Gordon [1961].

The conclusions reached in this chapter may be summarized as follows. There is no choice between earnings and dividends as the variable an investor takes as his expected future income for a share of stock. Only in the special case where earnings are equal to dividends may the former be used. It is nonetheless possible though unlikely that the price of a share is independent of the fraction of earnings the corporation pays in dividends. It is unlikely because the necessary condition is that the corporation's cost of capital be independent of the dividend rate. A corporation's retention rate and rate of growth in its dividend move together, and its cost of capital may rise or fall with the rate of growth in its dividend. The larger the increase in the uncertainty of a dividend with its time in the future and the larger the aversion to risk on the part of investors, the more likely it is that the cost of capital will increase with the growth in the dividend.

The stock price model developed in the preceding chapter incorporates the assumption that a corporation's cost of capital increases with the rate of growth in its dividend. The assumption cannot be proven true or false by deductive argument, but it would not be the least bit surprising to find that the empirical evidence agrees with it. We are, therefore, justified in exploring the usefulness of a stock price model that reflects this assumption.

Chapter 6

THE ALLOWANCE FOR RISK

The stock price model developed in Chapter 4 provides the value of a corporation's stock and the investment that maximizes its value under restrictive assumptions with respect to the corporation's expected financing policy. These assumptions will be in part relaxed in later chapters. However, with or without these financing assumptions, the use of the model requires numerical estimates of its cost-of-capital parameters, and the estimates from sample data with the model as it now stands imply that all corporations in the sample have the same degree of risk. That is, any two shares with the same dividend expectation, current value, and expected rate of growth should sell at the same price. On the contrary, it is widely accepted that two such shares may differ in risk and the riskier one should sell at a lower price. In other words, given its dividend expectation a corporation's cost of capital should vary with the uncertainty of the expectation. The purpose of this chapter is to establish and introduce into the model the variables other than the rate of growth in the dividend with which a corporation's cost of capital may be expected to vary.

Widespread acceptance of the proposition that a corporation's cost of capital varies with the uncertainty of its dividend or of its earnings expectation has been due more to the intuitive appeal of the proposition than to empirical evidence. Typical practice has been to account for risk by including in the stock price model one or more variables, with an index of earnings instability and the debt-equity ratio prominent among them, but the variables prove to have little influence on share price. At best the variation in share price with the variables is not material, and quite often the correlation is not significant or opposite in sign to that indicated by theory.[1]

[1] Some observations on why the debt-equity ratio behaves as poorly as it does are provided by Benishay [1960] and Usher [1960].

67

The disappointing results are due in no small part to the inherent difficulty of measuring the uncertainty investors attach to the future dividends of a corporation. However, the unsatisfactory results may also be due in some part to the *ad hoc* and crude manner in which the risk variables are empirically defined and included in the model. Our purpose in what follows is to arrive at a definition of a dividend expectation's uncertainty that is operational and has some theoretical content. Specifically, alternative definitions of an expectation's uncertainty will be posed, and they will be compared by reference to their performance in measuring the difference in risk among corporations under hypothetical situations considered relevant. The end result will be a definition sensitive, it is believed, to what investors consider in differentiating dividend uncertainty among corporations.

The propositions we will take as primitive are the following. A future payment may be looked on as a probability distribution with subjectively known mean and standard deviation. The standard deviation is looked on as an index of the expectation's uncertainty, and the attractiveness of a payment with a given mean is a decreasing function of its uncertainty.

6.1 The Single-Period Investment

As a start let us consider the definition of uncertainty for the simplest possible case—a firm that makes a single-period investment and liquidates at the end of the period. Assume four firms, F_1 to F_4, each with the initial net worth in the form of cash shown in the W row of Table 6.1. The expectation each firm obtains is a receipt R_a with a probability of .5 and R_b with a probability of .5. $\overline{R}$ is the expected value of the receipt. Y_a, Y_b, and $\overline{Y}$ are the comparable income figures, each being obtained from the indicated receipt by deducting W.

One measure of uncertainty is U_1, the standard deviation of the receipt or of the income, both being the same since the standard deviation of a distribution is unchanged by subtracting a constant from each possible event. Comparison of firms F_1 and F_2 illustrates the inadvisability of using U_1. The two firms differ only by a scale factor, but U_1 makes F_2 appear to be twice as risky as F_1.

An alternative definition $U_2 = \sigma/\overline{Y}$ is satisfactory on the above count, since $\overline{Y}$ serves as a scale variable to deflate σ. However, U_2 poses a problem when the firm F_3 is considered. F_3 has the same dispersion as F_1, but it is twice as profitable. The consequence is that U_2 is half as large for F_3 as for F_1. Similarly, F_4 is twice as profitable and twice as risky as F_1, but U_2 is the same for both firms. Using $\overline{Y}$ as a deflator makes the risk of a firm sensitive to its income or profitability.

We want a risk index to be insensitive to the profitability of the investment. Insofar as a higher income makes one expectation more attractive than another, this may be and usually is separately recognized through the inclusion of an income variable in the valuation of an expectation.

The use of $U_3 = \sigma/\overline{R}$ with the expected receipt as a deflator considerably reduces the sensitivity. The risk of F_3 is only slightly

TABLE 6.1

RISK POSITION OF ALTERNATIVE
SINGLE-PERIOD INVESTMENT FIRMS

Item	F_1	F_2	F_3	F_4
W = net worth...........	100	200	100	100
R_a = a receipt............	80	160	90	60
R_b = a receipt............	140	280	150	180
$\overline{R}$ = mean receipt.........	110	220	120	120
Y_a = an income...........	−20	−40	−10	−40
Y_b = an income...........	40	80	50	80
$\overline{Y}$ = mean income........	10	20	20	20
$U_1 = \sigma_R = \sigma_Y$	30	60	30	60
$U_2 = \sigma/\overline{Y}$...............	3.0	3.0	1.5	3.0
$U_3 = \sigma/\overline{R}$...............	.273	.273	.250	.500
$U_4 = \sigma/W$...............	.3	.3	.3	.6

below that of F_1, and for F_4 it is only slightly less than twice as large. With $U_4 = \sigma/W$ the investment is the deflator, and the risk index is completely insensitive to profitability. F_1 and F_2, which differ only by a scale factor, have the same risk index. F_3 with the same risk per unit of investment has the same risk value, and F_4 with twice the dispersion has a risk value twice that of F_1.

The conclusion suggested by these comparative situations is that U_4, the standard deviation of the receipt divided by the investment, is the best index of relative risk.

6.2 An Infinite Life Investment

The extreme opposite of a single-period firm is one with an investment that has an infinite life. The firm's receipts are obtained from the employment of the asset and not its sale, and the asset is not subject to depreciation.[2] In this case, the income and the receipt during a period are the same. Let the income during each period be a random variable Y_t with expected value $\overline{Y}_t$. Further, let $\overline{Y}_1 = \overline{Y}_2 = \cdots = \overline{Y}_t$, and let σ be the standard deviation of Y_1. We could take $U = \sigma/W$ as the uncertainty of the investment. Is this comparable with the $U_4 = \sigma/W$ established earlier for the single-period firm?

The comparability problem is due to the fact that $U = \sigma/W$ is based on the uncertainty of one receipt, the first in a series that extends indefinitely in time, while $U_4 = \sigma/W$ refers to the firm's position at the end of one period. A means of achieving comparability is to establish for the firm with an infinite life asset an index of uncertainty of position at the end of one period. What will be the net worth of the firm if it liquidates at the end of one period?

To answer this question let us assume that at the end of the first period the expected value of the income in each subsequent period $\overline{Y}_t$, $t = 2, 3, \ldots$, becomes equal to Y_1, the income realized during the period. Also the standard deviation of Y_2 remains equal to σ, the value for Y_1 at the start of the period.[3] Further, the reciprocal of the rate at which an earnings expectation with a one-period standard deviation of σ is capitalized by the market, $\nu = W/\overline{Y}_1$, is not expected to change. Under these assumptions, the firm's net worth at the end of one period will be $Y_1(1 + \nu)$, the income realized during the period plus ν times the income.[4] The variance of the receipt expectation, i.e., the net worth at the end of one period, is

$$\frac{\Sigma[Y_1(1 + \nu) - \overline{Y}_1(1 + \nu)]}{n} \tag{6.1}$$

The standard deviation of the net worth is

$$\sigma_W = \sigma(1 + \nu) \tag{6.2}$$

and a definition of uncertainty analogous to U_4 is

$$U = \frac{\sigma(1 + \nu)}{W} \tag{6.3}$$

[2] To make the situation concrete, let the asset be a stand of timber on which the government decides the cut each year with the objective of preventing any depletion of the natural resource. The owner allows a merchant to come in and make the government-allowed cutting at an agreed-upon price per ton of logs obtained. The merchant holds the logs one period for some reason and then sells them to pulp mills. He has no operating costs and is the single-period firm discussed earlier.

[3] When the text indicates t refers to a period in the future, Y_t is a random variable with a known frequency distribution. When t refers to a past period Y_t is the value actually realized.

[4] The order of magnitude of ν is about ten.

Therefore, under the assumptions stated, two firms, both with σ the one-period standard deviation of earnings, will differ in risk by a factor of $1 + \nu$ if one has an infinite life asset and the other a single-period asset.

The qualitative nature of the result seems plausible, but what may be questioned about Eq. (6.3) is the assumption that $\overline{Y}_t = Y_1$ as of the end of the first period. The opposite assumption is that $\overline{Y}_t = \overline{Y}_1$ regardless of the realized value of Y_1. Under this assumption the firm's net worth at the end of the period will be $Y_1 + \nu\overline{Y}_1$, and it is evident that $\sigma_W = \sigma$. Hence,

$$U = \frac{\sigma}{W} \tag{6.4}$$

It is plausible to believe that at the end of the first period $\overline{Y}_t$ will be some average of $\overline{Y}_1$ and Y_1. Hence, a reasonable compromise between Eqs. (6.3) and (6.4) is

$$U = \frac{\sigma(1 + \beta\nu)}{W} \tag{6.5}$$

β is a smoothing constant between zero and one that reflects the weighting of $\overline{Y}_1$ and Y_1 in arriving at $\overline{Y}_t$ as of the end of the first period.

We have just demonstrated that with the level and variability of income the same, a firm with a single-period asset has a smaller U than one with an infinite life asset. The economic rationale is that a firm with a single-period asset may change the employment of its capital if the current employment becomes unprofitable. Income on a single-period asset is defined as being net of capital recovery. Hence, if the investment of W_0 with the expectation of earning $\overline{Y}_1$ proves to be less profitable than expected, the firm takes $W_1 = W_0$ out of the operation and employes it elsewhere. By contrast, a firm with an infinite life asset has its technology fixed. If $Y_1 = R_1$ proves to be less than $\overline{Y}_1$, the firm cannot take $W_0 = \nu\overline{Y}_1$ out of the operation. The value of the asset will change from $\nu\overline{Y}_1$ to $\nu\overline{Y}_2$, with $\overline{Y}_2 \neq Y_1$ possible.

It may be argued that the results obtained were due to a difference in the definition of income on the two types of assets. Income on the infinite life asset was defined to exclude changes in the asset's value, i.e., changes in the assets expected future income. On the other hand, income on the single-period asset included capital gains and losses. In fact, income on the asset with one-period life is the change in its value. If capital gains and losses were accorded the same treatment in measuring the income on the two investments, they would be equally risky with the same σ for both.[5] However, the definitions used are correct because an estimate of σ for each firm derived from its historical data would be based on the definitions used and not on comparable definitions of income for the two firms.

6.3 A Simple Stock Price Model

The definition of uncertainty just established does not even begin to recognize all the dimensions of the variable, but it is desirable to pause and consider its use in the valuation of a share. For this it will be necessary to assume a universe of corporations for which the definition may be considered adequate.

Specifically, it will be assumed that corporations pay all income out in dividends, and given their initial stock financing, they engage in no further outside financing. It follows that if $\overline{Y}_1$ is the expected dividend in the first period, $\overline{Y}_t$, $t = 2, 3, \ldots$ are equal to $\overline{Y}_1$. It will be assumed further the corporation generates $\overline{Y}_t$ per share by means of an asset with an infinite life. A stock price model for a corporation with these properties is

$$P = \frac{\overline{Y}_1}{k} \tag{6.6}$$

The relative uncertainty of $\overline{Y}_t$ determines k, and using Eq. (6.5) we can write Eq. (6.6) as

$$P = \frac{\overline{Y}_1}{\alpha_0(1 + U)^{\alpha_3}} \tag{6.7}$$

α_0 is the rate of interest on a risk-free security, and k increases with U. The increase is by decreasing, constant, or increasing amounts, depending on whether α_3 is less than, equal to, or greater than one.

The definition of U established in the previous section would seem relevant for the valuation of a share in a corporation of the type described. Some may argue that in putting a value on the corporation as a whole, it does not seem appropriate to take as its risk the possible variation in its sale price one period in the future. The mar-

---

[5] E.g., the income on the single-period investment could be made comparable by defining it to include only the income on storage, etc., and to exclude the change in the market price of the commodity for other reasons.

ket for corporations is highly imperfect, and what they can be sold for rarely enters into a stockholder's calculations. However, the market for corporate shares is not imperfect, and a shareholder might reasonably use the one-period variation in a share's price as an index of its risk. Further, under the conditions stated, the yield at which a share sold might vary with earnings instability in the manner described.

However, looking more closely at the definition of $U = \sigma(1 + \beta v)/W$, problems in its implementation come to mind. It is difficult but conceptually possible to obtain an estimate of σ, but the same is not true of the other variables. In the definition of U, W is the market price (equal to cost) of a share. With U, we find k, and with k, we find P, the subjective value placed on the share by an investor. Our valuation model, however, defines P as the share's price and seeks only to explain or arrive at this quantity. We cannot use a share's price as an independent variable in a model the purpose of which is to predict a share's price. Reflection on the attributes of W that made it useful as a deflator in measuring uncertainty suggest that defining it as the book value per share may be satisfactory.

It will be recalled that v is the reciprocal of a corporation's cost of capital, and our definition of U takes it as known in arriving at k, which in this context is the subjective rate of profit an investor requires. Our valuation model does not treat k as a known independent variable. In fact, the determination of P is the same problem as the determination of k. The difficulty with respect to v is that a substitute for k is not as easily obtained as was the case with W. It may also be noted that β is not readily observed.

A course of action that leaves much to be desired, but which may be the only practical way out, is to drop βv from the definition of U. The resultant stock price model is

$$P = \frac{\bar{Y}_1}{\alpha_0(1 + \sigma/W)^{\alpha_3}} \tag{6.8}$$

The definition of U in Eq. (6.8) would be seriously in error if it were used to explain the valuation of a variety of assets, shares, commodities, etc., since βv can be expected to vary independently of σ among assets. However, we are concerned only with the valuation of common stocks. It is possible that βv is correlated with σ among shares, in which case dropping the term may not cause serious error.

6.4 Multiple Asset Firms

A share of stock has an infinite life, but the assets of a firm which generate the share's income rarely if ever consist of either a single-period or infinite life asset. Real firms have a complex of operating assets that range in lives from inventory with a single-period life to land with an infinite life. Included are machinery and buildings with lives that typically range from three to fifty years. Further, this entire complex of assets must be treated as a single entity in that the inventory, for example, cannot be liquidated without regard for the firm as a whole.

It seems reasonable to believe that the ability of a firm to change the technology and employment of its capital depends on its liquidity. That is, the shorter the expected lives of a firm's depreciable assets and the larger the fraction of inventory in the total, the more rapidly are the assets converted to liquid form and shifted to a new employment in response to a decline in profitability in their old employment. It would follow that with σ given, the earnings instability of a stock of operating assets is smaller the greater the flexibility of the stock. Further, the risk of a share should also vary inversely with the liquidity of the firm's assets.

This conclusion is supported by the fact that in arriving at a judgment as to the riskiness of a corporation, investment analysts look at the corporation's balance sheet structure, including the characteristics and relative amounts of its operating assets, as well as the instability of its earnings. Therefore, both deductive reasoning and observation of business practice support the hypothesis that these two pieces of information—operating asset characteristics and instability of earnings—are not alternative indexes of a firm's risk. They are more or less independent elements of risk, and some combination of the two should enter the measurement of a corporation's risk.

The first problem posed by the above conclusion is establishing a measurement definition of the liquidity or flexibility of a corporation's operating assets. An objective and correct definition is not immediately evident, but an arbitrary one based on informed judgment seems preferable to ignoring the influence of the variable. A corporation's operating asset liquidity index is defined as

$$\pi = \frac{7INV + 5OOA + 3PE}{5(INV + OOA + PE)} \tag{6.9}$$

In the above, INV = inventory, PE = plant and equipment net of depreciation, and OOA = other operating assets such as deferred charges and investments in other companies. The last are relatively small, and they typically fall between inventory and depreciable assets in liquidity.

A number of refinements could be introduced in the definition of π. For instance, the inventory coefficient could be a function of the product's demand elasticity, and the plant and equipment coefficient could be a function of the average depreciable life of the assets. These refinements will not be undertaken here, however.

The next task we face is to decide on the functional form of the relation between π and k. The most efficient and elegant course of action would be to redefine U to recognize its variation with π. For instance, we might define $U = (\sigma/W)\,\pi$. However, both σ/W and π are arbitrary indexes, and we have no a priori reason to believe that the scale of each will be consistent with taking their product as the risk variable. The safer alternative is to define a corporation's cost of capital as

$$k = \alpha_0\left(1 + \frac{\sigma}{W}\right)^{\alpha_3}(\pi)^{\alpha_5} \qquad (6.10)$$

In this form the variation in k with each variable is completely left to the data for determination.

6.5 Debt Financing: Some Simple Cases

A most interesting, important, and challenging problem in dealing with risk is the recognition of trading on the equity by the firm. In Chapter 8 our model will be enlarged to recognize debt financing on the part of a corporation. Part of the problem, however, the variation in k with trading on the equity, will be introduced here.

Let us begin with the single-period investment discussed earlier. Table 6.2 reproduces the data of Table 6.1 for the firms F_1 and F_2 and presents data for two new firms, F_5 and F_6. They each have a net worth of \$100, the same as F_1, but F_5 borrows \$100 at 4 per cent and invests \$200, while F_6 lends \$50 at 4 per cent and invests only \$50. All four firms invest in the same type of asset, and the receipt figures for F_5 and F_6 are after interest and principal received or paid.

The scale problem rules out the use of U_1. U_2 varies among the firms in a manner we would expect, since F_5 has a larger value and

F_6 a smaller value than F_1. However, the differences among them are due only to the fact that the interest rate is positive. With a zero rate of interest, U_2 would be the same for all three firms. In other words, with income the deflator, the firm's risk increases only with the requirement of the interest on its debt. The requirement that the much larger principle on the debt must be paid is completely ignored. The use of the receipt as the deflator corrects this. $U_3 = \sigma/\bar{R}$ varies over a wider range among the firms. However, U_3 as before is sensitive to the profitability of the investment. Raising the rate of

TABLE 6.2

RISK POSITION WITH TRADING ON THE EQUITY

Item	F_1	F_2	F_5	F_6
W = net worth............	100	200	100	100
R_a = a net receipt........	80	160	56	92
R_b = a net receipt........	140	280	176	122
$\bar{R}$ = mean net receipt.....	110	220	116	107
Y_a = an income..........	-20	-40	-44	-8
Y_b = an income..........	40	80	76	22
$\bar{Y}$ = mean income........	10	20	16	7
$U_1 = \sigma_R = \sigma_Y$	30	60	60	15
$U_2 = \sigma/\bar{Y}$...............	3.0	3.0	3.75	2.14
$U_3 = \sigma/\bar{R}$...............	.273	.273	.511	.140
$U_4 = \sigma/W$...............	.3	.3	.6	.15

interest and reducing the expected receipt net of interest raises the risk of the firm.

The definition of risk found best before, $U_4 = \sigma/W$, also works best here. F_5 with twice the debt of F_1 has twice the risk, and F_6 with half the debt has half the risk. These results are intuitively reasonable.[6] Our conclusion can be generalized as follows. If a firm's debt-equity ratio is $h = L/W$, the value of its uncertainty index is

$$U_4 = (\sigma/W)(1 + h) \qquad (6.11)$$

Turning now to the risk on an investment with an infinite life, let a firm with a net worth of W_0 borrow an amount equal to the fraction h of W_0 at an interest rate i. The firm invests the sum $W_0(1 + h)$ in an asset that will yield a receipt (or income) per period with an expected value of $\bar{Y}$ and a standard deviation of σ. We will let $\check{Y}$ and $\check{\sigma}$ refer to the values of the variables when $h = 0$,

---

[6] It could be argued that risk should increase somewhat with the rate of interest on the debt, but I believe it can be shown that this is not true. In any event the undesirable consequences of a higher interest rate are recognized in the income variable.

and the firm's investment is equal to W_0. As before it will be assumed that v, the ratio of W to $\check{Y}$, is not expected to change. Finally, it will be assumed that the firm's return on investment and the interest rate it pays are independent of the scale of its investment.

Under the conditions assumed, the expected value of the firm's net worth one period hence is

$$\overline{W}_1 = \overline{Y}(1 + v)(1 + h) - W_0 h(1 + i) \qquad (6.12)$$

The variance of W_1 is

$$\sigma^2(W) = \frac{\Sigma\left([\check{Y}(1 + v)(1 + h) - W_0 h(1 + i)] - [\overline{Y}(1 + v)(1 + h) - W_0 h(1 + i)]\right)^2}{n} \qquad (6.13)$$

Since $\check{Y}$ and $\check{Y}$ are both multiplied by the constant $(1 + v)(1 + h)$, the constant may be taken outside of the summation sign. The quantity $W_0 h(1 + i)$ may be dropped altogether since it is subtracted from both the $\overline{Y}$ and $\check{Y}$ terms. Hence,

$$\sigma^2(W) = \left[\frac{\Sigma(\check{Y} - \overline{Y})^2}{n}\right][(1 + v)(1 + h)]^2 = [\check{\sigma}(1 + v)(1 + h)]^2 \qquad (6.14)$$

The standard deviation of the firm's net worth one period hence is simply the square root of the above expression. It will be recalled that multiplying $\check{\sigma}$ by $1 + v$ assumes that the variability in net worth is proportional to the variability in one period income. In arriving at Eq. (6.5) we made the more realistic assumption that there will be some damping, and v was multiplied by the smoothing constant β. Using that constant again,

$$U = \frac{\check{\sigma}(1 + \beta v)(1 + h)}{W} \qquad (6.15)$$

is an uncertainty index for a firm with an infinite life asset and a debt-equity ratio of h.

6.6 Implications for the Required Rate of Return

The interesting feature of the result obtained in the previous section is that the recognition of trading on the equity resulted in a redefinition of U. It did not require the recognition of an additional variable in the definition of k. The latter becomes

$$k = \alpha_0[1 + \check{\sigma}(1 + \beta v)(1 + h)/W]^{\alpha_3} \qquad (6.16)$$

However, one may question the confidence that can be placed in this result.

Our deductive argument makes U a linear function of h. In contrast, it is argued in some financial circles that risk increases by increasing amounts with the debt-equity ratio. The reason frequently given is that the risk of insolvency increases more than proportionately with a firm's leverage. The conflict between our model and business judgment may be due to our assumption that the risk of an expectation may be represented by its standard deviation. σ is a linear function of h, but higher moments of a probability distribution may be nonlinear functions of h, and these higher moments may be more sensitive to the probability of insolvency.

The waters become even more muddied when we consider the relation between k and h implicit in Eq. (6.16). The coefficient of the variation in k with $1 + h$ is α_3, the same as the coefficient of the variation in k with $\breve{\sigma}(1 + \beta v)$. This may be true as the model stands and not be true when $1 + \beta v$ is dropped from U. The value of βv may vary among corporations. Hence, our definition of leverage-free risk at best has a scale error that will bias the estimated relation between k and leverage when Eq. (6.16) is used.

To pursue the thoughts on nonlinearity in the relation between k and leverage further, the frequency distribution of Y may be symmetrical about $\overline{Y}$ when $h = 0$ and skewed when $h \neq 0$. If that is true and if investors are concerned with the skewness as well as the variance of an expectation, k will not be independent of the combination of $\breve{\sigma}$ and $1 + h$ in the product $\breve{\sigma}(1 + h)$. Finally, we will see in a later chapter that theorems on the relation between k and h such as those advanced by Modigliani and Miller lead to still other functional relations among the variables.

The conclusion suggested by the above observations is that it may be advisable to treat $1 + h$ as a separate variable, the way π was treated, in the definition of k, and to let the data determine the relation between k and h.

As matters now stand, our definition of k for the valuation of a common stock that is expected to pay $\overline{Y}$ in perpetuity is

$$k = \alpha_0(1 + \breve{\sigma}/W)^{\alpha_3}(1 + h)^{\alpha_4}(\pi)^{\alpha_5} \tag{6.17}$$

For a corporation with an infinite life asset and a zero debt-equity ratio, an index of a share's earnings instability is $\breve{\sigma}/W$, the deflated one-period standard deviation of $\overline{Y}$, and k is simply an increasing function of $\check{\sigma}/W$. If the corporation has a complex of operating assets which vary in life, k is a decreasing function of π, an index of their average liquidity. Finally, k increases with the debt-equity ratio h employed to generate the expectation of $\overline{Y}$ per period.

A more efficient and elegant definition of k would define U as some combination of $\check{\sigma}/W$, π, and h, and would have k simply a function of U. Such a definition is theoretically possible as has been indicated in the preceding pages, but it is not practical without a more informed basis for combining the variables than we have been able to develop.

6.7 Debt Maturity

The above definition of k makes no reference to the maturity of a corporation's debt. It is widely accepted that the shorter the maturity of a firm's debt, the greater the risk associated with that debt. Notwithstanding the wide acceptance of this proposition as a practical matter, a demonstration of it will be useful.

Let a firm with a net worth of $100 borrow another $100 at 4 per cent interest and invest the $200 in an infinite life asset. The income on the asset in the first period before interest has an expected value of $20 on the basis of two equiprobable receipts of $13 and $27. The income in the second period has an expected value equal to the income realized in the first period and a standard deviation equal to that in the first period.

If the loan has a one-period maturity, the firm's net worth at the end of the period will be $170 or $30. That is, the asset will be sold for $270 or $130, depending on the outcome in the first period, and the $100 debt will be paid. If the loan has an infinite maturity, the income realized in the first period is the expected value of the income in each subsequent period.

It will now be shown that the firm's net worth at the end of one period has a greater variability under a one-period loan than an infinite maturity loan. If the $27 receipt is realized, and the loan has a one-period maturity, the $100 may be reborrowed at a lower rate of interest. The reason is that the creditor is more secure with an expected receipt per period of $27 covering his loan than with the receipt $20. On the other hand, if $13 is the receipt realized in the first period, the firm will be able to reborrow the $100 only at a much higher rate of interest, if at all. We see then that a one-period maturity makes a favorable outcome even better and an unfavorable outcome even worse than would be true with an infinite life maturity.

There is another way to look at the matter. The coefficients of variation of a firm's assets before debt and earnings before interest are the same. However, the interest rate at which a firm can borrow is below the rate of return it can expect to earn on investment. In consequence, the firm has a larger equity in its earnings than in its assets. On an infinite maturity debt the equity in earnings is relevant, whereas on a one-period maturity the equity in assets is relevant. With the equity in earnings larger than the equity in assets, its relative variability and risk is smaller.

It is reasonable to believe that the risk of a share in a corporation, as well as the corporation's risk, decreases as the maturity of the corporation's liabilities increase. The liabilities of a corporation vary over a wide range in maturity, and to include the variable in our definition of k, an index of a corporation's debt maturity must be established.

A firm's net debt is defined as

$$L = CL + ID + LD + LR + PS - CG - AR \qquad (6.18)$$

CL = current liabilities, ID = intermediate-term debt, LD = long-term debt, LR = liability reserves such as pension liabilities, PS = preferred stock, CG = cash and government bonds, and AR = accounts receivable. A firm's net debt which will also be referred to simply as debt is used in the definition of both debt maturity and the debt-equity ratio. The reason is that an increase in gross debt with a corresponding increase in monetary type assets involves considerably less risk than an increase in debt used to finance operating assets. As argued in Gordon [1960a], the consequence is to make net debt a superior measure of debt than gross debt.

A firm's net debt weighted to reflect the maturity of its liabilities is defined as

$$L' = CL + .8ID + .6LD + .5LR + .3PS - CG - .8AR \quad (6.19)$$

The maturity index for a firm is $\mu = (1 + L/W) / (1 + L'/W)$ so that μ increases with maturity.[7] The definition is arbitrary, and the arguments for and against it are similar to those involving π, a firm's operating asset liquidity.

[7] It is undesirable to have μ take a negative value. Since the lower limit of L/W and L'/W is minus one, the form of the definition avoids negative values for μ.

6.8   Retained Earnings and the Allowance for Risk

Up to this point it has been assumed that a corporation pays all of its earnings out in dividends. The fact that a corporation may retain some fraction of its income poses no problem. With a retention rate of b and a rate of return on investment of r, the initial dividend expectation is $(1 - b)\overline{Y}$, and br is the rate at which the dividend is expected to grow. The stock price model is

$$P = \frac{(1 - b)\overline{Y}(1 + br)^{\alpha_2}}{k} \tag{6.20}$$

with

$$k = \alpha_0(1 + \check{\sigma}/W)^{\alpha_3}(1 + h)^{\alpha_4}(\pi)^{\alpha_5}(\mu)^{\alpha_6} \tag{6.21}$$

When $b = 0$, the dividend and earnings are equal, the term in br disappears, and Eq. (6.20) is the same as Eq. (6.6), the valuation model developed earlier in this chapter. When $b > 0$, the current dividend is reduced, but P neither falls to $(1 - b)\overline{Y}/k$ nor remains $\overline{Y}/k$ with k unchanged. The dividend is expected to grow, and the influence of this on the value of the share is recognized by $(1 + br)^{\alpha_2}$. We saw in Chapter 5 that the risk of an expectation increases with its rate of growth. Accordingly, $(1 + br)^{\alpha_2}$ recognizes both (1) the increase in the value of a share due to a growth rate of br with the cost of capital given, and (2) the increase in the cost of capital due to the increased risk associated with a growth rate of br. Therefore, the risk associated with having the dividend differ from earnings has already been recognized.

In Chapter 4 we saw that the cost of capital on a share with a dividend rate of growth of br is

$$k = \frac{(1 - b)\overline{Y}}{P} + br$$

Using the expression for $(1 - b)\overline{Y}/P$ implicit in Eqs. (6.20) and (6.21),

$$k = \alpha_0(1 + \check{\sigma}/W)^{\alpha_3}(1 + h)^{\alpha_4}(\pi)^{\alpha_5}(\mu)^{\alpha_6}(1 + br)^{-\alpha_2} + br \tag{6.22}$$

When $b = 0$, k becomes equal to its value in Eq. (6.21).

6.9   Corporate Size

A lengthy and what may at times have seemed tedious argument was used to arrive at the recognition of investor uncertainty with respect to a share's dividend expectation reflected in Eq. (6.22). The objective was a theoretical basis for the variables included and the functional relation among them. This objective was not fully realized. There were gaps in the theory that could only be overcome by arbitrary but reasonable, it is hoped, assumptions. Even if the theory had been perfect, the empirical measurement problems leave the adequacy of a definition of risk open to question. This suggests that other variables which in prinicpal are irrelevant may in fact be used by investors to evaluate a corporation's risk, and they therefore should be included in a model designed to explain the variation in price among shares.

W. L. Crum [1934], among others, has shown that the stability of a corporation's earnings tends to increase with the size of the corporation. Insofar as this is true, it should be reflected in the value of σ for a corporation. However, if investors find it difficult to observe σ accurately, they may look at both σ and corporate size in evaluating a corporation's riskiness. There are other considerations supporting the inclusion of some index of corporate size among the independent variables. The market for a share in terms of its liquidity and investor interest may increase with the size of the corporation and have a favorable influence on the price. Therefore, our stock price model is

$$ P = \frac{(1 - b)\bar{Y}9(1 + br)^{\alpha_2}S^{\alpha_7}}{\alpha_0(1 + \breve{\sigma}/W)^{\alpha_3}(1 + h)^{\alpha_4}\pi^{\alpha_5}\mu^{\alpha_6}} \tag{6.23} $$

where S is an index of the corporation's size. The inclusion of S in the model is in recognition of the empirical limitations of the variables that in theory should make S redundant. Therefore, in certain theoretical discussions of the model, S will be excluded.

Chapter 7

INCOME CAPITAL AND
RATE OF RETURN

In the stock price model developed in Chapter 4, the dividend a corporation is expected to pay in each future period is given by Y_0, the corporation's current income, b, its retention rate, and r, its return on investment. This was made possible by the assumptions that at a point in time, call it the end of $t = 0$, b and r are expected to be the same in every future period, and the corporation is not expected to engage in outside financing. The outside financing assumption will be withdrawn in the next two chapters. A rationale of the retention rate assumption has already been presented. The assumption with respect to r, however, was acknowledged to be open to question, since r may be a function of the investment rate b, and even with the investment rate given, r may be expected to vary over time. The measurement of r from a theoretical point of view and the recognition of how it may be expected to vary with b and with time are a concern of this chapter.

The chapter will also be concerned with another related problem. In investigations such as the present one, it is not uncommon to costruct a theory on the basis of definitions considered valid from a theoretical point of view and then to proceed to empirical work that involves data reflecting accounting definitions of the variables. Accounting definitions of income, capital, rate of return, etc., are different than those of economic theory, and they are held in very low repute. The consequence is that relevance of the empirical work for the validity of theory and the usefulness of the theory for interpretation of the data are open to serious question. To avoid this state, we will construct definitions of our variables, particularly income, capital, and rate of return, that are consistent with the data of the variables that will be used later. Making explicit the definitions of these variables will serve the purpose stated earlier of establishing information on the behavior of r. It will also be of help in recognizing the relation of outside financing to the investment and valuation of a corporation.

Since the definition of income implicitly contains definitions of capital, rate of profit, and the other relevant variables, the discussion will be focused on the definition of income. The accepted definition under certainty will be reviewed, and possible extensions to an uncertain world will be presented. The resultant definitions prove to be of no practical value. Not only are they not observable, but they assume away the problem for which they are to be used rather than provide instruments for its investigation. We then turn to accounting theory and find that it provides a set of definitions for the variables, income capital, and rate of return that may be used to estimate a corporation's dividend expectation and meet the other needs of our theory.

With income and the related variables defined, the prediction of a corporation's return on investment is examined. A plausible functional relation between r and b is readily established, and it turns out that recognizing r is a function of b poses no problem for our theory. However, the theory requires that with the investment rate given, r is expected to be constant in successive periods of time. Although this may not be true, a plausible argument can be advanced in support of the hypothesis.

The data of our variables come from accounting practice and not accounting theory, and the rules of derivation we use in testing the theory must be objective. The consequence is that the values of Y_0 and r under our definitions may differ materially from investor estimates which are not subject to the same restrictions. The chapter closes with a discussion of the sources of differences between investor estimates of the variables and those we are forced to use.

7.1 Definition of Income under Certainty

An intuitively plausible definition of income is the amount a person can spend or a corporation can pay out in dividends during a period and be as well off at the end of the period as it was at the start. The measurement rules for implementing this definition of income have been well stated from a conceptual point of view by Hicks [1950] and other economists.

Briefly, the data assumed given for a firm at any point in time, say at the end of $t = 0$, are the future receipt stream $R_t, t = 1 \rightarrow \infty$ and a rate of interest i at which the firm can freely lend, borrow, and value its expectation. The firm's capital at the end of $t = 0$, W_0 is defined as the present value of $R_t, t = 1 \rightarrow \infty$ discounted at i. C_1, the depreciation in the capital during $t = 1$, is the amount by which W_0 exceeds the value that W_1 would have if R_1 is paid out in dividends. The firm's income in $t = 1$ is defined as

$$Y_1 = R_1 - C_1 \tag{7.1}$$

This definition satisfies the being-as-well-off requirement, since paying out Y_1 and reinvesting C_1 results in a capital stock at the end of the period, $W_1 = W_0$.

There is a more powerful sense in which paying out Y_1 will leave the person or firm as well off at the end as it was at the start of the period. It can be shown that if $R_t, t = 1 \rightarrow \infty$ has a present value W_0, and if i has the properties stated earlier, the firm is able to pay out $Y_1 = iW_0$ per period in perpetuity. Hence, if it actually pays out Y_1, during $t = 1$, the firm will continue to be able to pay out Y_1 per period in perpetuity.

The amount the firm actually does retain and invest will be $I_1 \gtrless C_1$. Then $W_1 = W_0 - C_1 + I_1$, and the "welloffness" of the firm at the end of $t = 1$ is W_1, or the ability to pay out $Y_2 = iW_1$ in perpetuity.

7.2 Definition of Income under Uncertainty

Few writers have gone very far in considering the problem of measuring income, capital, and rate of return under uncertainty, and those that have done so have not reached a consensus of opinion on the appropriate measurement rules.[1] The reasons for this become evident when we try to construct an uncertainty analogue to the measurement rules found satisfactory under certainty.

In this task we must become accustomed to dealing with "welloffness" as being an expectation with respect to future events and not a known set of future events. A person becomes more or less well off if he expects more or less in the future.

The essential feature of uncertainty is that with a given stock of assets the receipt expected in a future period will change with the

---

[1] The most ambitious discussion of the problems is contained in Alexander [1950].

passage of time. Hence $\overline{R}_{t,w,\tau}$ is the *receipt in period* t *on the capital stock at the end of* w *expected at the end of* τ. In other words, the receipt expected in some future period t depends on w, the capital stock that generates it, and τ, the time the expectation is held. At the end of $t = 0$, the firm expects to receive $\overline{R}_{t,0,0}$, $t = 1 \rightarrow \infty$, and discounted at the rate k_0, it expects to be able to pay a periodic dividend of $\overline{Y}_1 = k_0 W_0$ in perpetuity.[2]

We can if we wish define a firm's income in a period as being the amount it believes at the start of the period that it can pay out and be as well off at the end as at the start of the period. However, a definition of the income realized in a period that is independent of what actually takes place in the period does not seem right. Furthermore, this figure is not the amount the firm can pay out and actually be as well off at the end as it was at the beginning of a period. In general, R_1, the receipt actually realized during $t = 1$, will not be equal to $\overline{R}_{1,0,0}$. Also $k_1 \neq k_0$, and $\overline{R}_{t,0,1} \neq \overline{R}_{t,0,0}$. Hence, paying out $\overline{Y}_1$ and investing $\overline{C}_1$ will not realize $W_1 = W_0$.

An alternative approach is to define the income of a period as the amount a firm can pay out during $t = 1$ and actually be as well off at the end as at the start of the period. We look at R_1, $\overline{R}_{t,0,1}$, $t = 2 \rightarrow \infty$, and k_1, and with this information define $\overset{*}{C}_1$ as the investment during $t = 1$ that results in $W_1 = W_0$, where W_1 is $R_{t,1,1}$, $t = 2 \rightarrow \infty$ discounted at k_1. The income realized during $t = 1$ may be defined as $\overset{*}{Y}_1 = R_1 - \overset{*}{C}_1$.[3] It is evident that $\overset{*}{Y}_1 \gtrless \overline{Y}_1$. Nonetheless, the firm is as well off at the end as at the start of the period in the sense that $W_1 = W_0$.

However, "well off" may also be defined as the expectation of being able to spend $\overline{Y}_1 = k_0 W_0$ per period in perpetuity. $\overset{*}{Y}_1$ as defined above does not realize this. After paying out $\overset{*}{Y}_1$, a corporation expects to be able to pay out $\overline{Y}_2 = k_1 W_1 = k_0 W_0$ in perpetuity, but under uncertainty $k_1 \neq k_0$ is possible. With $k_1 \neq k_0$, the future dividend paying ability of the firm has changed. For $\overline{Y}_2 = \overline{Y}_1$, the dividend during $t = 1$ should be determined as follows. Given $\overline{R}_{t,0,1}$,

---

[2] $\overline{Y}_1$ is the income during $t = 1$ expected at the end of $t = 0$, while Y_1 is the income realized during $t = 1$. Under certainty the two are the same.

[3] Throughout this section Y_1 and C_1 refer to the values of the variables on the basis of information available at the start of the period, and $\overset{*}{Y}_1$ and $\overset{*}{C}_1$ reflect the information available at the end of the period.

$t = 2 \rightarrow \infty$, the depreciation and investment during $t = 1$ should realize

$$W_1 = \bar{Y}_1 / k_1 \tag{7.2}$$

It is evident that the retention and investment of $\overset{*}{C}_1$ so defined will result in $W_1 \gtreqless W_0$.

In the search for an analogue to the definition under certainty, we have developed three definitions for the income in a period when the future is uncertain. One is the dividend the firm believes at the start of the period that it can pay during the period and be as well off at the end as at the start of the period. The second definition is the dividend the firm can actually pay and have the same capital at the end as at the start of the period. The third is the dividend the firm can actually pay and have the same expectation as to the periodic future payment at the end as at the start of the period. We could go on to investigate the relative merits of the above three definitions. We will not, however, because the data provided by all three are not considered to be of any use in dealing with the problems that interest us in the definitions.

7.3 Problems Raised by Uncertainty

The contrast between the worlds of certainty and uncertainty is quite striking. We began with a general statement as to the definition of income that has considerable intuitive merit. For the world of certainty we then proceeded quickly and surely to a set of rules for the measurement of income, capital, and return on investment. By contrast with uncertainty the argument became highly involved, it was impossible to reach unique results, and worst of all the results obtained were based on untenable assumptions.

To realize the difficulties involved, consider what happens to a young man who goes into our uncertain world with an inheritance and the good intention of living on his income under any of the definitions stated in the previous section. He might be able to order his affairs so as to consume his income under the first definition—the amount he believes at the start of the period will leave him as well off at the end as at the start. Few would consider this a satisfactory implementation of his good intentions, since he might well be consuming his capital. Consuming his income under either of the other definitions would also pose some serious problems. For instance, under the second definition he consumes the amount that realizes $\overline{R}_{t,1,1}$, $t = 2 \to \infty$ discounted at k_1 equal to $\overline{R}_{t,0,0}$, $t = 1 \to \infty$ discounted at k_0. It is clear that in one year the resultant income may be so large that spending it would severely tax his sense of prudence and moderation, and in the following year his Spartan qualities could be presented with the challenge of living on a *negative* consumption.

The trials and tribulations of our virtuous young man may be dismissed as being merely the consequences of trying to follow an arbitrary decision rule. The usefulness of a definition for the realization of normative ends may be considered irrelevant to the definition's validity. However, we might wonder, is there any purpose in which these *definitions of income* are useful? Possibly a more serious objection is that the young man's or a corporation's ability to carry out the measurements necessary to obtain the data is open to serious question not only in fact but in theory as well.

What are the assumptions necessary for the measurement of income, capital, and return on investment under the above definitions. First, the firm is required to have an estimate of $R_{t,0,0}$, $t = 1 \to \infty$. Estimating the course of future events is a necessary condition for making economic decisions, and such estimates cannot in general be rejected on the grounds that the future is unknown. However, the requirement here is that a firm estimates its future receipts under the assumption that it undertakes no further net investment. We can be sure that a firm will not employ its existing stock of capital without making further investments, and estimating its future receipts under this assumption places a very unnatural demand on the firm.

The second assumption necessary for the employment of the definitions stated in the previous section is that the alternative investment opportunities available in a period and the receipt expectations associated with successive stocks in time all have the same degree of risk. In an uncertain world an element in the "welloffness" of a person or a corporation is the uncertainty of its receipt expectation. Therefore, it is not sufficient for the expenditure of $\overset{*}{Y}_1$ to realize either $W_1 = W_0$ or $\overline{Y}_2 = \overline{Y}_1$ for the corporation to be as well off at the end as at the start of the period. It is also necessary that the uncertainty of $\overline{R}_{t,0,1}$, $t = 2 \to \infty$ and of the incremental receipts due to the investment of $\overset{*}{C}_1$ to be equal to the uncertainty of $\overline{R}_{t,0,0}$, $t = 1 \to \infty$. In general, the above constancy of risk across investments and over time will not be realized. The problem is not peculiar to these measurement rules. Its solution requires a basis for converting an expectation with one level of risk to the equivalent amount for another level of risk. A line of attack for the solution of the problem has been suggested in Gordon and Gangolli [1961]. In what follows, however, we will assume that the problem is not quantitatively important.

The third assumption necessary for the definitions of the previous section was stated in developing them. It is that every investment available during a period is expected to earn the same rate of return. Obviously, if we take the investment opportunities available to a firm and find the discount rate that equates cost with the increment to the firm's receipts expected from each, the rate will vary among them. This fact can be reconciled with the assumption of a uniform rate of return equal to the required rate of return, but this reconciliation only reveals the most serious theoretical objection to the definitions.

It can be argued that if k_0 is the required rate of profit for the risk class in which the firm and its investment opportunities fall, no investment can be considered to have a higher rate of return than k_0. To the extent that the increments to the firm's receipts consequent on an investment exceed the amounts that provide a return of k_0, the excess represents quasi rents of the firm. For instance, consider a firm with mineral rights to a bare stretch of desert with a vast reservoir of oil below the surface. The considerable receipts from the sale of the oil should not, one can argue, be attributed to the oil field equipment necessary to remove it from the ground. Only the portion of the receipts needed to provide a fair return on the equipment should be attributed to the equipment. The balance represents the expected future receipts of the oil field in its virgin state, and these residual receipts discounted at the rate k_0 are the value of the field. They represent the $\overline{R}_{t,0,0}$, $t = 1 \to \infty$ and the W_0 stated earlier.

For certain purposes this statement is perfectly correct, e.g., for the purpose of arriving at a sale price for the oil field. For the purposes under consideration, however, it is quite worthless. We want to measure a firm's capital, the income on the capital, and the return on investment in order to obtain information that may be used in predicting its future income, financing, and investment. However, we are now told that $\overline{R}_{t,0,0}$ is obtained after first establishing the *optimum* investment in oil field equipment, deducting the cost of the investment from the resultant receipt expectation, and discounting the net expectation at the rate k_0. The very first step in measuring the firm's income during a period assumes that its investment and its cost of capital are already known. The only question that remains at issue, that may be answered with knowledge of the firm's income, is the financing of the investment. That is, how is the firm's income to be distributed between consumption and investment, and how much of the firm's investment which is already known is to be financed by borrowing?

What is really at issue in the definitions of the previous section is the assumption that there exists a discount rate k_0 with the properties ascribed to it. Let us examine a little more closely how the quantity W_0 is arrived at when quasi rents are imputed to the firm. Let the firm's stock literally provide the receipt expectation $\overline{R}_{t,0,0}$, $t = 1 \rightarrow \infty$. To this the receipt expectation on every investment opportunity in any future period that has a rate of return in excess of k_0 is added and the amount of the investment is deducted. The resultant net expectation is discounted at the rate k_0 to obtain W_0. We have just obtained the investment plan and the value of the firm at any point in time—and solved the problem to which this book is addressed. For this solution to be valid, however, the necessary condition is that investors in general can be expected to invest or disinvest in the firm to earn a return of k_0 on their investment regardless of the level and financing of the firm's investment. It has been and will be demonstrated further in the course of this book that a discount rate with these properties does not exist in an uncertain world. The attempt to make the transfer from a certain world where such a discount rate exists cannot survive exposure to the most elementary conditions that give substance to uncertainty.

7.4 A Cost-Oriented Basis of Measurement

We have met with failure in the attempt to devise rules for the measurement of income, capital, and return on investment in an uncertain world that are analogous to those found satisfactory for the world of certainty. The criterion we sought to satisfy was that the income in a period represented the amount a person or a firm could spend and be as well off at the end as at the start of the period. We found that the rules and assumptions needed to arrive at this income figure made its measurement extremely difficult. Further, we found that the figure is most unlikely to be a useful piece of information for expenditure and valuation decisions—a very important reason for wanting to know one's income. The definition of income assumes that the firm's cost of capital and its investment in operating assets over all future time, and its value, are independently known.

The purpose of this section is to present a set of rules for the measurement of income, capital, and return on investment that is free of the objections just raised to the previous rules. Let W_0, a firm's stock of capital at the end of $t = 0$, be historically given, meaning by this that the rules to be specified for arriving at W_1 were used to obtain W_0. Imagine the firm will annually invest an amount E_1. Given E_1 and $\overline{R}_1$, the estimated receipt on W_0 during $t = 1$, compute $\overline{Y}_1 = \overline{R}_1 - E_1$. Next, estimate $\overline{R}_2$ with the investment of E_1 added to the stock existing at the end of $t = 0$, and compute $\overline{Y}_2 = \overline{R}_2 - E_1$. Repeat these calculations for n, a large number of periods, and examine the $\overline{Y}_t$, $t = 1, 2, \cdots, n$. It is evident that if E_1 is "very small," the $\overline{Y}_t$ will fall as t increases. Similarly, if E_1 is "very large," the $\overline{Y}_t$ will rise. There is some value of E_1, designate it C_1, that will make the estimate of $\overline{Y}_t = \overline{R}_t - C_1$, $t = 1, 2, \cdots, n$, a constant.

C_1 is the depreciation during $t = 1$ on W_0, the capital stock existing at the end of $t = 0$. At that point in time $\overline{R}_1$ is the expected receipt and $\overline{Y}_1 = \overline{R}_1 - C_1$ is the expected income during $t = 1$. The actual receipt realized during $t = 1$ is R_1, and the actual income realized is defined as $Y_1 = R_1 - C_1$. The actual investment net of C_1 is I_1, and the capital stock at the end of $t = 1$ is $W_1 = W_0 + I_1$. Finally, the rate of return on the stock expected as of the end of $t = 0$ is $\overline{\eta}_1 = \overline{Y}_1/W_0$, and the rate of return realized during $t = 1$ is $\eta_1 = Y_1/W_0$. These definitions of the variables differ so little from accounting definitions that they may be looked on as such.

The above set of definitions for capital, income, and rate of return on capital may be questioned from a number of viewpoints. First, it may be argued that a periodic investment which satisfies the requirements of C_1 need not exist for a firm. For reasons that will become clear shortly, I do not consider this objection a serious one.

Second, it may be wondered how one arrives at C_1. This is a nice question that could be answered as follows. Investors buy and sell shares on the basis of their valuations of these shares, and if they act in the manner described by our theory, a difficult task they face is the estimation of C_1. The theory presumes that in the minds of investors a quantity that has the properties of C_1 exists, they estimate it, and there is a consensus of opinion among them as to its value for a share. Investors may go about the very difficult task of estimating C_1 in a variety of ways, and the need for advice on measurement rules in using the theory is reason for interest in how they do it. However, if the theory including the measurement rules explains the variation in price among shares, we may accept the presumptions stated above and the measurement rules used as true. We need not concern ourselves with how investors *really* go about estimating C_1. If the theory fails, which of the various presumptions entering into the theory was false is of interest only for the purpose of repairing the damage, i.e., modifying the theory, which includes the rules for measuring C_1.

However, data rarely give us a clear and simple yes or no answer to the question as to whether a theory is true. Hence, we also look at the intuitive merit of the argument on which the theory rests for information on its truth. This makes it desirable to consider how difficult it is for an investor or firm to estimate $\overline{Y}$, Y, W, $\overline{\eta}$, and η, and the uses to which he may put the data.

We saw earlier that under the definitions of neoclassical theory the firm knows the profitability of investment in each future period, *and it knows the investment that will be undertaken in each future period*. With this information the firm also knows $R_{t,0,0}$, $t = 1 \rightarrow \infty$, the receipt in each future period on the total of the existing stock and each future investment net of the cost of the investments. Finally, the firm knows a discount rate k with the property that $R_{t,0,0}$, $t = 1 \rightarrow \infty$ discounted at k is the value of the firm. The firm knows its investment in each future period because the investment forecast for each period is the amount that maximizes $R_{t,0,0}$, $t = 1 \rightarrow \infty$ discounted at k. Of course, k is independent of the investment in each future period.

Turning to the definitions proposed here, the quantities assumed known are $\overline{R}_1$ and C_1. These quantities, particularly the latter, are difficult to estimate, but they are not as formidable as the estimation of the firm's entire future investment plan *before* one knows its current income. The estimation of C_1 assumes that the profitability of investment in each future period is known, but it does not involve the logical problems one encounters with $R_{t,0,0}$. C_1 does not involve the assumption that the firm can freely invest or disinvest at a given cost of capital. A satisfactory estimate of C_1 is immediately obtained with the profitability of investment known.

On the use of the definitions proposed here, $\overline{Y}_1$ has whatever theoretical merits the neoclassical definition of income enjoys. As of the end of $t = 0$, $\overline{Y}_1$ is the firm's best estimate of the dividend it can pay during $t = 1$ and continue paying indefinitely thereafter. Under our definition of a firm's capital, W_0 is the investment in the firm at the end of $t = 0$, whereas under the neoclassical definition, W_0 is the value of the firm. The expected rate of return on the capital, $\overline{\eta}_1 = \overline{Y}_1/W_0$, is quite different than k. Depending on whether $\overline{\eta}_1$ is large or small, statements can be made on the profitability of the firm. That is, by contrast with k, it is possible to use $\overline{\eta}$ in evaluating the performance of the firm. Further, the realized values of the variables, Y_t and η_t, up through $t = 0$, represent a useful part, if not the total information, required to estimate C_1, $\overline{Y}_1$, and $\overline{\eta}_1$. In other words, our rules for measuring the variables create a historical record that may usefully be consulted in continuing their measurement. What is most important for our purposes, these definitions of the variables are independent of and find use for estimating a firm's investment, dividend expectation, cost of capital, and finally its value.

The last reveals most clearly the contrast between the neoclassical and accounting definitions of capital. Under the former definition, a firm's capital is the value of the firm, but how one uses and tests the definition is a mystery. Under the accounting definition, capital is the cost and not the value of the firm's assets, but this quantity and the related data may be observed and used to estimate the value of the firm.

7.5   The Return on Investment

We consider now the statements that can be made with respect to a corporation's return on investment. A capital budget of I_t consists of the most profitable investments a firm can make during t subject to the constraint that the total expenditure is I_t. I_t is the firm's net investment so that $I_t = 0$ implies an investment expenditure equal to the depreciation C_t. I_t expressed as a fraction of the income expected during t is $b_t = I_t/\overline{Y}_t$. The average rate of return on the investment in t when investment is at the rate b_t is r_t. That is, r_t is the discount rate that equates the increment to the firm's future receipts due to I_t with I_t.

How may r_t be expected to vary with b_t in a period t, and how may r_t be expected to vary with t for a given investment rate b? On the first question, let $r = f_t(b)$ be the functional relation between r

and b in the period t. In the absence of indivisibilities in investment opportunities, r should fall continuously as b increases. Indivisibilities do exist, so that for small b, the budget may include some investments less profitable than those that would be included under a larger b. The indivisibilities will in some part be absorbed by the gross investment equal to C_t when $b = 0$. Hence, if r rises at all it should only be for a short interval. The two alternative assumptions

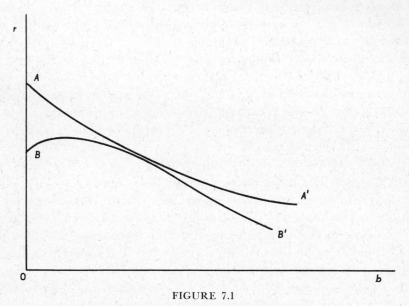

FIGURE 7.1

RELATIONS BETWEEN RETURN ON INVESTMENT AND INVESTMENT

with respect to the form of $r = f_t(b)$ are represented in Figure 7.1, and our belief is that the curve AA' which has r falling continuously as b rises is the more representative one.

We now consider how r_t may be expected to vary over time with b given. This is of interest because at $t = 0$ we estimate $\overline{Y}_t$, $t = 1$, $2, \ldots, n, \ldots$, and $\overline{Y}_t$ will depend on the return on investment in every period up through t. By assumption, at the end of $t = 0$, the investment in every future period is expected to be the fraction b of $\overline{Y}_t$, i.e., $b_0 = b_1 = b_2 = \cdots b_n = \cdots$. This implies that the absolute level of investment $I_t = b\overline{Y}_t$ will grow proportionately with $\overline{Y}_t$. The question of what happens to $f_t(b)$ as t changes is a difficult one. To be sure the question is understood, f_t is the relation between r and b in period t expected at the end of $t = 0$.

Investment in one period removes opportunities from the available list for the next period, but the passage of time opens up new opportunities. It is likely, therefore, that at least for one value of b, say $\overset{*}{b}$, $f_t(b) = f_{t-1}(b)$. A plausible argument is that for $b > \overset{*}{b}$, the exhaustion of investment opportunities will exceed discovery, and $f_t(b)$ will be to the left of or lower than $f_{t-1}(b)$. Conversely, the function will shift to the right for $b < \overset{*}{b}$. On the other hand, there is evidence that investment creates investment opportunities. Growing firms find ample investment opportunities, while stagnant ones are frequently at a loss to find profitable outlets for the little funds they wish to invest. Therefore, it is quite possible that as of the end of $t = 0$ the expectation $f_0(b) = f_1(b) = \cdots = f_t(b) = \cdots$ for any given value of b over a wide range. This is assumed to be true. Henceforth, $r = f_0(b)$ is the return on investment in every period $t = 0, 1, 2, \ldots$ expected at the end of $t = 0$ on an investment rate of b.

7.6 Problems of Accounting Practice

The previous pages have presented definitions of income, capital, and rate of return on investment and described their economic rationale. Our purpose in establishing these definitions is to estimate a corporation's future dividends, and they are useable for this purpose. That is, an individual can proceed on the basis of these definitions to estimate the values of the variables for a corporation on the basis of the available information. The forecast of the corporation's dividend that he derives does not involve contradictory or impossible assumptions, and if his estimates of the values of the variables are correct, the corporations future dividends will agree with his forecast.

However, two or more competent persons all with the same information might come up with different estimates, and each could believe his estimate is best. This means that for our purposes the definitions are still not satisfactory. To test the theory, we require definitions under which all competent persons arrive at the same data of the variables for a corporation. What makes the job difficult is that our definitions of the variables must not only be objective but they must also agree with the consensus of investor estimates of their values.

To restate our task, we want to estimate $\overline{D}_t$, $t = 1 \to \infty$, and under the assumptions established earlier with respect to the corporation's retention and return on investment rates.

$$\overline{D}_t = \overline{D}_0 e^{rbt} \tag{7.3}$$

An objective source of the values of these variables is the data of a corporation's financial statements. For $\overline{D}_0$ we could take D_0, the dividend actually paid during $t = 0$, for b we could use $b_0 = 1 - D_0/Y_0$, and for r we could use $\eta_0 = Y_0/W_{-1}$. Since a widely followed corporate practice is to pay a dividend that the corporation believes it can maintain, the rule for $\overline{D}_0$ seems reasonable for all but exceptional situations, the discussion of which can be reserved for Chapter 12. However, accounting practice and the economics of business operation make it unlikely that the consensus of investor estimates of $\overline{Y}_0$[4] and r for a corporation may be represented by the assumptions that $\overline{Y}_0 = Y_0$ and $r = \eta_0$.

The value of $\overline{Y}_0$ shall be considered first. Assume for the moment that accounting practice results in a value of C_0 that agrees with the definition of depreciation stated earlier. Then $\overline{Y}_0 = \overline{R}_0 - C_0$ is equal to $Y_0 = R_0 - C_0$, if $R_0 = \overline{R}_0$. $R_0 = \overline{R}_0$ will commonly not be true because transitory events cause year-to-year fluctuations in a firm's receipt before depreciation that are often quite material. This problem can be dealt with quite satisfactorily by using some average of the Y_t up through $t = 0$ in place of Y_0 as an estimate of $\overline{Y}_0$.

The chief problem in deriving from the accounting data an objective and correct estimate of $\overline{Y}_0$ centers around accounting practice in the measurement of depreciation. Under accounting practice the depreciation charge for a period is a portion of the cost of each asset not fully depreciated. At best the period charge for an asset is based on a reasonable allocation of the asset's cost over its expected life. In fact, bias in the estimation of asset lives exists, and the degree of accelerated depreciation varies among firms.

It is instructive to consider the error in accelerated depreciation under the assumption that absence of bias in estimating asset life results in *true depreciation*. Under steady state conditions the depreciation charge is the same regardless of the degree of acceleration.[5] The only consequence of accelerated depreciation is to reduce the

[4] $\overline{Y}_0$ is the income during $t = 0$ as of the end of $t = 0$ consistent with $\overline{Y}_1$, the income expected during $t = 1$. It will be explained further, shortly.

[5] Assume a firm with ten machines with the cost and life of each machine the same and with their ages evenly distributed between zero and nine years. Regardless of whether they are depreciated on a one-, ten-, twenty-, etc., year life, the depreciation charge will be 10 per cent of the cost of the ten machines. However, the net book value of the *ten* machines will differ depending on the assigned life. It will be 50 per cent of their cost under a ten-year write-off and 25 per cent with a five-year write-off.

net cost of the assets. However, steady state conditions are rarely realized. Assume that initially the depreciation charge is correct according to accounting practice and that the figure agrees with true depreciation, but the firm goes over to accelerated depreciation on all newly acquired assets. The depreciation charge will rise over time by increasing amounts for some number of periods and then fall towards its original level. However, to the extent that the firm's capital (measured under true depreciation) is growing, the fall in the charge will be delayed, and it will then only approach the true depreciation asymptotically. Therefore, when a firm is in transition to accelerated depreciation or when it is growing, accelerated depreciation results in a charge that exceeds the investment needed to maintain the firm's income at a constant level. The income reported by a corporation understates its true income or, what is the same thing, reported income is expected to grow with investment equal to the depreciation charge.

Possibly more important than accelerated depreciation is variation in the profitability of investment among firms as a cause of difference between true depreciation and the figure that is produced by accounting practice. It is evident that for a comparatively profitable firm, the correct accounting practice charge will exceed true depreciation, the periodic investment needed to maintain income at a constant level, and for a comparatively unprofitable firm, the depreciation charge will fall below the required amount. For a latter type firm, the periodic investment of the accounting practice depreciation charge will result in the decline of R_t and Y_t over time. Furthermore, there is evidence that accelerated depreciation is correlated with profitability, and there is some tendency for unprofitable firms to underestimate the lives of their assets. Therefore, acceleration and profitability probably combine rather than offset each other.

To further complicate matters, the prices of plant assets may be rising. Under accounting practice, depreciation is calculated on the historical and not the current cost of each asset. With all other causes of error absent, the historical cost depreciation charge will *understate* the true depreciation, the understatement varying with the rise in the price level and the age of the assets subject to depreciation. For a profitable firm this will tend to offset the overstatement caused by profitability and possibly also acceleration. However, insofar as the rate of investment varies with profitability, the firm's assets will on the average be younger and the offsetting error will be smaller than for unprofitable firms. For the latter, price level change and low profitability may both contribute to the understatement of depreciation and overstatement of income.

We can be sure that investors try as best they can to consider the factors mentioned above in estimating $\overline{Y}_0$, and an average of Y_t up to $t = 0$, our definition, will involve some error as a representation of the investor estimates of $\overline{Y}_0$. How large the error may be is only a matter of conjecture in the absence of some means for correcting the depreciation charge based on accounting practice. All we can say is that insofar as the theory fails to explain the variation in price among shares, this is one of the possible causes that should be given serious consideration.

An objective set of rules for measuring the return on investment that investors expect a corporation to earn is in many respects more difficult than a comparable set of rules for $\overline{Y}_0$. The only thing that makes the problem simple is the paucity of the available alternatives. Without the large body of information internal to the corporation, we cannot measure the variable directly. We could take the past *changes* in earnings and net worth as a measure of the variable, but this is a very dangerous course of action. The variable can take on fantastic values. A simple plausible course of action is to assume that $r = \overline{\eta}_0 = \overline{Y}_0/W_{-1}$. In other words, the corporation is expected to earn the same rate of return on investment as it is expected to earn on the existing stock. If the corporation's depreciation charge is in error, say understated, $\overline{Y}_0$ and hence $\overline{\eta}_0$ will be overstated. There may also be error, possibly in the same direction consequent on the assumption that $r = \overline{\eta}_0$. One reassuring thought is that when $\overline{Y}_0$ is understated, the overstatement of depreciation will also result in the understatement of W_{-1}, so that the bias in r may not be so great.

It still is true that a corporation that has been earning a high rate of return on existing capital is not necessarily expected to earn a high rate of return on investment, and vice versa. The primary consideration leading to the use of $\overline{Y}_0$ as we have defined it and the assumption that $r = \overline{\eta}_0$ is the likelihood that investors are strongly influenced by the historical data of a corporation in arriving at their estimates of the variables. Investors are unlikely to believe that true income is far different from normalized reported income or that return on investment is far different than return on stock for a well-established corporation. On the other hand, qualitative information such as new inventions, forecasts of the demand for the firm's products, and the vigor of management clearly influence expectations as to a corporation's return on investment as well as its return on stock. Insofar as investors take advantage of this information in their expectations, our empirical results will be impaired, and some means of incorporating it in the measurement of $\overline{Y}_0$ and r may be required.

Before closing, it should be noted that we have not abandoned the function $r = f_0(b)$. At the end of $t = 0$, investors have estimates of the investment rate and the rate of return on investment in every future period for a corporation. These estimates, b and $\overline{\eta}_0$, are all that appear in a model employed to explain the variation in price among shares. However, a corporation interested in the variation in the price of its stock with b may substitute $f_0(b)$ for r and use the information obtained to establish b. Subject to a lag associated with the problems of communication, a corporation may expect that investors will discover the change in b and the associated change in r and reappraise the share accordingly.

Chapter 8 DEBT FINANCING

The stock price model stated in Chapter 4 provides both (1) the value of a share given its dividend expectation, and (2) the investment rate that results in the dividend expectation which maximizes the share's value. The model realized these two objectives under certain restrictive assumptions: (1) that the corporation engages in no outside financing, and (2) that apart from their growth rates all shares have the same degree of risk.

To review the theory briefly, the parameters of

$$P = \alpha_0(1 - b)Y(1 + br)^{\alpha_2} \tag{8.1}$$

represent the valuation by investors of a dividend expectation with the initial value $(1 - b)Y$ and a rate of growth br.[1] A logarithmic form of Eq. (8.1) may be used to estimate the values of α_0 and α_2 under the two assumptions stated above. Given the valuation parameters α_0 and α_2, and given the function that the return on investment, r, is of the investment rate, b, Eq. (8.1) may also be used to find the investment rate that maximizes P.

The definition of risk established in Chapter 6 allows withdrawing the assumption that all shares have the same degree of risk, and the work of the previous chapter provides a more informed basis for making statements on the variation in a corporation's dividend expectation with its investment. The task we turn to in this chapter is withdrawing the assumption that the corporation engages in no outside financing. First, the valuation model will be enlarged to recognize the presence of debt financing. Next, our findings will be related to the Modigliani-Miller theorem that a corporation's cost of capital or price per share is independent of its reliance on debt

---

[1] In the last chapter we defined a corporation's dividend for the period $t = 0$ as $D_0 = (1 - b)\bar{Y}_0$. $\bar{Y}_0$ is the normalized income realized during $t = 0$. To avoid excessive notation we will write $\bar{Y}_0$ as Y where there is no ambiguity as to the meaning.

financing. The use of the model to find the investment and the financing, internal and debt, that maximize a share's value will be discussed. Extending the model to include outside equity financing will be examined in the next chapter.

8.1 Incorporation of the Debt-Equity Ratio in the Model

With the definition of k, the cost of capital, established in Chapter 6, the assumption that a corporation engages in no debt financing is unnecessarily restrictive. Our fundamental hypothesis is that the value of a share is determined by its dividend expectation and the uncertainty of the expectation. If a corporation with a debt-equity ratio of h is expected to maintain the ratio indefinitely,

$$P = \frac{(1 - b)Y(1 + br)^{\alpha_2}}{\alpha_0(1 + \check{\sigma}/W)^{\alpha_3}(1 + h)^{\alpha_4}\pi^{\alpha_5}\mu^{\alpha_6}} \tag{8.2}$$

provides the price at which the corporation's share will sell. This is true because the share's dividend expectation and its uncertainty with a debt-equity ratio of h are completely specified by the variables on the right side of Eq. (8.2). To demonstrate this conclusion more fully and to examine the variation in share price with the debt-equity ratio, Eq. (8.2) will now be restated in terms of the underlying finance-free variables.

With $h = 0$ a corporation's return on investment and return on common equity investment are the same. However, with h positive they are different. Henceforth $\check{r}$ will refer to the corporation's return on investment and the return on the common equity investment when $h = 0$. When $h \neq 0$, r will refer to the return on the common equity investment. With a leverage ratio of h a corporation's investment during a period t will be its retained earnings bY_t plus its borrowing which will be hbY_t. The corporation is expected to borrow hbY_t because this increase in its debt will maintain $h = L/W$ its debt-equity ratio. It follows that r, the return on the common equity investment when the corporation invests $b(1 + h)Y_t$, earns a rate of return of $\check{r}$ on the investment, and borrows at an interest rate i, is

$$r = \frac{\check{r}b(1 + h)Y_t - ihbY_t}{bY_t}$$
$$= \check{r}(1 + h) - ih$$
$$= \check{r}[1 + h - ih/\check{r}] \tag{8.3}$$

Turning to Y, the corporation's current earnings per share after interest on its debt, let $K = W + L$ be the corporation's operating assets per share. It is the sum of the net worth and the net debt per share. Also, let $\check{\eta}$ be a corporation's return on its existing net worth when $h = 0$. The income per share with leverage of $L = hW$ and $\check{r}$ the return on investment is

$$
\begin{aligned}
Y &= \check{\eta}W + \check{r}hW - ihW \\
&= W(\check{\eta} + \check{r}h - ih)
\end{aligned}
\tag{8.4}
$$

We will define $\check{Y}$ as the corporation's earnings per share when $h = 0$. When a corporation's return on stock and investment are equal, $\check{r} = \check{\eta}$ and $W = \check{Y}/\check{r}$. In this event

$$
\begin{aligned}
Y &= (\check{Y}/\check{r})(\check{r} + \check{r}h - ih) \\
&= \check{Y}(1 + h - ih/\check{r})
\end{aligned}
\tag{8.5}
$$

is the corporation's after interest earnings per share expressed as a function of its leverage free earnings, return on investment, leverage rate, and interest rate.

By means of Eqs. (8.3) and (8.4), Y and r may be specified for any value of h in terms of the underlying finance free variables and the interest rate. Making the indicated substitutions for Y and r, Eq. (8.2) becomes

$$
P = \frac{(1 - b)W(\check{\eta} + \check{r}h - ih)[1 + b\check{r}(1 + h - ih/\check{r})]^{\alpha_2}S^{\alpha_7}}{\alpha_0(1 + \check{\sigma}/W)^{\alpha_3}(1 + h)^{\alpha_4}\pi^{\alpha_5}\mu^{\alpha_6}}
\tag{8.6}
$$

The length of the above expression is somewhat burdensome, but it is quite easy to interpret when i and $\check{r}$ are assumed to be constants. In this event it may be presumed that $\check{r} > i$, in which case $1 + h - ih/\check{r}$ is an increasing function of h. Both the dividend and the growth rate, the two variables in the numerator, are therefore increasing functions of h, and through them an increase in leverage will tend to raise share price. On the other hand, $\alpha_4 > 0$, and a rise in h will tend to depress the price via the yield requirement on the share represented by the denominator. Whether price will rise or fall on balance as h increases will depend on the values of α_2 and α_4 given i and $\check{r}$.

More realistic than the assumption they are constants is the assumption that $\check{r}$ is a function of b and h, and i is a function of h, $\check{\sigma}/W$, π, and μ. These functions can be specified here only in a most general manner, and it would not be profitable to consider the variation in price with h further at this point. There is another reason for this conclusion. In Chapter 6 good theoretical grounds were established both for including risk variables in the denominator of Eq. (8.6) and for the definitions adopted for them. However, the same cannot be said for the functional relations assumed to hold between the variables and share price. The equation may therefore do reasonably well in explaining the variation in price among shares but at the same time yield incorrect generalizations on the variation in share price with leverage. The nature of the problem is indicated by considering the Modigliani-Miller theorem on the subject.

Before proceeding to the Modigliani-Miller theorem, some notice should be given to the fundamental assumption on which Eq. (8.6) is based. The assumption is that a corporation is expected to borrow a fraction h of the increase in its common equity in every future period. The assumption is similar to the retention policy assumption and is about as strong. There is evidence that corporations frequently follow a policy of establishing and maintaining a debt-equity ratio that is considered to provide a satisfactory level of security. See Gordon [1960a]. It is therefore plausible to assume that investors arrive at a value for h that they believe the corporation will maintain and use it in forecasting the corporation's dividend and risk. Although the forecast h may differ from the corporation's existing debt-equity ratio, without information to the contrary the existing h is likely to be used as the forecast.

8.2 The Modigliani-Miller Theorem

The Modigliani-Miller theorem is that a corporation's cost of capital is independent of its leverage or debt-equity ratio. This does not imply that a corporation's share price will remain unchanged as the corporation's debt-equity ratio is changed. Price may vary with the corporation's borrowing, but only as a consequence of the profitability of the investment financed with the debt. Their position is that if a corporation's return on investment is a constant equal to its leverage-free cost of capital, share price will remain unchanged as investment and debt are varied.

Modigliani and Miller made three assumptions in proving the theorem. One assumption was that corporations may be classified in equivalent return groups. Another was that corporations and persons may all lend and borrow freely at the same rate of interest. The third assumption was that investors are indifferent to the distribution of a corporation's income between dividends and retention.

The position taken in this work is that the last assumption is not true. However, it will be useful to first consider the theorem under an equivalent condition; viz., the corporation pays all of its earnings in dividends. We will then see what happens when the corporation retains some fraction of its income.

The second assumption is in fact not true. As Durand [1959] has noted, the rate of interest paid by individuals and corporations varies among them with their leverage-free risk attributes and it varies for each with the individual's debt-equity ratio.[2] However, in the range that leverage takes place, the interest rate may not vary materially among borrowers for the purpose of the theory, and a function of empirical research is to establish whether or not simplifying assumptions such as this one may be made.

The first assumption that corporations may be classified in equivalent return groups plays a rather curious role. The other two assumptions are all that is required for a satisfactory proof of the theorem. However, to test the theorem empirically, that is, to establish the truth of the interest rate assumption, some assumption such as the first is needed. A proof of the Modigliani-Miller theorem that makes no reference to the equivalent return group assumption will now be presented. I believe it does a somewhat better job of revealing the economic rationale of the theorem than their original proof.

What we will prove and what Modigliani and Miller proved in a different way is that leverage per se cannot influence share price because *an investor can obtain through leverage on personal account whatever a corporation can provide through leverage on corporate account.* Consider a corporation with no leverage, current earnings per share equal to the dividend of $\bar{Y}$, and a degree of risk such that $\check{k}$ is the yield at which the share is selling. With $\bar{Y}$ given, we may arbitrarily set W, the book value of the share, so that $\check{\eta} = \bar{Y}/W$ is equal to $\check{k}$, or $W = P$. Let an investor whose wealth is

---

[2] Modigliani and Miller [1958] acknowledged that insofar as there is variation among persons in the interest rates paid, the validity of the theorem is impaired. However, they maintained that variation in the interest rate with leverage does not qualify the theorem. In this they are wrong. What they maintain is that an x per cent interest in the equity and debt of a highly levered company involves no more risk than the same interest in an otherwise identical unlevered company. As they themselves recognized (see footnote, p. 274), the levered company is more likely to become insolvent.

equal to the price of one share borrow hW and invest $W(1 + h)$ in the share.[3]

Before interest the investor earns a return of $\check{k}$ on investment in the share. Hence, after interest the dividend he can expect with leverage of h and with $W = \check{Y}/\check{k}$ is

$$\begin{aligned} Y(h) &= \check{k}W + \check{k}hW - ihW \\ &= \check{Y} + h\check{Y} - ih/\check{k} \\ &= \check{Y}[1 + h - ih/\check{k}] \end{aligned} \qquad (8.7)$$

In other words, by varying his leverage on personal account the investor can obtain any dividend he wants subject to the risk associated with the leverage. For instance, if $\check{Y} = \$10$, $\check{k} = .10$, and $i = .04$, the investor can raise the income on his capital of $100 from $10 to $16 by leverage of $h = 1$. If the investor is more concerned with security than income, he may engage in negative leverage. For instance, $h = -.6$ implies that $40 is put in the share to earn $4.00, and $60 is put in risk-free bonds to earn $2.40.

It was shown in Chapter 6 that under reasonable assumptions, if $\check{\sigma}$ is the risk on a leverage-free investment, leverage raises the risk to $\sigma = \check{\sigma}(1 + h)$. Therefore, on a given capital an individual may obtain the income $Y(h)$ associated with any value of h he selects, subject to the condition that he bears the risk $\sigma(h)$ associated with the leverage required for $Y(h)$.[4]

There is an important conclusion to be drawn from the above analysis. We can look at each value of h associated with the share of stock as being a different share with income $Y(h)$ and risk $\sigma(h)$. Since each of these alternative dividend expectations can be obtained for the same price, $W = P$, they must all have the same value. The yield required on each "share" that satisfies this condition is

$$k(h) = \check{k}(1 + h - ih/\check{k}) \qquad (8.8)$$

The investor will pick the leverage on personal account given $\check{Y}$ and $\check{\sigma}$ that suits his preferences, but he still considers that all the alternatives have the same value. For an analogy, if drip and percolator ground coffee sell at the same price, they are worth the same to a consumer. He will, however, buy the grind that suits his preferences.

---

[3] Both assumptions, that $\check{\eta} = \check{k}$ and that the investor's wealth is equal to $P = W$ are not necessary for our proof of the Modigliani-Miller theorem. They only simplify the presentation of the argument.

[4] In practice there are conventional limits on leverage or margin trading, and our conclusions are valid only within those limits.

Let us now consider what happens if the corporation undertakes leverage of h. To neutralize the corporation's profitability of investment, assume that the corporation's rate of return on investment is $\check{r} = \check{k}$. Leverage on corporate account of h therefore will result in a periodic dividend of

$$\begin{aligned} Y &= \check{Y} + \check{k}hW - ihW \\ &= \check{Y}[1 + h - ih/\check{k}] \end{aligned} \tag{8.9}$$

This is exactly equal to the dividend the individual could have received by leverage on personal account. Furthermore, the risk of his dividend is also the same, equal to $\check{\sigma}(1 + h)$. Therefore, the price he is willing to pay for the share is not changed. If he owned the unlevered share with a leverage of h, he will change his investment from $W(1 + h)$ to W.

Consider now the investor who had an unlevered position in the unlevered share. When the corporation undertakes leverage of h, the investor can negate the corporate leverage by reducing his investment to the fraction $\dfrac{1}{1+h}$ of a share and putting the balance of W into bonds. His dividend plus interest in this event is

$$\begin{aligned} Y &= \left(\frac{1}{1+h}\right)\check{Y}[1 + h - ih/\check{k}] + \left(1 - \frac{1}{1+h}\right)iW \\ &= \check{Y} - \left(\frac{\check{Y}}{\check{k}}\right)\left(\frac{ih}{1+h}\right) + \left(\frac{1 + h - 1}{1+h}\right)iW \end{aligned} \tag{8.10}$$

Since $W = \check{Y}/\check{k}$, the investor's dividend plus interest is $\check{Y}$, and the risk of his expectation is $\check{\sigma}$. In general, let an investor own a share with personal leverage of h_p in a corporation that has leverage of h_c. It can be shown that if the corporation changes its leverage to h_c', the investor can find some leverage rate h_p' that maintains the income and risk on his capital. He cannot find an h_p' that raises his income and leaves his risk unchanged or reduces his risk and leaves his income unchanged.

The only possible objection to this conclusion given the assumptions stated at the start of the section is that the variation in risk with leverage is more complex than the Modigliani-Miller theory assumes. The standard deviation of a dividend, $\sigma = \check{\sigma}(1 + h)$, may not be a satisfactory measure of its risk. For instance, insofar as insolvency is a problem, personal leverage of $1/(1 + h)$ in a share with leverage of h does not result in a dividend with the same risk that could be obtained if the corporation had engaged in no leverage. Limited liability also qualifies the theorem.

This proof of the Modigliani-Miller theorem does not provide a basis for testing it, i.e., for establishing whether or not the assumptions are a satisfactory approximation of reality. The reason is that we cannot observe a corporation at two points in time with h different and everything else the same. To test the theorem, the concept of an equivalent return group must be introduced.

Assume that by some means we could identify a group of corporations for which we knew that with $h = 0$ the yield on each of the shares would be the same, equal to $\check{k}_j$. On the basis of Eq. (8.8), the price of a share in this equivalent return group is readily predicted. If the share has earnings (equal dividends) of Y obtained with a leverage of h,

$$P = \frac{Y}{\check{k}_j(1 + h - ih/\check{k}_j)} \tag{8.11}$$

The test of the theory is the correspondence between the actual prices and the prices predicted by Eq. (8.11) for the shares in the equivalent return group.

The problem is, how do we identify the return group to which a share belongs? Modigliani and Miller cautiously proposed that the corporation's industry be the basis for classification. Their caution is understandable. With imperfect and oligopolistic competition the corporations in most industries differ materially in their leverage-free risk. Therefore, investors are unlikely to assign the same $\check{k}$ to every firm in an industry, and a model that assumes they do is unlikely to provide an efficient test of the theory.

A more efficient basis for testing the theory is provided by the work of Chapter 6, which was devoted to establishing the variables with which the required yield on a share might be expected to vary. The argument of that chapter led to the following expression for the rate of profit required on a share.[5]

$$k = \alpha_0(1 + \check{\sigma}/W)^{\alpha_3}(1 + h)^{\alpha_4}(1 + br)^{-\alpha_2} + br \tag{8.12}$$

For the present our discussion of the Modigliani-Miller theory assumes that $b = 0$. If we also assume $h = 0$,

$$k = \check{k} = \alpha_0(1 + \check{\sigma}/W)^{\alpha_3} \tag{8.13}$$

---

[5] The variables π and μ included in Eq. (6.22) and S are dropped in Eq. (8.12) and in what follows to avoid cumbersome expressions.

Therefore, the theorem asserts that if we take a sample of corporations with risk and leverage (but not retention) varying among them, we would expect the price to be given by the expression

$$P = \frac{Y}{\alpha_0(1 + \check{\sigma}/W)^{\alpha_3}(1 + h - ih/\check{k})^{\alpha_4}} \tag{8.14}$$

with $\alpha_4 = 1$. The theory makes this statement, however, on the assumptions that corporations and persons both lend and borrow at the same risk-free rate of interest, insolvency is no problem, and, last but not least, corporations pay all their earnings in dividends.

8.3   Leverage and Growth

What are the consequences of withdrawing the assumption that the corporation pays all of its earnings in dividends? The problem is a difficult one, and a solution will be attempted along the following lines. We will assume a corporation with a retention rate of b and a return on investment that is a constant and fixed to neutralize the profitability of investment. The dividend expectation this corporation provides for an investor under a corporate debt-equity ratio of h will be established. Then the dividend expectation an investor can obtain with the corporation's leverage equal to zero and the leverage on personal account equal to h will be established. If the two expectations are the same, we may say as before that what corporate leverage accomplishes, the investor can obtain or avoid just as well by leverage on personal account, and leverage per se cannot influence share price. The two expectations do not prove to be the same, and after they are established, they will be examined to discover what can be said about the relation between leverage and the valuation of a share.

The dividend a corporation is expected to pay in time t with $h = 0$ and b given some positive value is

$$D_t = (1 - b)\check{Y}e^{b\check{r}t} \tag{8.15}$$

The profitability of investment will continue to be neutralized by assuming that at all levels of investment, the corporation's return on investment is a constant equal to $\check{k}$, the corporation's cost of capital when $h = 0$. Also, W will continue to be fixed so that $\check{\eta} = \check{k}$. Hence, $\check{\eta}$, $\check{r}$, and $\check{k}$ are equal and may be interchanged with each other.

If the corporation undertakes leverage of h, the dividend during t becomes

$$D_t = (1 - b)Y_0 e^{brt}$$
$$= (1 - b)\check{Y}_0(1 + h - ih/\check{k})e^{b\check{k}(1+h-ih/\check{k})t} \qquad (8.16)$$

Eq. (8.16) incorporates the substitution of the expressions for Y and r given by Eqs. (8.3) and (8.5) and the substitution of $\check{k}$ for $\check{r}$. An investor with a net worth of $W_0 = P_0$ who purchased a share of the stock at $t = 0$ would have, via the corporation, leverage of h on his capital, and the dividend he could expect in period t is given by Eq. (8.16).

Now assume that the corporation maintains a zero leverage, and the investor buys the unlevered stock with a leverage of h. His investment is $K_0 = W_0(1 + h)$. During $t = 1$ the share's dividend and price are expected to grow at the rate of $b\check{r} = b\check{k}$.[6] The investor's investment will also grow at this rate, and at the end of $t = 1$, $K_1 = K_0(1 + b\check{k})$. The entire increase in the investor's assets will accrue to his equity in the assets, so that $W_1 = W_0 + b\check{k}K_0$. Hence, to keep his leverage at h, the investor must borrow and add to his investment the fraction h of $b\check{k}K_0$. In other words, the investor's levered investment, K, grows at the rate $b\check{k}$ due to corporate growth and at the rate $hb\check{k}$ due to his leverage on the corporate growth. We may therefore write

$$K_t = K_0 e^{b\check{k}t} e^{hb\check{k}t}$$
$$= W_0(1 + h)e^{b\check{k}(1+h)t} \qquad (8.17)$$

as the investor's investment or assets at time t.

Since $W_0 = P_0$ and the dividend on one share during $t = 0$ is $D_0 = (1 - b)\check{k}P_0$, the dividend the investor expects during t is $D_t = (1 - b)\check{k}K_t$. Multiplying both sides of Eq. (8.17) by $(1 - b)\check{k}$, we obtain

$$R_t = (1 - b)\check{Y}_0(1 + h)e^{b\check{k}(1+h)t} \qquad (8.18)$$

the dividend the investor expects to obtain in t before deducting the interest on his debt.

The investor expects to have a debt of hW_t at time t. For the value of W_1 we saw earlier that he expects

$$W_1 = W_0 + b\check{k}K_0 = W_0[1 + b\check{k}(1 + h)] \qquad (8.19)$$

[6] If the dividend on the share during $t = 0$ was D_0, $D_1 = D_0(1 + b\check{k})$. The price at the end of $t = 1$ is expected to be $P_1 = P_0(1 + b\check{k})$.

In general the net worth he expects in period t is

$$W_t = W_0 e^{b\check{k}(1+h)t} \tag{8.20}$$

Therefore, the interest on his debt during t is expected to be

$$ihW_t = ihW_0 e^{b\check{k}(1+h)t} \tag{8.21}$$

Making use of the fact that $W_0 = \check{Y}_0/\check{k}$, and multiplying and dividing by $1 - b$, we have

$$ihW_t = \frac{ih\check{Y}_0(1 - b)}{\check{k}(1 - b)} e^{b\check{k}(1+h)t} \tag{8.22}$$

To obtain the dividend net of interest that the investor expects during t, we simply subtract Eq. (8.22) from Eq. (8.18). The result is

$$D_t = \left[1 + h - \frac{ih}{\check{k}(1 - b)}\right](1 - b)\check{Y}_0 e^{b\check{k}(1+h)t} \tag{8.23}$$

To compare the dividend provided by leverage on personal and corporate account, we compare the values of D_t in Eqs. (8.23) and (8.16).

The current dividend with corporate leverage, obtained by setting $t = 0$ in Eq. (8.16), is

$$D_0 = (1 - b)\check{Y}_0[1 + h - ih/\check{k}] \tag{8.24}$$

With personal leverage it is

$$D_0 = (1 - b)\check{Y}_0[1 + h - ih/\check{k}(1 - b)] \tag{8.25}$$

Since $(1 - b) < 1$, corporate leverage provides a larger current dividend than leverage on personal account.[7]

The opposite is true, however, on the rate of growth in the dividend. With corporate leverage, the rate of growth is $b\check{k}[1 + h - ih/\check{k}]$. With personal leverage, the rate of growth in the dividend

---

[7] This may be illustrated numerically as follows. Let $\check{\eta} = \check{r} = \check{k} = .10$, and $b = .5$. Also, let the price of a share be $P_0 = \$105$ at the end of $t = 0$. The investor's net worth is $W_0 = P_0$. With $\check{\eta} = .10$, the corporation earned $Y_0 = \$10$ during $t = 0$, retained \$5.00 and paid a dividend of \$5.00. The expectation with $\check{r}b = .05$ is $Y_1 = \$10.50$ and $D_1 = \$5.25$. With leverage on corporate account of $h = 1$, the corporation borrows \$105 at $i = .04$ at the end of $t = 0$. The first period earnings per share before interest becomes \$21. After interest of \$4.20, it is \$16.80, and with a 50 per cent dividend rate, the investor receives \$8.40 on his share. With corporate leverage of zero and personal leverage of $h = 1$, the investor borrows the \$105 at $i = .04$. At the end of the first period he obtains a dividend of \$10.50 on his two shares, pays interest of \$4.20, and nets \$6.30. The \$6.30 is smaller than the \$8.40 on corporate leverage.

net of interest is $b\breve{k}(1 + h)$. The latter is clearly the larger of the two.[8]

The conclusion to be drawn is that leverage on personal account is not an alternative to the same degree of leverage on corporate account when growth is present, even though the profitability of investment is neutralized. Contrary to the situation when $b = 0$, an investor cannot neutralize a change in leverage on corporate account by making the appropriate change in his leverage on personal account. Therefore, even a management that *is not concerned with the consequence of leverage for the corporation's own risk* cannot consider only the profitability of investment in deciding its leverage. Leverage per se may have an influence on share price.

8.4 The Influence on Share Price

Unfortunately, demonstrating that the Modigliani-Miller theorem may not hold when growth is present is an easier task than discovering the implications of the proof for the relation between leverage and share price. Our quandry may be stated as follows. On the one hand, the Modigliani-Miller theorem makes the crude relation between price and leverage stated in Eq. (8.8) suspect. On the other hand, the previous argument casts doubt on the exact statement contained in Eq. (8.14), since that statement is based on the assumption that growth is absent. As things stand now, the price of a share with $b > 0$ and $h \neq 0$ may be written

$$P(b, h) = \int_0^\infty (1 - b) Y e^{-t(k-rb)} dt$$

$$= \frac{(1 - b)Y}{k - rb} \tag{8.26}$$

With $\breve{r}$ allowed to assume any value and no longer fixed at $\breve{k}$, but keeping $\breve{\eta} = \breve{k}$, Eq. (8.26) is equal to

$$P(b, h) = \frac{(1 - b) W(\breve{\eta} + \breve{r}h - ih)}{k - b\breve{r}(1 + h - ih/\breve{r})} \tag{8.27}$$

[8] To illustrate this numerically we need only continue the previous illustration one more period. With corporate leverage, the corporation borrows $8.40 at the end of $t = 1$, and in $t = 2$ it earns $21 plus 10 per cent on $16.80, or $22.68. The interest rises to $4.54, and the dividend rises to .5 ($22.68 − $4.54), or $9.07. With leverage on personal account the investor borrows $10.50 at the end of $t = 1$, since the value of his two shares has gone up from $210 to $220.50. The $10.50 increases his holdings to 2.095 shares, and his dividend goes up to $11.55. Net of interest of $4.63 his dividend for $t = 2$ is $6.92. The rate of increase in his dividend is $.62/$6.30 ≈ .10. With corporate leverage, the rate of increase in the dividend is $.67/$8.40 ≈ .08.

The nasty problem is arriving at how k varies with both b and h.

The following is an attempt to answer this question in a manner that provides an operational stock price model, and that takes the maximum advantage of the knowledge we have acquired. When $b = h = 0$, the rate of profit required on a share is

$$k = \check{k} = \alpha_0(1 + \check{\sigma}/W)^{\alpha_3} \tag{8.28}$$

With $b = 0$ remaining but $h \neq 0$, the required rate of profit becomes

$$k = \overset{*}{k} = \check{k}(1 + h - ih/\check{k})^{\alpha_4} \tag{8.29}$$

With $b > 0$ and $h \neq 0$, the required rate of profit becomes

$$k = \overset{*}{k}(1 + rb)^{-\alpha_2} + rb \tag{8.30}$$

Written out in full, we have

$$k = \alpha_0(1 + \check{\sigma}/W)^{\alpha_3}(1 + h - ih/\check{k})^{\alpha_4}(1 + rb)^{-\alpha_2} + br \tag{8.31}$$

Substituting this expression for k in Eq. (8.26) and writing the numerator in the form of Eq. (8.27), we have

$$P = \frac{(1 - b)W(\check{\eta} + \check{r}h - ih)[1 + b\check{r}(1 + h - ih/\check{r})]^{\alpha_2}}{\alpha_0(1 + \check{\sigma}/W)^{\alpha_3}(1 + h - ih/\check{k})^{\alpha_4}} \tag{8.32}$$

What are the implications of Eq. (8.32) with respect to the variation in share price with leverage?

First, Eq. (8.32) is the same as Eq. (8.6) except for the substitution of $1 + h - ih/\check{k}$ for $1 + h$ as the leverage variable. The argument supporting the Modigliani-Miller theorem suggests that this change is an improvement. Second, when $\check{r} = \check{k}$, the leverage variable appears twice in the numerator of Eq. (8.32) and only once in the denominator. Hence, with the dividend coefficient equal to one, $\alpha_4 = 1$ implies that share price increases with corporate leverage. This should not surprise us, since we have seen that with growth in the dividend corporate and personal leverage are not substitutes, and $\alpha_4 = 1$ need not be true. Third, given the dividend and growth coefficients, α_4 would have a value that makes share price an increasing function of leverage under some combination of the following conditions. Investors prefer the high current dividend provided by corporate leverage; corporations can borrow at lower interest rates than individuals; and due to the inadequacies of our definition of risk, corporate leverage involves less risk to investors than personal leverage.[9]

Fourth, if the coefficients are such that price increases with leverage at $h = 0$, the increase continues for all values of h under the assumption that $\tilde{r}$ and i are constants. In fact, a finite amount of leverage will be optimal if for no other reason than $\tilde{r}$ falls as h rises and $\tilde{k}$ remains unchanged. It is also true that i should increase with leverage, but this raises a troublesome point with respect to the model. The rise in i lowers the leverage risk variable, implying that the required yield falls as the interest rate rises. Certainly, a risk-induced rise in i should not lower k, unless part of the equity risk is transferred to the creditors as leverage increases. There is another limitation to the model. It is widely believed that a little bit of corporate leverage is good and a lot is bad. If good and bad here refer to impact on share price, our model does not recognize this complex relation between price and leverage per se.[10]

A final point to note is that $\tilde{k} = z_0 (1 + \tilde{\sigma}/W)^{n_3}$ is an element in the leverage variable. This complicates our model from the viewpoint of empirical investigation, and some artifice will have to be used to estimate the coefficients of the model by the conventional methods of regression analysis.

[9] For reasons that may not be entirely psychological it is also possible that individuals prefer a portfolio consisting of bonds and highly levered shares to one consisting only of levered shares, or what is even worse a levered portfolio of very secure shares. In some circles corporate leverage is considered unwise, but personal leverage is considered immoral.

[10] The result is that the empirical use of the model may only reveal the relation between price and leverage either in the interval that it is "good" or in the interval that it is "bad." The former is more likely to be true.

Chapter 9   OUTSIDE EQUITY FINANCING

The major form of financing available to a corporation other than retention and borrowing is the sale of new common stock, and the task of the present chapter is to enlarge our theory to include this source of funds. In the analysis of debt financing, no distinction was drawn between the various forms of debt except insofar as the debt maturity index may be considered a crude attempt to deal with the problem. Such refinements as the differentiation among debentures, mortgages, preferred stock, etc., was not attempted. Similarly, we will not deal with the various ways a corporation may obtain funds through the sale of stock. It will be assumed that the source of equity funds is by sale of stock to the general public. Whether or not privileged subscriptions, stock warrants, or other means of obtaining new equity funds yield materially different results will not be considered.

The following section will review the rather limited existing theory on the subject. We will then construct a model for arriving at the relation between share price and new equity financing under highly simplified assumptions. The corporation is expected to undertake a single issue and engage in no subsequent financing of any sort. Notwithstanding the unrealism of these assumptions, the model carries the subject beyond the existing theory. On the basis of these findings Section 9.3 derives a stock price model in which the corporation is expected to engage in outside equity financing more or less continuously over time at some rate along with retention and debt. The last section deals with some problems in the empirical use of the model.

9.1 Existing Theory of Equity Financing

The question of outside equity financing is difficult, and its examination is not made easier by the fact that the existing theory on

114

the subject is still at a very elementary level. The theory can be stated quite briefly. If a corporation's stock is selling at an earnings yield y, and the corporation's return on investment $\check{r} > y$, the issue of new common stock will raise the price of the stock, and vice versa, if $\check{r} < y$. Modigliani and Miller would substitute for y the leverage-free earnings yield, $\check{y}$.[1] Otherwise this is their view of the matter.

The above conclusion involves a number of assumptions or qualifications, some of which have been recognized by its advocates. First and obviously, the return on investment must be calculated with the cost of floating the issue included. That is, if a corporation's stock is earning \$2.00 per share and is selling at \$20 per share, but the issue may be sold to an investment banker to realize only \$16, the latter must be used in calculating the required rate of return on investment. Hence, the investment must earn a return of at least 12.5 per cent and not 10 per cent so as to provide earnings of \$2.00 or more per new share issued.

Second, the conclusion assumes that the dividend rate has no influence on the valuation of a share. Third, it is assumed that the larger number of shares on the market consequent on the new issue will have no influence on the yield investors require. Whether or not the investment banker will permanently create a larger market for the stock at the same 10 per cent yield requirement is open to question. Even with these qualifications the theory does not predict the price at which the share will sell after the issue. The only statement made is that the price will be raised or lowered, depending on whether $\check{r} \lessgtr \check{y}$.

Durand (1952) has attempted to carry the analysis farther. Consider a corporation that wishes to undertake an investment which costs \$5,000,000, with the sale of stock through an investment banker the method of finance to be employed. Prior to the issue the stock is selling at \$23 per share and is earning \$3.00. The investment banker is willing to take the stock at \$20 and put it on the market at \$22. With \$20 per share the net proceeds to the firm, it must sell 250,000 shares to raise the \$5,000,000.

The question Durand asked was, what rate of return (RR) does the company have to earn on the investment to maintain the price of the stock at \$23? Under the assumptions stated earlier it is evident the price of the share will be maintained at \$23 if the earn-

---

[1] Alternatively, r, the rate of return on levered investment could be substituted for $\check{r}$. In other words, the corporation finances part of the investment by debt so as to maintain its leverage unchanged.

ings per share are maintained at $3.00. It immediately follows that the required rate of return is $750,000/$5,000,000 = 15 per cent. An increase of $750,000 in earnings due to the investment will provide $3.00 for each of the additional 250,000 shares. The RR of 15 per cent is higher than the current earnings yield of 13 per cent because of the $3.00 difference between the $23 price of the stock and the per share proceeds to the corporation on the new issue.

In his demonstration of the above, Durand first obtained the 13 per cent earnings yield at which the stock is currently selling and stated that it "provides a suitable multiplier if: (1) the market appraisal is considered correct; (2) the market is expected to continue to appraise the stock at the same rate after expansion (except possibly for a short period during the offering, when the stock may fall to about 22) ; (3) the dividend rate can be ignored; and (4) individual differences among stockholders, say tax status, can be ignored" [pp. 240–41]. The 13 per cent was then used in arriving at the 15 per cent RR. He explained, "The above calculations were made in a somewhat roundabout fashion to illustrate an important point: *For debt-free companies selling stock on the open market, the* RR *will be the same regardless of what capitalization rate is used*" [p. 242]. He then demonstrated that the 15 per cent would have resulted with any other capitalization rate. This is illustrated by the fact that we obtained the 15 per cent without reference to the 13 per cent earnings yield.

Durand attached great importance to his finding, because the choice of a capitalization rate is a very troublesome problem. However, it would seem to me that given the corporation's normal current earnings[2] and given the four assumptions above, we have the capitalization rate. Unless the earnings figure or some of these assumptions are made unnecessary, eliminating the task of finding the capitalization rate accomplished nothing.

Apart from the above question, what has Durand accomplished? He has found the rate of profit on investment that leaves share price unchanged—that leaves the existing stockholders indifferent to whether or not the proposed stock issue and investment should be undertaken. This is a break-even analysis that only establishes the break-even point. There is something anomalous about this formula-

---

[2] The earnings figure in Durand's illustration was the actual current earnings, but he was able to use it because of the *coincidence* that it agreed with the normal current earnings—what the corporation may be expected to earn on its existing capital.

tion of the problem—solving for the break-even rate of profit on the investment. An estimate of the rate of profit on the investment is known when it is proposed. If this figure had been 20 per cent, what would the price of the stock be after the issue?—before the issue? His model cannot answer these questions or the related question— what will the investment and financing do to the yield on the stock?[3]

Before proceeding it should be noted that the article cited by Durand was devoted primarily to debt financing, and the few pages devoted to stock financing were actually somewhat more precise than the usual treatment of the subject. He explicitly recognized the assumptions that the dividend does not enter into the valuation of the share and the valuation of earnings will be unchanged by the stock issue.

9.2 Solution to the Single-Issue Problem

Given the difficulty of the problem of stock financing, it may be adviseable to begin with the problem usually treated—the case where the corporation is not expected to engage in stock financing beyond the current issue. This is an unrealistic simplification, and the solution reached will simply indicate the nature of our task.

Consider a corporation that is initially expected to pay all its earnings in dividends and engage in no outside financing. Its dividend, equal to its earnings, is $\bar{Y}$, and it is selling at a yield of $\bar{k}$. The management suddenly announces the decision to raise Q dollars per share outstanding by the sale of stock and to use the proceeds to finance an investment that is expected to earn a rate of return of $\bar{r}$. Further, subsequent to this investment the corporation is expected to return to its previous dividend, outside financing, and investment policies.

The stockholders in the corporation may be presumed to reckon as follows. The investment of Q dollars will generate a periodic income of $Q\bar{r}$, but *on the assumption that the required yield on the share is not altered by the new issue,* the new investors need be given a periodic income of only $Q\bar{k}$ in return for their investment. Hence, $Q(\bar{r} - \bar{k})$ per period will accrue to the existing shareholders.

We may assume without loss of generality that there is initially only one share outstanding. The preannouncement price of the

---

[3] Modigliani and Miller [1958] answered this question under the assumption that the preissue price of the stock is independent of the investment opportunity.

share is $P = \breve{Y}/\breve{k}$, and the announcement of the new financing and investment will raise the price to

$$P' = \frac{\breve{Y} + Q(\breve{r} - \breve{k})}{\breve{k}} \tag{9.1}$$

The technical detail that must be settled is the establishment of n, the fraction of a share to be issued for Q dollars that provides the donor of Q dollars with a yield of $\breve{k}$ and raises the income per share on the existing stock to $\breve{Y} + (\breve{r} - \breve{k})\,Q$. The value of n must satisfy

$$\frac{n}{1 + n} = \frac{Q\breve{k}}{\breve{Y} + \breve{r}Q} \tag{9.2}$$

In other words, the equity of the new shareholder in the sum of his and the old shareholder's equity must be equal to the fraction his earnings are of the combined earnings on $1 + n$ shares. The solution for n is

$$n = \frac{Q\breve{k}}{Y + Q(\breve{r} - \breve{k})} \tag{9.3}$$

The sale of the fraction n of a share at Q dollars will satisfy all the compatability conditions. In particular, the issue will sell at the price P' and $nP' = Q$.[4]

A number of important points are illustrated by this example, simple as it is. First, the condition for the new issue to benefit the existing shareholders is that $\breve{r} > \breve{k}$. In general, the share in the corporation the new investor receives for a given Q varies inversely with $\breve{r} - \breve{k}$. Second, the postannouncement but preissue price of the stock should be the same as the postissue price; i.e., it should reflect the increase in the dividend expectation. Third, after the announcement of the new issue, the apparent yield on the share $\breve{Y}/P'$ will be below $\breve{k}$, the yield actually required. After the investment is made, the apparent yield $[\breve{Y} + Q\,(\breve{r} - \breve{k})]/P' = \breve{k}$.

Before leaving the illustration it should be noted that if the broader market required by the new issue can be obtained only by

---

[4] For a numerical illustration let $P = \$10$, $Y = \$1.00$, $\breve{k} = .10$, $Q = \$4.00$, and $\breve{r} = .15$. By means of Eqs. (9.1) and (9.3) we compute $n = .333$ and $P' = \$12.00$. The earnings on 1.333 shares are \$1.60—the old shareholder receives \$1.20 and the new receives \$.40. Both earn a return of $\breve{k}$ on the market values of their stock with $nP' = Q = \$4.00$.

raising the yield on the share to $k' > k$, the determination of P' and n should employ k' rather than k. We also have ignored the difference between the price of the stock and the price at which it can be given to an investment banker. The latter determines the proceeds to the corporation for investment. Including the commission in the model would have complicated it somewhat, but no important theoretical problems are involved.

9.3 Continuous New Equity Financing

The previous illustration makes clear that the valuation of a share should reflect the equity accretion shareholders expect as a consequence of new stock financing. What we shall now try to do is establish the value of a share when the corporation is expected to undertake new stock financing more or less continuously over time. This is a more realistic assumption than that on which the last section was based. We also will withdraw the assumptions that earnings are all paid out in dividends, and that the capitalization rate is independent of new financing.

It will be convenient to continue with the assumption that at $t = 0$ there is one share outstanding with book value W_0. The quantities W_t, Y_t, and D_t will refer to the book value, earnings, and dividend on a share of stock at time t. They of course will be the values at t for the share outstanding at $t = 0$. The book value, earnings, and dividend on *all shares outstanding* at time t will be designated W_t^*, Y_t^*, and D_t^*. An important assumption we will make is that the return on the book value of the corporation's capital is equal to its return on investment. That is, $Y_0/W_0 = Y_t/W_t = r$.[5]

Let the funds the corporation expects to obtain from new stock issues during t, $t = 1 \rightarrow \infty$, be $Q_t = qW_t$. The corporation's net worth at $t = 1$ will be

$$W_1^* = W_0 + bY_0 + qW_0 \qquad (9.4)$$

and since $Y_0 = rW_0$,

$$W_1^* = W_0 + rbW_0 + qW_0 = W_0[1 + rb + q] \qquad (9.5)$$

---

[5] I believe, but am not sure, that withdrawing this assumption does not materially alter the conclusions reflected in our final results. Without the assumption, the argument is a good deal more difficult. To justify the assumption, note we also assume that r, the return on investment in every future period, is expected to be the same as its value at $t = 0$, the value depending possibly on the expected annual rate of investment. We may arbitrarily set the book value of the corporation so that $\eta = Y_0/W_0 = r$.

If internal growth and new financing take place continuously, the corporation's net worth at t will be

$$W_t{}^* = W_0e^{brt}e^{qt} = W_0e^{t(br+q)} \tag{9.6}$$

In each period the net worth is raised by the fraction br due to retention and the additional fraction q due to stock issues.

What will be the net worth in any future period of a share with W_0 the net worth at the end of $t = 0$? Let v be the fraction of Q_t, the stock issue during $t + 1$, that accrues to the stockholders at the end of t. The equity of the existing stockholders will be increased by $vQ_t = vqW_t$. To elaborate, the initial book value per share of W_0 is raised by bY_0 due to retention and by vqW_0 due to stock issue. Hence, at $t = 1$, the equity of the shareholder at $t = 0$ is

$$\begin{aligned} W_1 &= W_0 + bY_0 + vqW_0 \\ &= W_0 + brW_0 + vqW_0 \\ &= W_0(1 + br + vq) \end{aligned} \tag{9.7}$$

since $Y_1 = rW_0$.

Dividing both sides of Eq. (9.7) by r we have

$$Y_1 = Y_0(1 + br + vq) \tag{9.8}$$

The dividend during t, with growth taking place continuously, will be

$$D_t = (1 - b)Y_0e^{t(br+vq)} \tag{9.9}$$

Hence, the value of a share at $t = 0$ with the expectation of stock financing at the rate q and equity accretion at the rate v is

$$\begin{aligned} P_0 &= \int_0^\infty (1 - b)Y_0e^{(br+vq)t}e^{-kt}dt \\ &= \frac{(1 - b)Y_0}{k - br - vq} \end{aligned} \tag{9.10}$$

It turns out then that on this level of generality the only change in the model brought about by the recognition of outside equity financing is to raise the rate of growth in the dividend from br to $br + vq$.

We have defined v as the fraction of the funds invested by new shareholders during a period that accrues to the equity of the existing shareholders at the start of the period. It can be explained further as follows. Let there be one share outstanding at the end of $t = 0$; let n_1 be the fraction of a share issued at the start of $t = 1$ in return for $Q_1 = qW_0$; and let W'_1 be the book value per share after the issue. After the issue there will be $1 + n_1$ shares oustanding. Hence, v can be described as the amount invested by new stockholders less the amount that accrues to their equity divided by the amount invested, or $(Q_1 - n_1 W'_1)/Q_1$.

Since the price of the share outstanding at $t = 0$ will reflect the expectation that funds will be raised from new issues at the rate q, the current issue will not raise the price per share. Consequently, $Q_1 = n_1 P_0$ as well as qW_0. Therefore, we may write

$$v = \frac{Q_1 - n_1 W'_1}{Q_1} = 1 - \frac{n_1 W'_1}{n_1 P_0} \tag{9.11}$$

Also, it is evident that

$$W'_1 = \frac{W_0 + Q_1}{1 + n_1} \tag{9.12}$$

Substituting the above expression for W'_1 in Eq. (9.11) and simplifying results in

$$v = 1 - \frac{1}{P_0}\left(\frac{W_0 + Q_1}{1 + n_1}\right)$$
$$= 1 - \frac{W_0 + Q_1}{P_0 + Q_1} \tag{9.13}$$

Therefore, given W_0, P_0, and the expected outside financing rate, the value of v may be obtained.[6]

There is an alternative approach to the relation between share price and new equity financing that may provide additional insight into the economic relations involved. The number of shares given to new shareholders during $t = \tau$ in return for Q_τ dollars must satisfy two conditions. One condition is that the new issue is sold at the market price of the stock.[7] The other condition is that the dividend expectation the new shareholders receive should have a present value

[6] A numerical illustration may be helpful. Assume a corporation with ten shares outstanding, $W_0 = \$20.00$, $P_0 = \$30.00$, and $Q_1 = \$45.00$. On a per share basis $Q_1 = \$4.50$, $q = \$4.50/\$20.00 = .225$, and $n_1 = \$4.50/\$30.00 = .15$. The equity accretion rate is

$$v = 1 - \frac{\$20.00 + \$4.50}{\$30.00 + \$4.50} = .29$$

The book value per share rises to $W'_1 = W_0(1 + vq) = \$20.00(1 + .065) = \$21.30$. The equity of the purchaser of n_1 shares is $Q_1(1 - v) = \$3.20$, and the book value of 1.15 shares is $W'_1 (1 + n_1) = W_0 + Q_1 = \$24.50$.

[7] There will be some flotation costs, but on a publicly traded issue they should be small and they will be ignored. The model can be readily adjusted to include them, however.

equal to Q_τ when discounted at the rate k. With r the corporation's return on investment, b its retention rate, and $(1 - v) Q_\tau$ the equity in the corporation obtained by the new shareholders, the initial dividend the new shareholders will receive is

$$(1 - b)r(1 - v)Q_\tau \qquad (9.14)$$

Their dividends, like those of the existing shareholders, should grow at the rate $rb + vq$, and the yield they require on their stock is also k. Hence, the above two conditions are satisfied if

$$Q_\tau = \int_{t=\tau}^{\infty} (1 - b)r(1 - v)Q_\tau e^{(t-\tau)(k-rb-vq)}dt$$

$$= \frac{(1 - b)r(1 - v)Q_\tau}{k - rb - vq} \qquad (9.15)$$

An expression for v is provided by the value that satisfies the above equation. Dividing both sides of Eq. (9.15) by Q_τ and rearranging terms we find that

$$v = \frac{r - k}{r - rb - q} \qquad (9.16)$$

is the value of v that satisfies Eq. (9.15). This value may be substituted for v in Eq. (9.10).

Eq. (9.16) provides some information on the properties of v. Assume first that the denominator is positive. Then v is positive if $r - k$ is positive, and it increases with $r - k$. This, as we noted earlier is quite reasonable. Looking at the denominator we find that given r and k, with $r > k$, v increases with b and q. This also is quite reasonable since the dividend expectation that the new stockholders receive from a given share in the company will vary with the internal growth and new issue rates. Hence, the share that has to be given to him in relation to his investment is reduced. However, it should be noted that as q increases, $r - k$ should fall, since r should fall and k should increase.

The interpretation of Eq. (9.16) becomes somewhat involved when the denominator is negative. A negative numerator simply implies that the new issues are causing equity dilution. All we will say on the question of a negative denominator is that it is most unlikely. We should expect $(r - rb) > q$ to be true. For this not to be true, both b and q would have to be very large, in which case $r - k$ would also be negative. Both numerator and denominator negative does not appear to be a case of much practical interest.

On the basis of the above analysis the following conclusions may be reached on the variation in a share's price with outside financing. Our model is Eq. (9.10) with Eq. (9.16) substituted for v.

$$P_0 = \frac{(1 - b)Y_0}{k - rb - q(r - k)/(r - rb - q)} \tag{9.17}$$

With $q = 0$, P_0 is determined by Y_0, b, r, and k. If $r > k$ at $q = 0$, price initially rises with q. As q rises, the annual rate of investment rises, and r may tend to fall, in which case the rise in P_0 with q is reduced and ultimately P_0 will reach a maximum. P_0 will reach a maximum for some q apart from r, which may be independent of the annual rate of investment. There are two reasons why the required yield on the share will rise as q increases. First, the increase in P_0 with q takes place because the rate of growth in the dividend is increasing, but as the rate of growth rises, k, the required yield on the dividend, also goes up. Second, increasing q implies that existing stockholders must be persuaded to increase their holdings of the stock and/or new investors must be brought into the corporation. Other things the same, this can be accomplished only by making the share more attractive, i.e., by raising the yield on the share.

9.4 Empirical Representation of the Theory

Eq. (9.17) cannot be used to predict the price at which a share will sell. The only new variable is q, and we may be able to estimate it from past data as b and h are estimated. However, k cannot be observed directly, and its determination has been made more complicated. Looking back at Eq. (9.10) we see that it has not been radically altered by the recognition of outside equity financing. All we have done is add vq to the denominator, so that the yield based on the current dividend has become $D/P = k - br - vq$ and the required rate of profit has become $k = (D/P) + br + vq$. The yield based on the current dividend may still be expected to fall as the rate of growth, $br + vq$, in the dividend rises, and the required rate of profit may be expected to vary with growth in the same way as before. However, apart from its influence on the rate of growth in the dividend, outside equity financing may raise the required yield, i.e., have a depressing influence on share price. Accordingly, the model as it stood at the end of the last chapter, Eq. (8.31), may be enlarged to recognize stock financing by adding vq to the growth variable and adding $1 + q$, a stock financing variable. We have

$$P = \frac{Y_0(1 - b)(1 + rb + vq)^{\alpha_2}S^{\alpha_7}}{\alpha_0(1 + \check{\sigma}/W_0)^{\alpha_3}[1 + h - ih/k]^{\alpha_4}\pi^{\alpha_5}\mu^{\alpha_6}(1 + q)^{\alpha_8}} \qquad (9.18)$$

$Y_0(1 - b)$ is the current dividend, and the rest of the expression is the yield at which it is selling. $(1 + rb + vq)^{\alpha_2}$ is the amount by which the dividend yield is reduced due to the expected rate of growth $rb + vq$. The variables with the coefficients α_3 to α_6 and α_0 represent what the yield would be with $b = 0$ and $q = 0$. They reflect the risk of the share with zero growth. To the extent that the growth $rb + vq$ is obtained by outside equity financing, the price is further depressed by the need to bring in new stockholders, and that is recognized by the presence of $(1 - q)^{\alpha_8}$ in the denominator. We would expect $\alpha_8 > 0$.

The nasty problem posed by Eq. (9.18) is obtaining the data of v and q for a corporation. For q we would want the expected reliance by the corporation on new equity financing—not the optimum amount. This quantity may be estimated from past data on such financing, although the infrequency and irregularity of such financing makes the margin of error in the estimate large. For v historical values may also be obtained given the book and market values of the stock. In other words, an estimate of v is Eq. (9.13). The margin of error here would also be large, possibly larger. A problem is that W_0 should be equal to Y_1/r, the current earnings divided by the expected rate of profit on investment. It is widely believed that accounting practice and inflation tend to make W_0 smaller than Y_1/r in varying degrees for corporations. This of course also results in bias in our estimate of a corporation's internal rate of growth br as noted in Chapter 7.

The major problem posed by using Eq. (9.13) as our definition of v is that P_0, our dependent variable, appears on the right side of the equation. This of course makes any empirical results obtained suspect, but I know of no other way to handle the problem.

In view of the difficulties involved in including outside equity financing in the model, it may be wondered whether doing so would contribute to the explanation of share prices. The alternative is to maintain that reliance on outside equity financing by corporations, particularly those engaged in manufacturing, is so small and infrequent that with minor exception stockholders ignore it in valuing a share. This would justify ignoring the variable in a stock valuation model.

Chapter 10

THE QUESTION OF TAXES

We will now consider a problem that some may feel should have occupied our attention a good deal sooner. Up to this point our theory has been developed on the assumption that income taxes, corporate and personal, did not exist. In fact, corporations and persons give considerable thought to the tax consequences of their decisions, and the question this poses for us is, what changes if any must be made in our models for use in a world where corporate and personal income are subject to tax?

The following section will show that for our simple models, where the corporation engages solely in retention or solely in debt financing, we may simply use the after-tax values of the variables. We will then investigate the implications for a corporation's optimum debt-equity ratio of a corporate income tax with interest on debt deductible as a business expense. Our examination of the corporate income tax concludes with a discussion of its implications for the general model established in Chapter 9.

It appears from the analysis described above that the corporate income tax poses no serious threat to our theory, and those for whom this appears self-evident may pass over these sections. The same cannot be said for the personal income tax. The questions posed by a personal income tax with capital gains subject to preferential tax treatment will be examined in the balance of this chapter.

10.1   The Corporate Income Tax

The first problem we will consider is the changes if any that must be made in the models of the preceding chapters because of the corporate income tax. That is, we assume as before the investor buys a dividend expectation that extends into the indefinite future, and the price he will pay for it depends on the expectation and on the rate of profit he requires. The last of course depends on the risk attributes of the corporation's dividend expectation. Clearly, if the corporation is subject to an income tax, the tax will have some influence on the dividends an investor expects to receive from the corporation. May we simply take the after-tax values of the variables contained in our models and proceed as if the income tax is nothing more or less than a business expense?

To answer our question, let the variables as defined in the previous chapters refer to their pretax values. Next let the subscript λ on a variable refer to its value in a system where corporate income is subject to income tax. The corporate income tax rate is assumed to be $1 - \lambda$. Finally, λ times a variable will denote the indicated multiplication. To illustrate what we are about, assume a corporation that pays all of its earnings in dividends and engages in no outside financing. In a world without income taxes, our theory is that the value of a share in the corporation is

$$P = \frac{Y}{k} \tag{10.1}$$

With a corporate income tax the investor buys the after-tax dividend, which is expected to be Y_λ in every future period, and

$$P_\lambda = \frac{Y_\lambda}{k_\lambda} \tag{10.2}$$

It is evident that $Y_\lambda = \lambda Y$. Hence,

$$P_\lambda = \frac{\lambda Y}{k_\lambda} \tag{10.3}$$

and the corporate income tax poses no problem. Our model is unchanged except for the fact that we use the after-tax value of the current dividend. Notice the valuation parameter k_λ is estimated on the basis of the dividend after taxes. What k would be if there were no income tax we cannot know. For certain purposes it is useful to label as the pretax value of the required rate of profit, the quantity that equates the pretax dividend with the price. In the present case $k = k_\lambda/\lambda$.

Assume now that the corporation engages in no outside financing but retains the fraction b_λ of its income after taxes.

$$b_\lambda = \frac{Y_\lambda - D_\lambda}{Y_\lambda} \tag{10.4}$$

We have seen that $Y_\lambda = \lambda Y$, and it is evident that

$$D_\lambda = \lambda Y(1 - b_\lambda) \tag{10.5}$$

Furthermore, since the pretax and after-tax retention rates are the same, $b_\lambda = b$ and $D_\lambda = \lambda D$.

With the corporation subject to an income tax, the income it is expected to earn during $t = 1$ is $Y_{0\lambda}$ plus a return of r_λ on $bY_{0\lambda}$, the income of $t = 0$ retained. Hence,

$$Y_{1\lambda} = Y_{0\lambda} + r_\lambda b Y_{0\lambda} \tag{10.6}$$

The after-tax rate of return on investment $r_\lambda = \lambda r$, and hence

$$Y_{1\lambda} = \lambda Y_0 + \lambda r b \lambda Y_0 = \lambda Y_0(1 + \lambda r b) \tag{10.7}$$

Therefore, on an after-tax basis

$$P_\lambda = \frac{D_\lambda}{k_\lambda - r_\lambda b} = \frac{\lambda Y(1 - b)}{k_\lambda - \lambda r b} \tag{10.8}$$

It would seem that our empirical valuation model should be

$$P_\lambda = \alpha_0 \lambda Y(1 - b)(1 + \lambda r b)^{\alpha_2} \tag{10.9}$$

Eq. (10.9) is the same as Eq. (4.13) with the after-tax values of the earnings and rate of return on investment values used instead of the pretax values.

Now let the corporation pay all of its earnings in dividends but have a debt-equity ratio of h that it is expected to maintain. As in previous chapters we assume that $\hat{\eta}$, the corporation's return on stock, is equal to $\check{k}$, the leverage free required yield. Therefore, the pretax dividend is the income on the stock of W plus the leverage of hW less the pretax interest on hW, or

$$D = Y = W(\hat{\eta} + \check{r}h - ih) \tag{10.10}$$

The after-tax dividend is simply

$$Y_\lambda = \lambda Y = \lambda W(\hat{\eta} + \check{r}h - ih) \tag{10.11}$$

The value of a share in the corporation is

$$P_\lambda = \frac{\lambda Y}{k_\lambda} = \frac{\lambda W(\hat{\eta} + \check{r}h - ih)}{k_\lambda} \tag{10.12}$$

with k_λ some function of h or of h, i, and $\check{k}_\lambda$, depending on whether or not we use the Modigliani-Miller theorem on the variation in the cost of capital with h.

10.2 Optimum Leverage with a Corporate Income Tax

In Chapter 8 we saw that in a system without a corporate income tax, the yield investors require on a share with $\check{k}$ the leverage-free required yield, h the leverage rate, and $b = 0$, is

$$k = \check{k}(1 + h - ih/\check{k}) \tag{8.8}$$

The reasoning under which we reached this conclusion may be summarized as follows. If the corporation had $h = 0$, its periodic dividend of $\check{Y}$ would sell at a yield of $\check{k}$. Through leverage on personal account the investor can obtain a periodic dividend net of interest equal to $\check{Y}(1 + h - ih/\check{k})$. The discount rate that equates this dividend with the share's price (the shareholder's investment) is Eq. (8.8). Under the assumptions of the Modigliani-Miller theory, corporate leverage of h involves the same risk as personal leverage, and the dividend the corporation can provide with leverage of h will be discounted at the same rate k.[1]

What happens under a corporate income tax? The leverage-free corporate dividend is $\check{Y}_\lambda = \lambda\check{Y}$. Through personal leverage of h on an investment of P the investor obtains $\lambda\check{Y}$, plus the dividend on his debt of hP, less the interest on hP. Since the share is selling at a yield of $\check{k}_\lambda = \lambda Y/P$, the dividend on the debt financed investment is $\check{k}_\lambda hP$, and the dividend net of interest the shareholder expects on his levered investment of P is

$$\begin{aligned} D &= \check{k}_\lambda P + h\check{k}_\lambda P - ihP \\ &= \lambda\check{Y} + h\lambda\check{Y} - ih\lambda\check{Y}/\check{k}_\lambda \\ &= \lambda\check{Y}(1 + h - ih/\check{k}_\lambda) \end{aligned} \tag{10.13}$$

The yield that equates this dividend with P is

$$k_\lambda = \check{k}_\lambda(1 + h - ih/\check{k}_\lambda) \tag{10.14}$$

Corporate leverage of h is assumed to involve the same degree of risk as personal leverage. Therefore, with $\check{k}_\lambda$ the yield investors require on a leverage free dividend, a corporation with leverage of h will have its dividend discounted at the rate k_λ given by Eq. (10.14).

A corporation with a pretax leverage free rate of return on stock of $\check{\eta}$ and a rate of return on investment of $\check{r}$ that engages in leverage of h will raise its after-tax dividend to

$$D_\lambda = Y_\lambda = \lambda W(\check{\eta} + \check{r}h - ih) \tag{10.11}$$

---

[1] An investor will pay no more or less, i.e., use the same discount rate on a dividend with a given degree of risk regardless of whether it arises through personal or corporate leverage.

Since a dividend with leverage of h will be discounted at the rate given by Eq. (10.14),

$$P_\lambda = \frac{\lambda W(\check{\eta} + \check{r}h - ih)}{\check{k}_\lambda(1 + h - ih/\check{k}_\lambda)}$$

$$= \frac{\lambda W\check{\eta} + \lambda \check{r}hW - \lambda ihW}{\kappa_\lambda(1 + h - ih/\check{k}_\lambda)} \tag{10.15}$$

is the price at which the share will sell.

The interesting point to note with respect to Eq. (10.15) is that the interest rate, i, in the numerator is after taxes while in the denominator it is before tax. It will be recalled that without an income tax, share price is independent of leverage if $\check{r} = \check{k}$. Of course, $\eta = \check{k}$. Now, however, with $\lambda\check{r} = \check{k}_\lambda$, price increases with leverage. The reason is that the net interest cost of borrowing is smaller with corporate than personal leverage.

The above conclusion on the effect of a corporate income tax on the attractiveness of corporate leverage is generally accepted as correct. Our demonstration of it serves two purposes. First, we have gone beyond the general qualitative conclusions on the subject and established how share price varies with leverage in a system that contains a corporate income tax. Secondly, though there is no basic disagreement between our analysis of the question and that of Modigliani and Miller [1958], the form in which we pose and solve the problem is different and possibly more informative.

It may be advisable at this point to summarize our conclusions on the influence of leverage per se on share price. Under the assumptions (1) corporations and persons all borrow at the same rate of interest, (2) investors are indifferent as between leverage on personal and corporate account, (3) corporations pay all earnings in dividends, and (4) there is no corporate income tax, we reached the conclusion that leverage per se has no influence on share price. However, not one of these assumptions is in fact true. For all but the third, withdrawing the assumption commonly has the consequence of making share price an increasing function of leverage, and the consequence of withdrawing the third assumption is not clear. Therefore, it should not surprise us to find empirical results which suggests that share price increases with leverage.

10.3 The General Valuation Model

In Section 1 above we considered the implication of the corporate income tax for the measurement of the variables under two types of financing assumptions. We saw that if the corporation either (1) relies solely on retention or (2) relies solely on debt financing, the dividend variable is simply the after-tax dividend and the growth rate variable is simply the product of the after-tax rate of return on investment and the retention rate. The pretax and post-tax retention rates are the same.

On the valuation of a share under a corporate income tax, we reached the following conclusions. In the absence of leverage we simply proceed as before using the after-tax values of the variables, and the qualitative nature of the results, e.g., the variation in price with retention, is the same as it would be in the absence of a corporate income tax. In the last section we analyzed the behavior of share price for a firm that retains nothing but has a debt-equity ratio of h, and we found that here the symmetry between the no-tax and post-tax solution ends. On a post-tax basis the corporation can borrow at a lower rate of interest than the individual, and a corporate income tax makes share price an increasing function of leverage with all the other conditions for independence satisfied.

The reader may wonder at the practice we have followed of investigating a problem under the unreal assumptions that the corporation engages only in internal financing or that the corporation engages only in debt financing. It might seem more expeditious to proceed immediately to the general case where the corporation engages in all forms of financing. There are important benefits, however, in first reaching solutions for these somewhat unreal special cases. Clear and exact solutions are reached under the simplifying assumptions, and they facilitate understanding and sometimes reaching a solution for the general case. It is also true that each of the special cases closely approximates the financing constraints under which large groups of corporations operate. Therefore, each has empirical interest in its own right.

With this explanation for proceeding so methodically, we turn now to the general case where all forms of financing may be used. The stock value model reached at the close of Chapter 9 with some of the risk variables ignored is

$$P = \frac{(1 - b)W(\mathring{\eta} + \check{r}h - ih)(1 + br + vq)^{\alpha_2}}{\alpha_0(1 + \sigma/W)^{\alpha_3}(1 + h - ih/\check{k})^{\alpha_4}} \tag{9.18}$$

The variables excluded, π, S, and μ, are the same on an after-tax as on a no-tax basis. The same is also true of vq as well as b.

With a corporate income tax rate of $1 - \lambda$, and the investor buying the after tax dividend expectation

$$P_\lambda = \frac{(1 - b)\lambda W(\mathring{\eta} + \mathring{r}h - ih)(1 + b\lambda r + vq)^{\alpha_2}}{\alpha_0(1 + \lambda\check{\sigma}/W)^{\alpha_3}(1 + h - ih/\mathring{k}_\lambda)^{\alpha_4}} \qquad (10.16)$$

In other words, we take advantage of the results represented by Eqs. (10.9) and (10.15) and simply substitute the after-tax values of the current dividend and rate of return on investment.

In what follows we will make no further use of λ to refer to the after-tax values of the variables. That is, with the exception of i, the variables D, Y, $\check{r}$, $\check{k}$, and so on will refer to their after-tax values. Our stock value model is

$$P = \frac{(1 - b)W(\mathring{\eta} + \mathring{r}h - \lambda ih)(1 + br + vq)}{\alpha_0(1 + \check{\sigma}/W)^{\alpha_3}(1 + h - ih/\mathring{k})^{\alpha_4}} \qquad (10.17)$$

The interest rate is multiplied by λ in determining D and r because i is the interest rate gross of the corporate income tax.

10.4 The Personal Income Tax

Unfortunately when we turn to the personal income tax the analysis is not as simple as that involved in the corporate income tax, and more troublesome questions with respect to the validity of our theory are raised. The important characteristics of the personal income tax are (1) the tax rate on dividend income varies among persons with the level of income, and (2) a capital gain, the excess of the sale price of a share over its cost, is tax free until realized and then taxed at a flat rate that is usually lower than the marginal rate on dividend income. The second problem will be considered first. All investors are assumed to be subject to a tax rate on dividend income of $1 - \lambda_1$ and a tax rate on capital gains of $1 - \lambda_2$. The after-tax income on a dollar of capital gain is greater than the after-tax income on a dollar of dividends, i.e., $\lambda_2 > \lambda_1$.

A fundamental hypothesis of our theory is that an investor buys the future payments he expects to obtain. The investor may contemplate selling the share after n periods, in which case the payments are the dividends for n periods plus the price of the share at the end of the n periods. Nonetheless, we took as the payment expectation he expects the dividend expectation for all future time. Our basis for doing this was that the price at the end of n periods is expected to be equal to the dividend for $t = n + 1 \to \infty$ discounted back to

$t = n$. This substitution, however, may not be legitimate, particularly in a system where personal income is taxed in the manner described above.

The first problem in the way of developing a theory of share valuation based on the future payments the investor actually expects to receive is arriving at his time horizon. A model that allows the time horizon to vary depending on the investor does not seem feasible. Instead, we assume that in placing a value on a share, every investor acts as if he expects to sell it one period hence. Next, in the analysis that follows we will differentiate between V_0, the value an investor places on a share at $t = 0$, and P_0, the market price which the investor takes as given. Finally, it will be assumed for the present that all the elements of the payment expectation are discounted at the same rate k.

The value the investor places on a share is

$$V_0 = \frac{\lambda_1(1 - b)Y_0(1 + rb)}{1 + k} + \frac{\lambda_2(P_1 - P_0)}{1 + k} + \frac{P_0}{1 + k} \quad (10.18)$$

The first term on the right side is the after-tax dividend the investor expects to receive at the end of the period discounted back to its value at $t = 0$. D_1 is expected to be larger than $D_0 = (1 - b)Y_0$ by the percentage rb due to the expected growth in the dividend. The second term is the after-tax amount of the expected capital gain discounted back to its value at $t = 0$, and the last term is the tax-free capital recovery discounted back to its value at $t = 0$.

On the assumption that the expected rate of growth in the price of the stock is the same as the rate of growth in the dividend, Eq. (10.18) may be written

$$V_0 = \frac{\lambda_1(1 - b)Y_0(1 + rb)}{1 + k} + \frac{\lambda_2 P_0 rb}{1 + k} + \frac{P_0}{1 + k} \quad (10.19)$$

Clearly, other assumptions with respect to the increase in price are possible, and the reader may if he wishes explore the consequences for the analysis that follows of any alternative he considers superior. The assumption that the investor expects $P_1 = P_0(1 + rb)$ is clearly a reasonable one, and it is convenient as will be seen.

It would seem that for an investor to be in equilibrium $V_0 = P_0$ should be true, and we may ask first how is this equilibrium brought about? A plausible hypothesis is that as an investor's holdings of a stock increase, the advantages of diversification make each additional share less and less attractive.[2] In other words, the three payments in Eq. (10.19) associated with the mth share in the investor's portfolio are discounted at the rate k_m. If the result is $V_0 > P_0$, he considers share $m + 1$. The numerator of every term on the right side of Eq. (10.20) is unchanged as the investor considers share 1, 2, $\cdots$, m, $\cdots$, but the denominator k rises due to the advantages of diversification. We will designate as the jth share of a stock the one for which the discount rate k_j realizes $V_0 = P_0$.

We may visualize that given P_0 there is some desired holdings of a share for each investor, and the aggregate of this quantity over all investors is the demand for the share at the price P_0. If the demand is equal to the supply, the latter being number of shares outstanding, P_0 is an equilibrium price. If the demand differs from the supply, say exceeds the supply, $V_0 > P_0$, and the price will rise. The rise in P_0 will induce a rise in V_0 because the tax-free capital recovery, P_0, and the capital gain, $P_0 r b$, both increase with P_0. However, it is possible that P_0 will rise more rapidly than V_0, so that an equilibrium price is reached. First, the last two terms of Eq. (10.19) may rise proportionately with P_0, but the dividend will remain unchanged. In this event the induced change in V_0 is a smaller percentage of its value than the change in P_0. Second, as P_0 rises, the portion of the investor's portfolio in the share rises, and the advantages of diversification will raise k. Third, in our model rb and with it the expected rate of increase in the price are independent of the past changes in price, but contrary to this assumption it is possible that the expected future increase in the price falls as the past increase rises. On the other hand, really nasty problems of price stability are created if the expected rate of change in price is correlated with its rate of change in the immediate past.

It should be evident already that our model is not a very effective one from a practical point of view. It predicts the subjective valuation by an investor of his marginal share. We cannot observe this quantity, and, therefore, our theory cannot be tested. All we have to rely on for the validity of our conclusions is the intuitive merit of our assumptions. Furthermore, we are interested in the price of a share and not its subjective value. What can this model tell us about the price of a share? Given the existing price and certain

---

[2] The advantages of diversification include the desirability of holding part of one's portfolio in monetary assets or of not borrowing beyond some point. For an ingenious use of the principle see Markowitz [1952].

other objective variables, it tells us the value of a share. If one of the other variables changes and our assumptions are correct, we obtain the change in the value of the marginal (and any intramarginal) share on the assumption that the price remains unchanged. However, the price will not remain unchanged. It will move with the subjective value, and this is what the model tells us: the direction in which price will move in response to a change in one of the other variables.

The model does not really even tell us the value of a share. The model predicts V_0 given P_0 and the other objective variables, but if $V_0 \neq P_0$, P_0 will change and V_0 will change. Where the two will come to rest we do not know. Since $V_0 = P_0$ is a necessary equilibrium condition, if we could predict what happened to one we would also know the other. As just stated, all the model can tell us is the direction in which price will change in response to a change in one of the other objective variables.

The model is not very powerful, but I know of no alternative methods for dealing with the problem that are superior. Our purpose in exploring it is to discover the limitations, if any, in the theory of the preceding chapters when it is recognized that investors have a finite time horizon and they are subject to personal income tax. Notwithstanding the limitations of the model, its employment may provide some information on this question. Also, examination of the analysis that follows may suggest improvements to others that will make this approach to the problem of stock valuation more effective that it now appears.

10.5 The Optimum Retention Rate

Let us consider now the consequence of a change in the retention rate for the value of a share when personal income is subject to tax as described above. It might seem that all we need do is take the derivative of V_0 with respect to b. Doing so we obtain

$$\frac{\partial V_0}{\partial b} = \frac{-\lambda_1 Y_0(1 + rb) + \lambda_1 Y_0(1 - b)r + \lambda_2 P_0 r}{1 + k}$$

$$= \frac{-\lambda_1 Y_0(1 + 2rb - r) + \lambda_2 P_0 r}{1 + k} \tag{10.20}$$

Setting this expression equal to zero and solving for b results in

$$2rb = \frac{\lambda_2 P_0 r}{\lambda_1 Y_0} - 1 + r \tag{10.21}$$

and

$$b = \frac{1}{2}\left[\frac{\lambda_2 P_0}{\lambda_1 Y_0} - \frac{1}{r} + 1\right] \tag{10.22}$$

Broadly speaking, the solution seems reasonable. The optimum retention rate increases with λ_2/λ_1, with P_0/Y_0, and with r.

However, the solution is not consistent with the conclusions on the role of retention established in Chapters 4 and 5. To proceed as we did there, let us neutralize the other variables by setting $\lambda_2/\lambda_1 = 1$ and $P_0/Y_0 = 1/r$. The first assumption eliminates the tax influence, and the second assumes that the required rate of profit is a constant and equal to the rate of return on investment. Under these conditions the investor who buys a dividend expectation is indifferent to the dividend rate, but now the value of a share is maximized at $b = \frac{1}{2}$.[3]

Fortunately, the conclusion is incorrect due to a very subtle error contained in the application of Eq. (10.20) to finding the variation in V_0 with b. To establish the error, assume we are looking at a share on the morning of the last day of the year, i.e., just before the dividend for the year is declared and paid. Immediately after the dividend payment, the price will drop by about the amount of the dividend.[4] In other words, the difference between the price before and after it goes exdividend represents a variation in price with b. No one questions this variation in V_0 and P_0 with b, but it has nothing to do with the influence on current price of variation in the dividend and price appreciation one year hence. It is quite evident, however, that in arriving at Eq. (10.22) we have assumed that P_0 is independent of the retention of *last year's* earnings and that this assumption is not true. We would like to abstract from this variation in P_0 with b, that is from the drop in P_0 as the current dividend is raised.

Constructing a model that deals with the above considerations rigorously proved to be extremely difficult and it did not result in a manageable solution. Instead we will keep P_0 a constant and intro-

---

[3] If growth and discounting were assumed to take place continuously, i.e., e^k and e^{rb} were substituted for $1 + k$ and $1 + rb$, the ½ would disappear from the right side of Eq. (10.22). The optimum retention rate would be $b = 1$.

[4] For a further discussion of the ex-dividend behavior of a share's price, see Durand and May [1960].

duce a compensating error in the dividend variable. I am quite sure that the resultant value model is correct for our purposes.[5] It is

$$V_0 = \frac{\lambda_1(1 - b)Y_0}{1 + k} + \frac{\lambda_2 P_0 r b}{1 + k} + \frac{P_0}{1 + k} \qquad (10.23)$$

Taking the derivative with respect to b, we obtain

$$\frac{\partial V_0}{\partial b} = \frac{-\lambda_1 Y_0 + \lambda_2 P_0 r}{1 + k} \qquad (10.24)$$

What we now have is that the value of a share is independent of the retention rate when the neutrality conditions, $\lambda_1/\lambda_2 = 1$ and $Y_0/P_0 = r$, are satisfied.

In Chapters 4 and 5 we established that an investor who values a share on the basis of the dividend in $t = 1 \rightarrow \infty$ is indifferent to the corporation's dividend rate when taxes are ignored and when r and k are constants and equal. We have just shown that an investor who buys a share for capital appreciation is similarly indifferent to the dividend rate under the same conditions. In both models the value of a share increases with the retention rate if r and k are constants but $r > k$. A contribution of this model is to make clear that with $r = k$ and constant V_0 increases with b when $\lambda_2/\lambda_1 > 1$, i.e., when capital gains are taxed at lower rates than dividend income.

Our next task is to look a little more closely at the discount rate used in the previous analysis. The value of a share established in Eq. (10.23) assumes that the three elements of the receipt one period hence may all be discounted at the same rate k. With the capital appreciation and the capital recovery one period hence separated, the former is likely to be considered more uncertain, and it should be discounted at a higher rate. Comparing the dividend expected for the coming year with the capital appreciation, no deep reflection is required to realize that the former is much less uncertain. Since the capital appreciation has a much greater dispersion around its expected value than the dividend, the capital appreciation should be discounted at a considerably higher rate. We argue that Eq. (10.23) should be written

$$V_0 = \frac{\lambda_1(1 - b)Y_0}{1 + k_1} + \frac{\lambda_2 P_0 r b}{1 + k_2} + \frac{P_0}{1 + k_3} \qquad (10.25)$$

[5] The same result is obtained by looking at the share after the current dividend is declared and by assuming that b and D_1 are determined not by D_0 but by a verbal announcement on the part of the corporation.

with $k_2 > k_1$ and probably $k_2 > k_3$ as well. The change in V_0 with b is

$$\frac{dV_0}{db} = -\frac{\lambda_1 Y_0}{1 + k_1} + \frac{\lambda_2 P_0 r}{1 + k_2} \qquad (10.26)$$

on the assumption that k_1, k_2, and r are independent of b.

Inspection of Eq. (10.26) reveals that with taxes and the profitability of investment neutralized, $\lambda_1 = \lambda_2$ and $Y_0 = P_0 r$, we no longer have the value of a share independent of b. V_0 falls as b increases because $k_2 > k_1$. It does not follow, however, that V_0 is a function of b in the way it is under our dividend expectation model. None of the quantities on the right side of Eq. (10.25) are functions of b. Hence, given $\lambda_1 Y_0$, k_1, $\lambda_2 P_0$, and k_2, there is some value of r for which $dV_0/db = 0$, as can be seen by reflection on Eq. (10.26).

We have assumed in carrying out the operation represented by Eq. (10.26) that as b increases and the distribution for an investor's income between dividend and capital appreciation change, the investor remains indifferent. That is, when $b = 0$ and all of next year's income is dividend, the investor discounts an increment to the capital appreciation component of his expected income at the same rate as he will discount the increment obtained by eliminating the last penny of dividends. I believe it more likely that as b rises and the distribution of income shifts from dividend to capital appreciation, k_1 falls and k_2 rises.[6] In this event, k_1 and k_2 are functions of br, and dividend policy is a factor in the valuation of a share.

The influence of dividend policy on the value and price of a share is even stronger when we undertake a dynamic aggregate extension of our model and recognize that λ_1 differs among investors. Assume that for the initial value of the retention rate b_0, the supply and demand for a share are equal. That is for each investor V_0, the value of his marginal share, is equal to P_0, the current price. Now let the corporation raise b to b_1. Every investor recomputes the value of the jth share, including investors for which $j = 0$. Investors in the higher tax brackets, for which λ_2 is much greater than λ_1, will find that the value of the marginal share has gone up more than investors in the lower brackets. Some of the latter may even find that the value has declined as a result of the rise in b.

We saw earlier that with $V_0 > P_0$ for every investor, the price of

[6] The increased coverage of the dividend as b rises makes it more secure. At the same time the rise in capital appreciation as a fraction of the investor's total income makes the total income less secure.

the share is bid up, both V_0 and P_0 rise, but P_0 rises faster, so that at $b = b_1$ there is an equilibrium reached at $V_1 = P_1$. Now, however, the rise in price is moderated by the fact that some investors find $V_0 < P_0$ at $b = b_1$ and they reduce their holdings. As b rises, the attractiveness of the share for low-income small investors falls, and its attractiveness for high-income large investors rises. The holding of the stock is concentrated in a smaller number of investors, and their holdings increase in size.

The interaction of the forces at work may be summarized as follows. As b rises, the sale of the stock by small stockholders has a depressing influence on price. As the large stockholders increase their holdings of the share, the value of k_2 for each rises, due to the increase in the portion of the stockholder's portfolio in the share. The fraction of his portfolio in the share increases both because of the larger number of shares held and because of the rise in the share's price. Finally, k_2 for the share goes up, because the portion of the stockholder's income expected in the form of capital appreciation has gone up. The combination of these forces are such that given the tax rates and the profitability of investment for the corporation, and given k_1 and k_2 for investors such that $dV/db > 0$ at $b = b_0$, there is some finite b at which $dV/db = 0$. Notice this conclusion was reached with r a constant.

What are the conclusions to be drawn from the analysis of share price determination presented in this chapter? First, the treatment of the problem leaves much to be desired. Th deductive argument has been in very general terms, sometimes vague, and it is quite possible that in many spots the argument is open to question. Further, the models suggested by the theory cannot be employed in empirical work to test, enrich, and use the theory. Nonetheless, the analysis is justified on two accounts. First, the approach to the problem is richer and more ambitious than that employed in the previous chapters. The analysis does not only recognize the differential tax treatment of capital gains and dividend income. Differences among investors in tax status and other relevant variables are recognized and incorporated in a model that determines stock price through the supply and demand decisions of investors acting on subjective valuations. It is possible that some ideas have been raised which will assist further research along these lines.

The other and more immediate justification of the analysis lies in its implications for the model developed in the preceding chapters. What we did there was arrive at statements on the variables that influence share price and on the form of the relation between price and these variables under the assumption that the investor buys an infinite stream of dividends. In this chapter we have assumed that the investor buys the dividend for one period and the price at the end of the period. The analysis of this problem revealed that the same variables—dividend, rate of growth, and instability— are considered by investors in arriving at the value of a share. We have not been able to show that the structure of the appropriate model is the same under both assumptions. However, we have seen that there is enough similarity in behavior under the two assumptions to justify proceding with our model.

Chapter 11 : REVIEW OF PRIOR STATISTICAL WORK

The theory of investment, financing, and valuation stated in the preceding seven chapters was developed over a number of years, and in its development there was considerable interaction with empirical research. The statement of the theory did not incorporate this historical development, because doing so would only have complicated the presentation of the argument. When we turn to empirical verification, matters are somewhat different. Different and often more sophisticated rules of measurement for the variables as well as refinements in the model were adopted as the statistical work proceeded over time. The measurement rules and model finally adopted may seem extremely complicated, and the deductive arguments that can be presented in their support may not be impressive. Comparative performance in explaining the behavior of stock prices is often the only convincing evidence, and the evidence is to be found in the historical development of the research.

It can be argued that an investigator is free to define his variables in the manner he considers appropriate for the problem, and no defense is necessary. Information on the comparative performance of the measurement rules is nonetheless of interest, because some workers in this area have been prone to look on such problems as being of secondary importance. Theory construction is a far more satisfying task than implementation, but it will become evident in what follows that a theory is no better than the rules employed for observing the variables. There is another reason for reviewing the statistical work leading up to the theory presented here. Some of the issues between the theory and its alternatives are illuminated or resolved by the review of the prior statistical work.

11.1 A Linear Model

My earliest empirical work in the area was reported in a paper, "Dividend, Earnings and Stock Prices" [1959]. At the time the work was done it was believed that an issue really existed between the use of dividends and earnings in the valuation of a share, and the purpose of the paper was to establish whether one, the other, or a combination of the two best represented investor behavior.

The hypothesis that investors use earnings alone or that they

TABLE 11.1

REGRESSION OF PRICE ON DIVIDEND AND INCOME

	Chemical	Food	Steel	Machine Tool
1951				
Constant term	−7.0	.1	5.5	2.4
Dividend:				
Coeff.	−.8	7.0	6.6	12.0
S.E.	(5.2)	(1.5)	(1.8)	(1.2)
Earnings:				
Coeff.	16.7	5.5	2.0	.8
S.E.	(3.1)	(.9)	(.6)	(.5)
Coeff. of Det., R^2	.865	.810	.740	.810
1954				
Constant term	−3.0	−.4	8.7	6.3
Dividend:				
Coeff.	25.7	10.4	8.4	5.5
S.E.	(5.2)	(2.2)	(1.7)	(1.4)
Earnings:				
Coeff.	.3	5.6	2.0	4.1
S.E.	(3.3)	(1.0)	(.8)	(.6)
Coeff. of Det., R^2	.846	.828	.884	.792

use both earnings and dividends were both tested by means of the linear function

$$P = \alpha_0 + \alpha_1 D + \alpha_2 Y \qquad (11.1)$$

P is the year-end price, D is the dividend, and Y is the earnings paid during the year. Parameter estimates were obtained for eight samples derived from four industries and two years.[1] Table 11.1 presents the least-squares estimates of the parameters, their standard errors, and the sample coefficients of determination, i.e., the multiple correlation coefficients squared.

[1] The years were 1951 and 1954, and the industries with the number of firms in each were: chemicals, 32; foods, 52; steel, 34; and machine tools, 46.

Under the earnings hypothesis, a share's price should be independent of the dividend given the earnings of a firm.[2] Accordingly, the dividend coefficient should not be statistically significant. Clearly the data offer no support for the hypothesis. The dividend coefficient is large and statistically significant for seven of the eight samples. This, however, may not be an adequate test of the earnings hypothesis. As Modigliani and Miller [1959] have argued, earnings fluctuate considerably from one year to the next, and investors may use the dividend as a surrogate for a corporation's normal current earnings.

The hypothesis that investors buy both earnings and dividends represents a fairly low order of heuristic reasoning. It is evident that investors *look* at both variables, and in the absence of a theory on how investors use the information, one may simply include both among the independent variables. The only possible justification for this type of model is that it works for some purpose, but a look at the data makes it difficult to imagine a purpose in which the model would work better than possible alternatives. The high intercorrelation between the independent variables makes the coefficients highly unstable. They vary over a very wide range from one sample to the next, and they cannot be used to make reliable statements on the variation in share price with each variable.

A crude representation of the dividend hypothesis is provided by the expression

$$P = \alpha_0 + \alpha_1 D + \alpha_2 (Y - D) \tag{11.2}$$

The reasoning is that the investor buys the dividend, but the price he is willing to pay for the current dividend varies with its expected rate of growth. Retained earnings, $Y - D$, is an index of the expected rate of growth, since it will vary with the fraction of income a corporation retains, other things the same.[3]

Table 11.2 presents the parameter estimates for Eq. (11.2). Notice that the dividend coefficient in this table is the sum of the dividend and earnings coefficients in Table 11.1, while the earnings and retained earnings coefficients are the same. This is a consequence

---

[2] It has been shown in Chapter 5 that investors buy the dividend, and the real issue is whether or not its valuation depends on its rate of growth. The advocates of the earnings hypothesis answer no, in which case earnings, what the dividend would be if all earnings were paid out, is all that investors consider in valuing a share. Hence the model remains of some interest even under this more sophisticated statement of the issue.

[3] Other things are not the same. In particular, two companies with the same retained earnings may enjoy different rates of return on the investment of the retained earnings. Therefore, the model is a crude implementation of the theory.

of the mathematical relation among the two equations under least-squares estimates of their parameters. However, it does not in any way detract from the considerable improvement in the results. Both the range of variation in the dividend coefficient and its standard error are materially reduced. The use of Eq. (11.2) to say how price will vary with the dividend *given a corporation's retained earnings* yields more reliable and also more plausible statements than the use of Eq. (11.1) to say how price will vary with the dividend *given the corporation's earnings*.

TABLE 11.2

REGRESSION OF PRICE ON DIVIDEND AND RETAINED EARNINGS

	Chemical	Food	Steel	Machine Tools
		1951		
Constant term	−7.0	.1	5.5	2.4
Dividend:				
Coeff.	15.9	12.5	8.6	12.8
S.E.	(2.7)	(1.1)	(1.5)	(1.0)
Retained earnings:				
Coeff.	16.7	5.5	2.0	.8
S.E.	(3.1)	(.9)	(.6)	(.5)
Coeff. of det., R^2	.865	.810	.740	.810
		1954		
Constant term	−3.0	−.4	8.7	6.3
Dividend:				
Coeff.	26.0	16.0	10.4	9.6
S.E.	(2.6)	(1.5)	(1.4)	(1.2)
Retained earnings:				
Coeff.	.3	5.6	2.0	4.1
S.E.	(3.3)	(1.0)	(.8)	(.6)
Coeff. of det., R^2	.846	.828	.884	.792

The value and the standard error of each retained earnings coefficient is the same as the corresponding earnings coefficient. The coefficients appear low, and in some cases they are not statistically significant. However, on the theory that they represent what investors are willing to pay for growth in the dividend, they are not completely ridiculous, particularly when the crudeness of the model and of the measurement of the variable are recognized. As earnings coefficients they are most discouraging.[4]

On the supposition that the poor results for retained earnings

---

[4] Uncertainty in the growth of the dividend might limit the price investors will pay for it to very low values, but if investors buy earnings, they must certainly pay more than the coefficients suggest.

were due to wide year-to-year changes in the variable, parameter estimates were also obtained for the equation

$$P/W = \alpha_0 + \alpha_1 \bar{D}/W + \alpha_2\left[\frac{D}{W} - \frac{\bar{D}}{W}\right] + \alpha_3\bar{g} + \alpha_4(g - \bar{g}) \quad (11.3)$$

D/W is the dividend divided by book value in the current year; $\bar{D}/W$ is the average over the five prior years of D/W; g is current year retained earnings divided by book value; and $\bar{g}$ is the average of g over the five prior years. The deflation by book value was undertaken for a number of reasons, including the desire to avoid bias in

TABLE 11.3
DEFLATED REGRESSION OF PRICE ON AVERAGE DIVIDEND AND
RETAINED EARNINGS AND THE DIFFERENCE BETWEEN CURRENT
VALUES AND THE AVERAGE FOR THE VARIABLES

	Chemical	Food	Steel	Machine Tools
		1951		
Constant term	−.23	.04	.15	.12
Dividend, $\bar{D}/W$:				
Coeff.	12.42	14.04	9.88	12.62
S.E.	(2.63)	(1.04)	(1.05)	(1.17)
Dividend change, $\frac{D}{W} - \frac{\bar{D}}{W}$:				
Coeff.	9.79	8.06	6.38	5.93
S.E.	(5.98)	(2.49)	(1.87)	(2.75)
Growth, $\bar{g}$:				
Coeff.	18.74	3.16	1.45	.12
S.E.	(5.96)	(1.39)	(1.09)	(.99)
Growth change, $g - \bar{g}$:				
Coeff.	14.36	4.57	.41	1.11
S.E.	(5.60)	(1.58)	(1.06)	(.80)
Coeff. of det., R^2	.640	.810	.874	.828
		1954		
Constant term	.54	−.03	.18	.05
Dividend, $\bar{D}/W$:				
Coeff.	17.38	15.51	9.69	11.65
S.E.	(2.92)	(1.04)	(.99)	(1.16)
Dividend change, $\frac{D}{W} - \frac{\bar{D}}{W}$:				
Coeff.	12.71	8.74	3.85	6.06
S.E.	(8.93)	(2.82)	(1.13)	(1.74)
Growth, $\bar{g}$:				
Coeff.	.12	5.15	2.02	3.70
S.E.	(6.39)	(1.66)	(.68)	(1.12)
Growth change, $g - \bar{g}$:				
Coeff.	3.44	5.96	2.85	1.92
S.E.	(4.78)	(1.67)	(.67)	(1.04)
Coeff. of det., R^2	.624	.846	.828	.757

the average for a firm due to trend in the variables. The basic theory is the same as that underlying Eq. (11.2), but in arriving at the current dividend and its growth, investors are assumed to look at the averages of the variables over the prior five years and the amount by which the current values depart from the averages. As can be seen by inspection of Table 11.3, there is a slight improvement in the dividend coefficient, both in statistical significance and in the range of fluctuation of the coefficient among the samples.[5] The growth coefficient, however, remains disappointing, and it cannot be said that averages of the sort used in the present model yield reliable estimates of what investors are willing to pay for retained earnings or growth. The constant term, it may also be noted, should be equal to zero, but it is quite large in some samples and it varies over a wide range.

11.2   A Nonlinear Model

The results obtained on the first test of a model similar to that developed in Chapter 4 were reported in a paper "The Optimum Dividend Rate." [1960b] The estimating equation including risk variables that were simply added to the equation is

$$P/W = \alpha_0[(1 - b)Y/W]^{\alpha_1}\alpha_2^{br}S^{\alpha_3}\alpha_4^{u}L^{\alpha_5} \tag{11.4}$$

P/W and $(1 - b)Y/W$ are the year-end price and the current dividend deflated by the book value per share. For b and r, the current retention rate, $(Y - D)/Y$, and return on net worth rate, Y/W, were used. S, u, and L are a size index, an uncertainty index, and the debt-equity ratio, respectively.

The deflation of the price and dividend by book value were for the purpose of eliminating correlation due to scale.[6] In this model price is an exponential function of br, but br is close to zero so that $br \approx ln(1 + br)$, and $ln\alpha_2$ in Eq. (11.4) is about equal to α_2 in Eq.

[5] Other things being the same, investors should not be willing to pay more or less for a dividend expectation in one corporation than they would be willing to pay for the same expectation in another corporation. Other things do not remain the same between industries and between years. Hence, we would expect some differences among industry year samples in the coefficients. In particular, we would expect that in a model without risk variables the dividend coefficients would be smaller the riskier the industry. By and large, the order of the coefficients is what one would expect, the food and chemical coefficients being larger than those for the steel and machine tool industries. On the other hand, a wide range of fluctuation in the coefficients, particularly from one year to the next, should make the accuracy of the results questionable.

[6] The consequences of the deflation are uncertain since the regression is on the logarithms of the variables. It turned out that the variance of $Ln(P/W)$ was greater than the variance of LnP. What the deflation did was make stocks selling at a high ratio of price to book "high-priced" shares, and vice versa.

(4.13). For S, the corporation's net worth was used. The uncertainty variable is the standard deviation of the corporation's return on net worth over the period 1934–54. For L, the ratio of a corporation's net worth plus its long-term debt to its net worth was used.

The sample data is the same as that described earlier to com-

TABLE 11.4

REGRESSION OF PRICE ON DIVIDEND, GROWTH RATE,
AND UNCERTAINTY VARIABLES

	Food	Chemical	Steel	Machine Tool
		1951		
Dividend:				
Coeff.	1.023	.825	.733	.874
S.E.	.063	.132	.095	.078
Growth rate:				
Coeff.	5.51	4.56	2.10	1.54
S.E.	1.07	2.29	.90	.82
Size:				
Coeff.	.024	.077	.002	.041
S.E.	.026	.038	.029	.042
Uncertainty:				
Coeff.	−.283	−.081	−.002	−.085
S.E.	.064	.104	.132	.082
Coeff. of det., R^2	.865	.757	.740	.757
		1954		
Dividend:				
Coeff.	.953	.822	.835	.694
S.E.	.055	.130	.091	.081
Growth rate:				
Coeff.	3.87	−.11	3.71	3.24
S.E.	1.08	1.92	.85	.87
Size:				
Coeff.	.084	.088	.022	.028
S.E.	.024	.039	.021	.044
Uncertainty:				
Coeff.	−.165	−.018	.136	−.131
S.E.	.057	.100	.098	.089
Coeff. of det., R^2	.903	.792	.846	.774

pare the dividends and earnings hypothesis,[7] and the sample statistics appear in Table 11.4. Notice that the debt-equity ratio is not among the variables included in the table. The reason is that of the eight samples, four had positive and four had negative correlation between price and the debt-equity ratio. The variable was statistically signifi-

---

[7] However, corporations with a dividend less than 2 per cent of book value per share in a sample year were deleted. The model cannot handle a corporation with a zero or very small dividend.

cant at the 5 per cent level in only three samples, and two had the wrong sign.

Since α_0 is the dividend multiplier, $\alpha_1 = 1$ is predicted by the theory. The coefficients are highly significant and fluctuate in a narrow range. All but two fall between .82 and 1.02, and the other two are over .69. However, all but one are less than one, and it does not seem that the dividend is just a scale variable. A possible explanation is that investors believe that the likelihood a corporation will increase its dividend declines as it increases in relation to some normal value, with the normal value some percentage of book value. Alternatively, the independent variable may not be free of error in its measurement, in which case the estimate of its coefficient, α_1, would have a downward bias[8] and $\alpha_1 = 1$ is in fact the best estimate.

The growth rate coefficients are materially better than those obtained with the linear model, all but one being statistically significant at the 5 per cent level. Nonetheless, they remain disappointing. Eq. (11.4) may be solved for the dividend rate that maximizes the price of a share, and if r is a constant, it is

$$1 - b = \alpha_1/rln\alpha_2 \qquad (11.5)$$

However, under any plausible assumption with respect to the value of r, the values of $ln\alpha_2$ are so low that the data tell us every corporation should pay more than its earnings in dividends. In other words, every corporation should liquidate in short order to maximize the price of its stock.

The size and uncertainty variables strike a positive note. The size coefficient has the right sign in each of the eight samples, and it is significant at the 5 per cent level or better in three. The uncertainty coefficient has the right sign in all but one of the samples, and it is significant in three. The weight of the evidence is that in valuing a dividend expectation, investors will pay more the larger the corporation and the more stable the historical earnings record. However, the absolute magnitudes of the coefficients are small in relation to the range of variation in the variables, so that the data do not indicate material variation in a corporation's cost of capital with investor uncertainty as to the dividend expectation. A more likely explanation for the failure of the variables to be material is that S and u do not do a very good job of measuring the uncertainty investors find in a dividend expectation.

[8] For a further discussion of this problem, see page 179.

It may have been noted the coefficients of determination are not materially larger and in some cases are lower than those in Table 11.2. It does not follow that the simpler model, Eq. (11.2), on which Table 11.2 was based, performed as well as Eq. (11.4). Eq. (11.2) is linear in the variables, and the coefficients of determination obtained are materially increased by the variation in scale among the shares. The same values for the coefficient of determination obtained with an equation in which the relation between price and dividend is linear in the logarithms represent a higher level of performance in explaining the valuation of shares.

11.3 Exponentially Weighted Averages of the Variables

The findings reported in the previous section make it evident that some improvement in the measurement of the expected growth in the dividend is necessary for the theory to realize its potential. Although the experience with averages in Eq. (11.3) was not at all encouraging, one cannot avoid the conclusion that year-to-year fluctuations in a corporation's dividend and in particular its earnings make the use of their current values highly suspect as basis for investor estimates of the expected current dividend, the retention rate, and the return on investment.

Three factors may combine to explain the unimpressive results obtained with averages in Eq. (11.3). First, the linear relation among the variables assumed in the model and other of its properties have poor theoretical foundations. Second, the weights assigned to different years, roughly .5 to the current year and .1 to each of the five prior years, may not be representative of investor behavior. Third and probably most important, the deflation of dividends and particularly retained earnings by book value prior to averaging had peculiar consequences. Many corporations had extraordinarily large earnings in relation to their net worth per share in the early postwar period. The earnings were for the most part retained for the replacement of old fully depreciated plant. The consequence was that book value per share rose sharply from 1946 on, while earnings showed no comparable trend. With the intensification of competition in the postwar period, a decline in earnings was not at all uncommon. It was possible therefore for a corporation with a dividend that rose slightly in the period through 1951 and 1954 and earnings that remained stable or even declined to show a high rate of growth in the dividend. To see this, recall that the definition of the average value used was

$$\bar{g} = \frac{1}{5} \sum_{t-5}^{t-1} \frac{Y_t - D_t}{W_t} \tag{11.6}$$

A large Y_t relative to D_t combined with an abnormally small W_t for an early year would result in a most unrealistically large value of $\bar{g}$ for a corporation.

Empirical work with the definition of the variables designed to make them free of the above objections was reported in a paper, "The Savings, Investment, and Valuation of a Corporation" [1962]. The model employed was

$$P = \alpha_0[(1 - b)Y]^{\alpha_1}(1 + br)^{\alpha_2}S^{\alpha_3}(1 + u)^{\alpha_4} \tag{11.7}$$

It is Eq. (4.13) with size and uncertainty variables added. A debt-equity ratio variable was not included since a solution to the problems that caused its failure in Eq. (11.4) had not been found.

To improve the estimates of the current dividend and its expected growth rate, it was decided that exponentially weighted averages of the dividend and earnings should be used in their measurement. Accordingly, the normal dividend and earnings in period t were defined as

$$\bar{D}_t = \lambda_1 D_t + (1 - \lambda_1)\bar{D}_{t-1} \text{ and } \bar{Y}_t = \lambda_2 Y_t + (1 - \lambda_2)\bar{Y}_{t-1} \tag{11.8}$$

The expected rate of growth in the dividend is

$$br = (\bar{Y}_t - \bar{D}_t)/W_t \tag{11.9}$$

The problem that remained was to arrive at the values of λ_1 and λ_2. $\lambda = 1$ implies that only the most recent value of the variable is used, and $\lambda = 0$ implies that the variable is a constant independent of its history. It was decided that one of the combinations

(1) $\lambda_1 = 1.0$; $\lambda_2 = 1.0$ (2) $\lambda_1 = .8$; $\lambda_2 = .7$
(3) $\lambda_1 = .8$; $\lambda_2 = .5$ (4) $\lambda_1 = .8$; $\lambda_2 = .3$
(5) $\lambda_1 = .6$; $\lambda_2 = .5$ (6) $\lambda_1 = .6$; $\lambda_2 = .3$

would be used, and the choice among them would be the set that does the best job in explaining the variation in stock prices.

In this statistical work the samples used were from only two industries, food and machinery, and for four years, 1954 through 1957. Also, new samples were used. In the previous study a sample contained all corporations in related industry categories filing annual reports with the Securities and Exchange Commission in 1951 that satisfied the following conditions: (1) listed on any security exchange; (2) published income and net worth data starting in 1934;[9] and (3) paid a dividend of 2 per cent or more of the net worth per share in 1951 and 1954. In the present study a sample contained all corporations in related industry categories of the Value Line Investment Survey that satisfied the following conditions: (1) published the required data starting in 1947; (2) was not subject to abnormal market interest during the sample years; and (3) failed to pay a dividend in no more than two of the years 1951–58. A more detailed statement of these conditions, some additional ones of secondary importance, and a list of the corporations are contained in Appendix A. It may be noted here, however, that a large number of corporations were common to both the earlier and the present food and machinery samples. The change in the population from which the samples were drawn tended to eliminate a few small corporations with a narrow market interest, and it thereby may have improved the findings slightly.

The definitions of the other two variables, size and earnings instability, were also changed. A corporation's size was defined as the sum of its net working capital and net plant account. The change here was for ease in obtaining the data, and it probably had no influence on the findings. The instability of a corporation's earnings was defined as the average of the year-to-year change in income (without regard to sign) over the period 1947 to the sample year divided by the book value per share. The rationale for simplifying the definition of earnings instability was that the great pains taken to go back to 1934 and thereby include a large number of observations and to use the standard deviation, a sophisticated measure of dispersion, did not pay off. It was believed that even if the definition adopted did not do as well as the previous one, nothing much would be lost.

11.4 Improvement in the Findings

Comparison of the alternative possible values for λ_1 and λ_2, the smoothing constants to be employed in arriving at a corporation's normal current dividends and earnings, revealed that $\lambda_1 = .6$ and

[9] This condition was dictated by the desire of having a fairly large number of observations for calculating the standard deviation of earnings.

$\lambda_2 = .5$ were the best pair.[10] Table 11.5 presents the regression statistics of Eq. (11.7) with these weights employed to arrive at $\overline{D}$ and $br = (\overline{Y} - \overline{D})/W$. The results obtained are superior to those of Eq. (11.4) on all counts, and the improvements cannot be attributed to the changes in the samples. The dividend coefficients remain significantly below one, but their spread is now smaller and their average

TABLE 11.5

Regression of Price on Exponentially Averaged Dividend and Growth Rate and on Risk Variables*

Ln Price Mean	$Ln\alpha_0$	$Ln\overline{D}$		$Ln(1 + br)$		$Ln (1 + u)$		LnS		R^2
		Mean	Coeff.	Mean	Coeff.	Mean	Coeff.	Mean	Coeff.	
				Food Sample						
1954.....3.70	2.55	.671	.83	.039	11.80	.031	−5.49	4.36	.071	.904
.57	.15	.494	.06	.021	1.49	.024	1.31	.85	.036	
1955.....3.69	2.56	.672	.93	.040	9.87	.029	−4.23	4.41	.055	.931
.59	.13	.503	.05	.021	1.29	.022	1.23	.84	.032	
1956.....3.59	2.62	.654	.92	.042	8.76	.027	−4.44	4.47	.027	.912
.54	.14	.500	.05	.020	1.34	.020	1.35	.84	.032	
1957.....3.54	2.49	.600	.83	.042	9.87	.026	−6.21	4.51	.065	.931
.52	.12	.488	.05	.018	1.25	.019	1.20	.85	.026	
				Machinery Sample						
1954.....3.53	2.42	.609	.88	.047	4.16	.035	−1.97	3.68	.122	.799
.47	.22	.412	.09	.025	1.32	.023	1.61	.73	.045	
1955.....3.62	2.57	.619	.83	.045	6.07	.035	−2.32	3.76	.093	.869
.51	.19	.465	.07	.022	1.39	.020	1.48	.75	.039	
1956.....3.67	2.41	.553	.82	.054	7.68	.035	−1.77	3.87	.116	.912
.55	.17	.518	.05	.024	1.12	.019	1.40	.77	.034	
1957.....3.36	2.23	.557	.85	.055	3.91	.033	−4.52	3.98	.149	.893
.52	.17	.518	.05	.021	1.25	.017	1.60	.81	.033	

* The figure below each mean or coefficient is its standard deviation or standard error.

is closer to one. All are .82 or larger. The growth coefficients are all substantially larger in absolute size than in Table 11.4, and they are now all statistically significant at the 1 per cent level or better. The values of the size and the earnings instability coefficients are also significantly improved. All have the right sign, and six of the eight size and five of the eight uncertainty coefficients are statistically sig-

10 For the analysis employed to reach this conclusion see Gordon [1962].

nificant at the 5 per cent level or better. Finally, in the industry year samples that are comparable, the coefficients of multiple determination, are materially larger in Table 11.5.

The use of weighted averages of dividends and earnings in arriving at investor estimates of a corporation's current dividend and its rate of growth has materially improved the performance of the model in explaining the variation in price among industrial common stocks. It is not only a matter of the higher multiple correlation and greater statistical significance of the parameter estimates. These estimates approach being reasonable in that the food sample values of α_1 and α_2 yield estimates of the optimum dividend rate that call for earnings retention on the part of a profitable corporation.

Nonetheless the parameter estimates remain far from being completely satisfactory. The growth coefficients for the machinery samples are substantially below the values for the food sample, and the dividend rates that they indicate are optimal are not within the bounds of reason. This is not the only reason for questioning the parameter estimates. The risk variables included in the model should account for the variation in share price with the uncertainty of the dividend expectation, and the growth coefficient should not vary materially between the food and machinery samples. The large spread in α_2 between the food and machinery samples and within the machinery samples may be due to a number of reasons, among which only two will be noted here. First, the failure to allow for trend in obtaining $\overline{D}$ and $\overline{Y}$ from weighted averages of past data may have left material error in the values of $\overline{D}$ and br used as investor estimates. Second, it does not appear that the size and instability of earnings variables measured investor uncertainty as to a corporation's future dividends with a high degree of accuracy. The variables are statistically significant, but given their values, the size of the parameter estimates obtained lead to the suspicious conclusion that uncertainty does not materially influence the value of a share.

Two observations of a statistical nature are also of interest. First, since the dependent variable, share price, was not deflated, it is possible that the residuals were heteroscedastic, i.e., correlation existed between the square of the residuals and an independent variable.[11] The test was only applied to the food samples, and for it correlation between the residuals and the two important independent

---

[11] Heteroscedasticity impairs the reliability of the parameter estimates. For a further discussion of the subject, see Hoel [1947, p. 106].

variables, the dividend and the growth rate, was significant at the 5 per cent level only for the dividend in 1954. Therefore, the use of an equation in which the relation between the variables is linear in the logarithms avoided the problem of heteroscedasticity.

Another cause for concern is a phenomenon that has been labeled "firm effects" by Kuh [1959]. If the average of the residuals for a firm in successive cross-section samples over time departs significantly from zero, they are not due to random disturbances. Instead, there is some variable stable in value for each firm, or there is a different variable peculiar to each firm that contributes materially to the determination of the dependent variable. When such firm effects are present, there is the possibility that inclusion in the model of an additional variable or that a different method of estimation will improve the reliability of the parameter estimates. Analysis of the food samples for the presence of firm effects revealed that they were highly significant.

The conclusion to be reached from the empirical work reported in this chapter is that the share price model based on our theory is a superior instrument for explaining the variation in share price among corporations than previous models. The parameter estimates for the dividend and growth variables are highly significant and fluctuate in a comparatively modest range among the samples. Also, the performance of the risk variables represents a material improvement over the previous attempts to recognize their influence on share price. Nonetheless, considerable room for improvement remains. It is possible that more accurate measurement of the variables and the more sophisticated treatment of leverage and risk proposed in the prior chapters will secure the improvement.

Chapter 12 PERFORMANCE OF THE MODELS

The purpose of this chapter is to test the stock valuation models developed in Chapters 8 and 9. The method of testing and parameter estimation to be employed is least-squares regression or correlation analysis. The parameter estimates will be presented and examined for statistical significance, size, stability, and other attributes that are indicative of the theory's performance. The sample data are the same as those used for Eq. (11.7) in the preceding chapter and described in some detail below and in Appendix A. Basically, there are two samples, one of 48 food and the other of 48 machinery corporations, but data for each sample have been obtained to run cross-section regressions for the years 1954–58. Therefore, for each of the model equations we will have ten sets of parameter estimates.

The next two sections will present in some detail the measurement rules employed to obtain the data for the regression equation that represents Eq. (8.6). To provide some feel for the data, the means and standard deviations of the variables for each sample will also be presented and discussed. The following section will report and evaluate the estimates of the regression coefficients for Eq. (8.6). We will then go on to the more ambitious models represented by Eqs. (8.32) and (9.18). The methods by which the data of the additional variables were obtained will be stated, and the empirical results will be reported and analyzed.

12.1 Measurement of the Variables: Price, Dividend, and Growth

Eq. (8.6) is the stock price model that did not take advantage of the Modigliani-Miller theorem on leverage and disregarded outside equity financing. In logarithmic form it is

154

$$LnP = ln\hat{\alpha}_0 + \alpha_1 lnD + \alpha_2 ln(1 + br) + \hat{\alpha}_3 ln(1 + \breve{\sigma}/W)$$
$$+ \hat{\alpha}_4 ln(1 + h) + \hat{\alpha}_5 ln\pi + \hat{\alpha}_6 ln\mu + \alpha_7 lnS \quad (12.1)$$

The variables with the coefficients α_3 through α_6 along with α_0 appeared in the denominator of Eq. (8.6), to avoid confusion with respect to sign we have set $\hat{\alpha}_0 = 1/\alpha_0$, $\hat{\alpha}_3 = -\alpha_3$, $\hat{\alpha}_4 = -\alpha_4$, etc. The rules by which the value of each variable for a corporation was obtained are stated and explained below.

$P = Price$. For the dependent variable, the value used was the price on the third Friday in January of the year following the cross-section year.[1] The alternative to taking the price on one day was to take an average of the price over some time period. This seemed to raise more problems than it solved, particularly since our objective was to explain the price prevailing at some point in time. The date selected was guided by the objective of having a price based on the information contained in the values of the independent variables used and not on subsequent values of the variables.

The information problem is posed largely by dividends and earnings. The price on the third Friday in January of the year following the cross-section year precedes the publication of the corporation's earnings for the year. However, a date following publication of the year's earnings would also follow the first quarterly dividend in the next year, and it would be undesirable to use a price that had reacted to this information. The price on the date used was reconciled with use of annual report earnings and other data by assuming that quarterly reports, preliminary estimates, and other sources of information provide investors with reliable estimates of the year's earnings and other financial report statistics prior to the date used for the share price.

Table 12.1 contains the mean and standard deviation of the natural logarithms of share price for the ten samples. The mean and standard deviation of the price are also shown. The average over the five food samples of the means is $39.47, and data for the average of the standard deviations is also shown.[2] The corresponding machinery

---

[1] E.g., if the dividend and other variables are for 1954, the price is on the third Friday of January, 1955.

[2] Strictly speaking, the figure for the mean price is the antilog of the mean of the logarithms of price. The standard deviation was obtained as follows. The mean of the logarithms, e.g., 3.702 for the 1954 food sample, was increased by one standard deviation and reduced by one standard deviation to obtain 4.269 and 3.135. The antilogs of these two figures are $71.42 and $22.98, and the amount by which each differs from $40.55 was calculated. The two figures obtained, written 31/18, appear as the standard deviation.

TABLE 12.1

MEAN AND STANDARD DEVIATION OF PRICE, DIVIDEND, AND GROWTH

Food Sample

	1954	1955	1956	1957	1958	*Average*
Ln price.............	3.7015	3.6911	3.5898	3.5360	3.8341	3.6703
S.D...............	.5673	.5826	.5380	.5115	.4977	.5394
Price...............$40.55		$40.08	$36.19	$34.31	$46.23	$39.47
S.D............... 31/18		32/18	26/15	23/14	30/18	28/18
Ln dividend..........	.6511	.6929	.6801	.6213	.6378	.6566
S.D...............	.5170	.5179	.5005	.5097	.5236	.5137
Dividend.............$ 1.92		$ 2.00	$ 1.97	$ 1.86	$ 1.89	$ 1.93
S.D...............1.30/.78		1.36/.81	1.29/.77	1.24/.64	1.30/.77	1.29/.78
Dividend yield........	.047	.05	.054	.054	.041	.049
Ln(1 + *br*)..........	.0415	.0384	.0384	.0384	.0381	.0390
S.D...............	.0188	.0179	.0170	.0147	.0147	.0166

Machinery Sample

	1954	1955	1956	1957	1958	*Average*
Ln price.............	3.5387	3.6293	3.6702	3.3673	3.6233	3.5658
S.D...............	.4668	.5029	.5456	.5191	.5052	.5019
Price...............$34.42		$37.69	$39.26	$29.00	$37.45	$35.56
S.D............... 20/14		25/15	28/17	20/12	25/15	23/14
Ln dividend..........	.6027	.6306	.5651	.5643	.4063	.5538
S.D...............	.4322	.4812	.5468	.5238	.5626	.5093
Dividend.............$ 1.83		$ 1.88	$ 1.76	$ 1.76	$ 1.50	$ 1.74
S.D...............99/.65		1.16/.76	1.28/.74	1.21/.72	1.13/.64	1.16/.69
Dividend yield........	.053	.05	.045	.061	.04	.049
Ln(1 + *br*)..........	.0482	.0432	.0460	.0473	.0421	.0454
S.D...............	.0209	.0171	.0180	.0180	.0143	.0177

sample figures are slightly smaller. The changes in these variables over the five years are not particularly significant because they are influenced by stock splits and stock dividends as well as changes in the value of the shares.

$D = Dividend$. With the qualifications to be noted, the dividend is the amount paid during the calendar year, or the amount declared if the payment of the fourth quarterly dividend falls shortly after the end of the year. However, if the last two quarterly dividends taken in conjunction with the prior dividend payments indicate that the annual dividend has been changed during the year, the indicated annual dividend as of the year end is used. On the same principle, a year-end extra that investors are likely to consider a true extra, i.e., not repeated, is excluded from D. Stock dividends were of course also excluded.

Unlike the income figure to be described shortly, the dividend is the current value and not an average of two or more years. It is widely believed that corporations follow a policy of paying a stable dividend, i.e., the dividend is typically changed in response to long-run developments and not year-to-year changes in earnings and other variables. Averaging would therefore do more harm than good. There is one exception to this generalization. When income falls sharply and/or the firm feels a strong temporary need for cash, the dividend may be cut sharply as a temporary expedient. To deal with these situations 2 per cent of the book value per share was used whenever the dividend was below this figure.

Turning to Table 12.1, the five-year averages of the dividend are $1.93 for the food samples and $1.75 for the machinery samples. The dividend fluctuates in a narrower range and not always in the same direction as the price. The year-to-year changes, like those of price, are due to stock splits and dividends as well as actual changes in the dividend. A point worth noting is that percentage-wise the variation in the dividend among the corporations is almost as great and in some years greater than the variation in price.

A statistic of some interest is the dividend yield, the mean dividend divided by mean price, and it also appears in Table 12.1. For the food sample, it rises between 1954 and 1957 from .047 to .054, and in 1958 it falls sharply to .041. The machinery sample yield by contrast falls from .053 to .045 between 1954 and 1956, rises sharply in 1957 to .061, and falls sharply in 1958 to .04.

$br = Growth\ Rate$. The expected rate of growth in the dividend is the product of b, the retention rate, and r, the rate of return on investment. The latter is assumed to be equal to the return on the existing common equity. Hence,

$$br = \left(\frac{\bar{Y} - D}{\bar{Y}}\right)\left(\frac{\bar{Y}}{W}\right) = \frac{\bar{Y} - D}{W} \tag{12.2}$$

or retained earnings divided by book value per share. Unlike D and W, $\bar{Y}$ is not the value for the cross-section year but an exponentially smoothed trend adjusted average of earnings for 1947 through the cross-section year.

$\bar{Y} = Earnings$. The earnings per share for a cross-section year were obtained as follows. Let $Y_t =$ actual, $\tilde{Y}_t =$ smoothed, and $\bar{Y}_t =$ smoothed trend adjusted earnings for year t. For 1946 both $\tilde{Y}_t$ and $\bar{Y}_t$ were arbitrarily set at 1.5, the 1947 dividend. The smoothed earnings in each subsequent year were obtained recursively from the equation

$$\tilde{Y}_t = .3Y_t + .7\tilde{Y}_{t-1} \tag{12.3}$$

The trend rate of growth in earnings was arbitrarily set at .03 for 1946, and for each subsequent year it was obtained from the expression

$$G_t = \frac{.3(\tilde{Y}_t - \tilde{Y}_{t-1})}{\tilde{Y}_{t-1}} + .7G_{t-1} \tag{12.4}$$

The smoothed trend adjusted earnings is

$$\bar{Y}_t = .3Y_t + .7\tilde{Y}_{t-1}(1 + G_t) \tag{12.5}$$

In words, $\bar{Y}_t$ is an average of the current value and the smoothed value for the prior year with the latter raised by the average trend increase in earnings.[3]

A point to note is that in the computation of br, the values of Y_t, D_t, and W_t used were the equivalent amounts per share outstanding at the end of 1958 and not the actual amount for year t. That is, the current values were adjusted for stock splits and stock dividends to make the values over the period 1947–58 comparable. On the other hand, P and D are the current values of the variables. Shares that have experienced a considerable increase in dividend and price are more likely to have been split and, expressed in 1958 shares, the values of P and D for these high-growth stocks would have had low values in the early years. The resultant parameter estimates would have been biased.

Table 12.1 contains the mean and standard deviation of ln $(1 + br)$. Since br is so close to one, $br \approx ln$ $(1 + br)$. The average of the food growth rates, 3.9 per cent, was below the 4.5 per cent of the machinery samples. The food mean fell from 4.2 per cent to 3.8 per cent between 1954 and 1955 and then remained at that level. By contrast, the mean for the machinery samples fluctuated between 4.2

---

[3] There may be some objection to this method of handling trend, but I don't believe that the work on exponential smoothing has solved the problem satisfactorily. Cf. Brown [1959] and Winters [1960].

per cent and 4.8 per cent. The higher average level and greater fluctuation over time for the machinery sample seems reasonable.

12.2   The Risk Variables

$\check{\sigma}/W$ = *Earnings Instability Index.* The quantity σ/W is an index of the variability in a corporation's earnings, and $\check{\sigma}/W$ is the value σ/W would have in the absence of leverage. For the first step in obtaining $\check{\sigma}/W$, the earnings in t expected at the end of $t - 1$ was defined as

$$\hat{Y}_t = \bar{Y}_{t-1}(1 + G_{t-1}) \tag{12.6}$$

The absolute difference between the earnings in t expected at the end of $t - 1$ and the earnings actually realized in t is $|\hat{Y}_t - Y_t|$, and

$$\triangle_t = \frac{|\hat{Y}_t - Y_t|}{W_t} \tag{12.7}$$

The value of σ/W for 1954 is an exponentially weighted average of $\triangle_t$ for 1947 through 1954. For each subsequent year

$$\left(\frac{\sigma}{W}\right)_t = .3\triangle + .7\left(\frac{\sigma}{W}\right)_{t-1} \tag{12.8}$$

is the value of the variable.

In Chapter 6, it will be recalled we defined $(\sigma/W)_t$ as the standard deviation of the return on net worth in t expected in $t - 1$. For our estimate of this quantity, we take the difference between the actual return on net worth during a period and the return expected at the start of the period and obtain a weighted average of this difference over the years 1947 through t. A point to note is that the symbol σ is used in our definition of the variable, but the average and not the standard deviation of the actual around the expected values is employed.

For a leverage-free earnings instability index, we should have used earnings plus net interest paid in the numerator and the sum of net worth and net debt in the denominator of Eq. (12.7). However, a corporation's interest paid net of interest earned is hard to obtain, particularly with current liabilities and monetary assets included in its net debt, and a simpler course of action is possible. Net interest paid is likely to be small and stable, so adding it to $\hat{Y}_t$ and Y_t will not materially change $\hat{Y}_t - Y_t$. The denominator of $\triangle_t$ is what will differ: in one case it is W_t, and in the other it is $W_t + L_t$. Therefore, an index of leverage-free earnings instability may be obtained by adding L_t to the denominator of Eq. (12.7) and using this quantity in Eq. (12.8) to calculate $(\check{\sigma}/W)_t$. Unfortunately, this was not done. Instead the quantity used was

$$(\check{\sigma}/W)_t = (\sigma/W)_t \left(\frac{W_t}{W_t + L_t} \right) \tag{12.9}$$

TABLE 12.2

MEAN AND STANDARD DEVIATION OF THE RISK VARIABLES

Food Sample

	1954	1955	1956	1957	1958	Average
$Ln(1 + \check{\sigma}/W)$	.0268	.0255	.0235	.0255	.0224	.0247
S.D.	.0163	.0153	.0138	.0125	.0120	.0140
$Ln(1 + h)$	.1748	.1628	.1826	.1729	.1414	.1669
S.D.	.3103	.3002	.2983	.2958	.2890	.2987
$Ln\pi$	−.0252	−.0270	−.0320	−.0369	−.0379	−.0318
S.D.	.1609	.1586	.1574	.1592	.1602	.1593
$Ln\mu$	.1070	.0950	.0881	.0879	.0778	.0912
S.D.	.1006	.0905	.0920	.0850	.0808	.0898
LnS	4.3623	4.4143	4.4734	4.5136	4.5603	4.4648
S.D.	.8375	.8296	.8310	.8459	.8566	.8401
Size (000,000)	78.45	82.62	87.66	91.25	95.61	87.12
S.D.	103/44	107/47	113/49	121/52	130/55	114/50

Machinery Sample

	1954	1955	1956	1957	1958	Average
$Ln(1 + \check{\sigma}/W)$	.0399	.0398	.0384	.0365	.0406	.0390
S.D.	.0203	.0205	.0188	.0181	.0206	.0197
$Ln(1 + h)$	−.0579	−.0705	−.0301	−.0192	−.0598	−.0475
S.D.	.2784	.2719	.2649	.2600	.2709	.2692
$Ln\pi$	.0380	.0328	.0313	.0254	.0134	.0282
S.D.	.0852	.0882	.0932	.0915	.0943	.0905
$Ln\mu$	.0492	.0103	.0027	.0113	.0273	.0202
S.D.	.0775	.0653	.0793	.0719	.0648	.0718
LnS	3.6845	3.7667	3.8756	3.9763	4.0036	3.8613
S.D.	.7292	.7518	.7709	.8150	.8223	.7778
Size (000,000)	39.82	43.23	48.21	53.32	54.80	47.88
S.D.	43/21	50/23	56/26	67/30	70/31	56/26

The error in this definition was not considered great enough to justify computing the values under the superior definition.

Table 12.2 presents the sample means and standard deviations of $ln\,(1 + \check{\sigma}/W)$. The average of the food sample means, .024, is considerably lower than the .039 for the machinery sample. For the food sample, $\check{\sigma}/W$ fell continuously over the five years, while the machinery sample value turned up in 1958. As one might expect the variability in $\check{\sigma}/W$ among the corporations, as well as the average level in each year, is considerably higher for the machinery than for the food corporations. To interpret the level of the variable, let $\check{r} =$ .10 and $\check{\sigma}/W = .03$ for a corporation. *Roughly speaking,* there is a probability of one half that $\check{r}$ will fall between .07 and .13 in the next period.

$h = L/W = Debt\text{-}Equity\ Ratio.$ It will be recalled that a firm's debt, L, was defined as all of its liabilities, including preferred stock less its monetary assets, cash, accounts receivable, and government bonds. The reason for this definition was that current liabilities are an important source of leverage, and firms incur varying amounts of debt to hold monetary assets rather than engage in leverage. Inspection of the data suggested a further refinement in the definition. Inventory often fluctuated materially from one year to the next in response to short-term changes in market conditions, and these short-term inventory fluctuations were highly correlated with changes in cash or current liabilities. They therefore were responsible for large year-to-year fluctuations in L. It is likely that these fluctuations are ignored by investors in arriving at a firm's net debt or leverage. Accordingly, a firm's net debt was defined as

$$L = CL + ID + LD + LR + PS - CG - AR - \widehat{INV} \quad (12.10)$$

For the definitions of the variables other than $\widehat{INV}$, see page 80.

The quantity $\widehat{INV}$ is the amount by which the firm's actual inventory exceeds its normal inventory. Abnormal inventory is treated as a monetary asset on the reasoning that the commitment of funds is temporary and will be withdrawn shortly. $\widehat{INV}$ is defined operationally below.

Table 12.2 contains the sample means and standard deviations of $ln\,(1 + h)$. The food sample means fluctuate slightly over the five years around their average, .167, while the machinery sample means fluctuate somewhat more around their average, $-.048$. It appears that machinery corporations as a group offset their higher earnings instability by engaging in considerably less trading on the equity than food corporations. In fact on the average their leverage is negative. In both industries, the variation in leverage among the corporations in a sample is quite large. The averages of the standard deviations are .299 and .269 for the food and machinery samples.

$\pi = $ *Operating Asset Liquidity Index.* It will be recalled that this quantity was defined on page 74 as

$$\pi = \frac{7INV + 5OOA + 3PE}{5(INV + OOA + PE)} \tag{6.9}$$

The index varies with the relative importance of inventory and plant in the firm's operating assets, and as argued in Chapter 6, share price should vary with π. On the basis of the reasoning in the previous paragraph, the actual inventory is replaced by $\overline{INV}$, the normal inventory. To obtain $\overline{INV}$ for each year we began by obtaining

$$\overline{inv}'_{53} = \sum_{t='50}^{'53} \frac{INV_t}{CE_t} \tag{12.11}$$

where $CE = $ common equity. For each subsequent year

$$\overline{inv}_t = .4INV_t/CE_t + .6\,\overline{inv}_{t-1} \tag{12.12}$$

Finally $\overline{INV}_t = \overline{inv}_t CE_t$. In words, the normal inventory during a period is an exponential average of the inventory to common equity ratios up through the current period multiplied by the current common equity. The abnormal inventory used in the measurement of L is $\widehat{INV}_t = INV_t - \overline{INV}_t$.

The data of the asset liquidity index for the two industries provide an interesting contrast. For the food industry, the log of the index is negative, meaning that plant assets exceeded inventory, and the fall in the index over the five years reveals that inventory fell in importance relative to plant assets. The positive value of the index for the machinery index reveals that inventory outweighed plant, but the relative importance of inventory declined over the five years here also. For both industries the means are close to zero, meaning that plant and inventory are about equal in amount on the average. However, the large standard deviations indicate considerable variation in the variable among corporations.

$\mu = Debt\ Maturity\ Index.$ The quantity was defined in Chapter 6, page 80, as

$$\mu = \frac{1 + L/W}{1 + L'/W} \tag{12.13}$$

with L' a sum of the items comprising L weighted according to their maturity. With abnormal inventory considered a monetary asset, L' becomes L' as defined in Eq. (6.19) minus $.7INV$.

The values of $ln\mu$ in Table 12.2 require some interpretation. For a firm with cash the only monetary asset and with all liabilities current, we would have $ln\mu = 0$. As the maturity of the liabilities is raised, L'/W would fall, and $ln\mu$ would rise, indicating a stronger liquidity position. Shifting monetary assets into receivables and excess inventory will reduce the liquidity of the firm. Accordingly it will leave L unchanged and raise L', thereby reducing the value of $ln\mu$. The values of $ln\mu$ for the food sample are considerably higher than the machinery sample values, which indicates that their debt on the average has the longer maturity. This is due primarily to the more limited use of long-term debt financing by the machinery corporations.

$S = Size.$ Our final variable, the size of the corporation, is the sum of its assets less current liabilities. Other measures of size might seem more attractive, but they are unlikely to yield materially different results, and this one was found convenient in collecting the data. The average of the sample means was $87,120,000 for the food corporations and $47,880,000 for the machinery corporations. The variation in size around the sample means was large in both industries, and it may also be noted that on the average the machinery corporations grew in size at a faster rate than the food corporations.

12.3   The Simple Leverage Model

Table 12.3 contains the sample estimates of the regression statistics for Eq. (12.1). The data are the estimates of the coefficients, their standard errors, and R^2, the coefficient of determination, for the ten samples comprising two industries and five years. The results shown in Table 12.1 will be compared with the data of Table 11.5 which contains the data based on Eq. (11.7). The latter, it will be recalled, contained no leverage variable, and for purposes of identification, it will be called the Nolev model. Eq. (12.1) will be called the Simlev model.

TABLE 12.3

REGRESSION STATISTICS FOR THE SIMLEV MODEL

Food Sample

	1954	1955	1956	1957	1958	Average
Const. term, $ln\hat{\alpha}_0$	2.488	2.458	2.584	2.553	2.668	2.550
S.E.	.170	.146	.169	.134	.158	.155
Dividend, α_1	.784	.859	.885	.789	.711	.804
S.E.	.066	.058	.064	.049	.056	.059
Growth, α_2	10.972	10.854	8.946	10.114	10.199	10.217
S.E.	1.870	1.508	1.789	1.849	1.930	1.789
Earn. inst., $\hat{\alpha}_3$	−5.619	−4.442	−3.885	−8.562	−3.661	−5.234
S.E.	2.127	1.812	2.432	2.201	2.440	2.202
Leverage, $\hat{\alpha}_4$	−.522	−.416	−.255	−.343	−.175	−.342
S.E.	.159	.151	.163	.120	.147	.148
Asset liq., $\hat{\alpha}_5$	.322	.343	.175	.285	.164	.258
S.E.	.197	.181	.202	.156	.186	.184
Debt mat., $\hat{\alpha}_6$	.008	−.019	−.286	−.247	−.572	−.223
S.E.	.462	.412	.425	.374	.478	.430
Size, α_7	.114	.094	.051	.087	.106	.090
S.E.	.038	.034	.037	.029	.035	.035
Coeff. of var., R^2	.913	.939	.904	.933	.901	.918

Machine Sample

	1954	1955	1956	1957	1958	Average
Const. term, $ln\hat{\alpha}_0$	2.516	2.533	2.205	2.337	3.019	2.522
S.E.	.182	.176	.163	.174	.176	.174
Dividend, α_1	.845	.813	.858	.919	.824	.852
S.E.	.079	.067	.052	.058	.056	.062
Growth, α_2	7.468	7.619	8.819	4.370	2.197	6.095
S.E.	1.415	1.742	1.495	1.618	2.157	1.685
Earn. inst., $\hat{\alpha}_3$	−3.112	−3.317	−.854	−3.880	−.625	−2.358
S.E.	1.711	1.576	1.638	1.862	1.887	1.735
Leverage, $\hat{\alpha}_4$	.119	−.202	.026	.255	.162	.072
S.E.	.149	.169	.153	.173	.172	.163
Asset liq., $\hat{\alpha}_5$	−.400	−.337	−.016	−.094	.602	−.049
S.E.	.370	.352	.300	.321	.312	.331
Debt mat., $\hat{\alpha}_6$	−.088	.161	−.628	−1.029	.456	−.226
S.E.	.458	.663	.495	.574	.627	.563
Size, α_7	.082	.101	.158	.117	.048	.101
S.E.	.047	.047	.040	.045	.047	.045
Coeff. of var., R^2	.851	.880	.913	.890	.881	.883

The dividend coefficients once again are highly significant, fluctuate in a narrow range between years, and are significantly less than one for both industries. On the average, the food sample coefficients are somewhat lower than the machinery sample. In comparison with the Nolev model, the Simlev coefficients are slightly, almost imperceptibly lower. Apart from the introduction of additional variables, the reason why the dividend coefficients in the Simlev model may be different is the current dividend rather than an exponentially smoothed average of the dividend was used as the variable. It would seem that the only basis for choice between the two measurement rules is computational ease, in which case the current dividend should be used.

Turning to the growth variable, the parameter estimates for the food samples once again are highly significant and vary little over the five years. Their average level is slightly higher than in the Nolev model, but their standard errors are also higher. Once again the machinery sample does not perform as well as the foods. Not only are the parameter estimates considerably lower, but in 1957 and particularly 1958, they fall disastrously. In the latter year α_2 is not even statistically significant at the 5 per cent level. By comparison with the Nolev model, the Simlev model values of α_2 are higher, strikingly so in 1954. It would seem that measurement rules employed for the growth rate in this model are slightly superior than the Nolev model's. However, it seems that there are problems in measuring return on investment for machinery corporations that are still unsolved.

The earnings instability parameter estimates all are negative as expected, but α_3 is not statistically significant for two of the five food samples and three of the five machinery samples. Further, in two of the machinery samples, α_3 is less than its standard error. In both samples, α_3 fluctuates over a wide range, but the average level is considerably higher for foods. Comparison of α_3 with the corresponding parameter estimates in the Nolev model reveals some increase in their level but a considerable fall in their significance, i.e., they are smaller multiples of their standard errors. This is not surprising. In the Nolev model u is the instability in levered earnings, and the variable represents the combined effect of leverage and leverage-free earnings instability. In the Simlev model, $\check{\sigma}/W$ reflects the leverage-free instability of earnings. Without the refinements discussed earlier in measuring $\check{\sigma}/W$, I don't believe the results would have been as good as those obtained.

The remaining variable common to both models, corporate size, continues to perform well. In every sample, α_7 has the right sign and only the 1956 foods and the 1958 machinery estimates are not statistically significant at the 5 per cent level. The level and statistical significance of the food coefficients are considerably better than in the Nolev model, while the machinery coefficients are about the same. It appears that the additional risk variables included in the Simlev model do not weaken the importance of a corporation's size as an index of security and the liquidity of its shares.

The performance of the leverage variable is quite uneven. The food sample coefficients all have the right sign, and three of the five values of α_4 are significant at the 5 per cent level. On the other hand, in the machinery samples, α_4 has the right sign in only one year, and that coefficient is not even significant. I find the food sample results more a source of pleasure than the machinery sample results a source of disappointment. Failure to obtain inverse correlation between share price and leverage is typical.[4] One possible reason is that the earnings instability variable is based on levered earnings usually. With leverage recognized both directly and indirectly through earnings instability, the correlation with each variable is impaired. Another possibly more important reason is that secure profitable corporations are more likely to go into debt than insecure profitable ones. Insofar as this is true, the leverage variable tends to measure security and profitability instead of leverage with everything else the same.

In order to observe the inverse correlation between share price and leverage that we may presume exists, the influence of return on investment and earnings instability must be adequately recognized through other variables. Our efforts to accomplish this appears to have met with some success in the food samples but not in the machinery samples. If return on existing stock is not considered a reliable indicator of future investment profitability while leverage is looked on as an indicator for some of the corporations, the behavior of the machinery sample will be the result.

The other two risk variables, asset liquidity and debt maturity, performed poorly. Both $\hat{\alpha}_5$ and $\hat{\alpha}_6$ should be positive. All estimates of $\hat{\alpha}_5$ for the food samples were positive, with three almost twice their standard errors and the other two almost equal to their standard errors. However, only the 1958 machinery value of $\hat{\alpha}_5$ is satisfactory;

---

[4] Cf. the results obtained by Benishay [1960].

the other years all have the wrong sign. The values of $\hat{\alpha}_6$ for both industries have the wrong sign and/or do not differ significantly from zero. It appears that the errors in the measurement of these variables and/or the little influence they have on share price results in little or no contribution to the model.

12.4   The Modigliani-Miller Leverage Variable

The Modigliani-Miller theorem on leverage suggests that $1 + h - ih/\check{k}$ be substituted for $1 + h$ as the leverage variable in our model. Doing so and dropping μ, the debt maturity variable, on the grounds that there is no evidence investors use it in valuing a share, we have

$$LnP_0 = ln\hat{\alpha}_0 + \alpha_1 lnD + \alpha_2 ln(1 + br) + \alpha_3 ln(1 + \check{\sigma}/W) \\ + \hat{\alpha}_4 ln(1 + h - ih/\check{k}) + \hat{\alpha}_5 ln\pi + \alpha_7 lnS \quad (12.14)$$

The problem in testing this model, which will be called the Adlev model, is observing the leverage variable, in particular the value of $\check{k}$.

In the argument leading up to Eq. (8.13) we established that the value of k when $h = b = 0$ is

$$\check{k} = \alpha_0(1 + \check{\sigma}/W)^{\alpha_3}\pi^{\alpha_6}S^{-\alpha_7} \quad (12.15)$$

Therefore, give the values of the α and the values of the variables in Eq. (12.15) for each corporation, $\check{k}$ for each firm may be obtained. For an alternative course of action, rearrange the terms of Eq. (8.6) so that the terms on the right side of Eq. (12.15) are on one side. The remaining terms equal to $\check{k}$ are

$$\check{k} = \frac{(1 - b)Y}{P}(1 + br)^{\alpha_2}(1 + h)^{-\alpha_4} \quad (12.16)$$

What this expression does is adjust a corporation's dividend yield to the value it would have if h and b were equal to zero for the corporation. This is our definition of $\check{k}$.

Objections can be raised against both of the above alternatives, and some may feel that the strongest apply to the course of action taken, a variant of the second.[5] The major objection, however, is

---

[5] The expression actually used was

$$\check{k} = \frac{(1 - b)Y}{P}(1 + h)^{-\alpha_4} + br$$

Adding br yields about the same result as multiplying by $(1 + br)^\alpha$.

common to both in that both assume share price is known (directly or indirectly in the form of the α) to obtain an independent variable of a model in which share price is the dependent variable. Our defense is that the knowledge about P employed in obtaining $\check{k}$ will not materially influence the correlation obtained between P and the leverage variable. In other words, $\check{k}$ plays a relatively minor role in $1 + h - ih/\check{k}$, and P plays a relatively minor role in $\check{k}$. Therefore, the results that are obtained with the leverage variable are not dependent on the method by which $\check{k}$ was obtained. A method free of these objections will yield results that are better if they differ at all.

Two further statements are needed to fully specify the method of obtaining the leverage variable. First, $\check{k}$ was computed for each corporation on the basis of its values for D/P, h, and br, and with $\alpha_4 = .3$. Second, in obtaining the leverage variable, the interest rate $i = .045$ was used for all corporations in all years. It is possible that better results could be obtained by using the sample estimate of α_4 for each sample and by varying i among corporations with their leverage.

Table 12.5 presents the sample means and standard deviations of $ln(1 + h - ih/\check{k})$. As we would expect, $ln(1 + h - ih/\check{k})$ is smaller than $ln(1 + h)$. On the average, $\check{k}$ is about twice i, so that the Adlev leverage variable averages a little more than one half of Simlev variable. Also, the standard deviation of the former is about half that of $ln(1 + h)$.

Table 12.4 presents the sample estimates of the coefficients for the Adlev model. The striking feature of the results is the dramatic improvement in the food sample estimates of α_4. The coefficient has gone up from an average over the five years of .34 to .85, and its range of variation over the five years was materially reduced. Further, in the Simlev model α_4 is over two times its standard error in three of the five samples, while in the Adlev model it ranges from three to five times its standard error. This improvement cannot be attributed to the change in the scale of the variable. If we had divided each value of the Simlev leverage variable by two, we would expect α_4 to double, and we would also expect its standard error to double. However, we did not simply change the scale of the variable, and α_4 increased by a factor of 2.5 while its standard error rose by only one third.

The Modigliani-Miller theorem clearly provides a better basis for measuring the influence of leverage on share price than the use

TABLE 12.4

REGRESSION STATISTICS FOR THE ADLEV MODEL

Food Sample

	1954	1955	1956	1957	1958	Average
Const. term, $ln\hat{\alpha}_0$	2.454	2.435	2.545	2.541	2.632	2.521
S.E.	.158	.142	.168	.126	.150	.149
Dividend, α_1	.790	.855	.874	.787	.708	.803
S.E.	.058	.055	.063	.044	.051	.054
Growth, α_2	12.401	11.609	8.959	10.442	10.038	10.690
S.E.	1.640	1.449	1.725	1.535	1.685	1.607
Earn. inst., $\hat{\alpha}_3$	−5.427	−3.977	−3.312	−8.675	−4.000	−5.078
S.E.	1.872	1.678	2.258	1.988	2.251	2.009
Leverage, $\hat{\alpha}_4$	−1.062	−.854	−.617	−.834	−.852	−.844
S.E.	.195	.200	.223	.171	.222	.202
Asset liq., $\hat{\alpha}_5$	−.272	.342	.222	.283	.245	.273
S.E.	.161	.155	.182	.131	.154	.157
Size, α_7	.107	.091	.056	.085	.113	.090
S.E.	.034	.032	.036	.026	.033	.032
Coeff. of var., R^2	.925	.942	.904	.941	.911	.925

Machinery Sample

	1954	1955	1956	1957	1958	Average
Const. term, $ln\hat{\alpha}_0$	2.556	2.523	2.238	2.330	2.975	2.524
S.E.	.179	.178	.166	.181	.178	.176
Dividend, α_1	.844	.815	.851	.875	.832	.843
S.E.	.077	.066	.052	.059	.056	.062
Growth, α_2	7.207	7.442	8.846	3.758	2.176	5.886
S.E.	1.375	1.705	1.517	1.638	2.135	1.674
Earn. inst., $\hat{\alpha}_3$	−3.163	−3.351	−.274	−4.317	−.788	−2.379
S.E.	1.542	1.542	1.650	1.992	1.995	1.744
Leverage, $\hat{\alpha}_4$	−.337	−.353	−.096	−.118	.428	−.095
S.E.	.325	.276	.274	.295	.379	.310
Asset liq., $\hat{\alpha}_5$	−.337	−.250	.061	.052	.666	.038
S.E.	.325	.314	.283	.331	.334	.317
Size, α_7	.076	.106	.142	.131	.064	.104
S.E.	.045	.044	.039	.046	.046	.044
Coeff. of var., R^2	.857	.878	.909	.882	.879	.881

of the debt-equity ratio alone. Also, using their variable and possibly also dropping the debt maturity variable has brought about some slight improvement in the significance of the other coefficients, particularly the asset liquidity coefficient. In the Adlev model, every α_5 exceeds its standard error, and two are significant at the 5 per cent level.

Almost as striking as the improvement in the food sample values of α_4 is the failure of the machinery sample values to respond to the change in the leverage variable. Three of the five years have the right sign, but only in one year does α_4 exceed its standard deviation. The Modigliani-Miller leverage variable is not powerful enough to solve the problems presented by the machinery sample.

12.5 Outside Equity Financing

Eq. (9.18) represents the enlargement of our model to include outside equity financing. It is the Adlev model with vq, the equity accretion rate, added to the growth variable and q, the outside financing rate, a new variable. It will be called the Eko model, and in logarithmic form, the equation is

$$LnP = ln\hat{a}_0 + \alpha_1 lnD + \alpha_2 ln(1 + br + vq) + \hat{\alpha}_3 ln(1 + \breve{o}/W)$$
$$+ \hat{\alpha}_4 ln(1 + h - ih/k) + \hat{\alpha}_5 ln\pi + \alpha_7 lnS + \hat{\alpha}_8 ln(1 + q) \quad (12.17)$$

The measurement rules for obtaining v and q will be stated, their sample values will be stated and discussed, and the parameter estimates will be presented.

The actual outside financing rate in a year is defined as the funds obtained from stock issued divided by the net worth at the start of the year. Stock issued includes shares issued for property and for conversion of convertible prior securities. It does not include shares arising from stock splits and stock dividends. The funds actually obtained on each stock issue is a hard figure to obtain, and $n_t P_{t-1}$, with n_t the number of shares issued for money or property and P_{t-1} the price of the stock at the start of the year, was considered a satisfactory approximation. Therefore, the outside financing rate is

$$q_t = \frac{n_t P_{t-1}}{N_{t-1} W_{t-1}} \quad (12.18)$$

where N is the number of shares outstanding and W is the book value or net worth per share. The issue of stock for money or property takes place very irregularly over time, and the normalized or average rate of financing is

$$\bar{q}_t = \beta q_t + (1 - \beta)\bar{q}_{t-1} \qquad (12.19)$$

For 1954, $\bar{q}_t$ is a weighted average of q_t for 1951–54, and for subsequent years it was obtained by the above formula with $\beta = .3$. In what follows q_t refers to the normalized value of the variable.

The value of v, the fraction of the funds invested by new stockholders that accrues to existing stockholders, presents the same problems of observation as $\bar{k}$. The only simple and straightforward solu-

TABLE 12.5

MEAN AND STANDARD DEVIATION OF CERTAIN VARIABLES

Food Sample

	1954	1955	1956	1957	1958	Average
Leverage,						
$ln(1 + h - ih/k)$ ...	.0907	.0841	.0965	.0876	.0556	.0829
S.D.	.1656	.1532	.1582	.1479	.1261	.1502
Stock issue, $ln(1 + q)$ ...	.0058	.0080	.0098	.0089	.0109	.0087
S.D.	.0143	.0229	.0202	.0163	.0215	.0190
Growth, $ln(1 + br + vq)$	.0429	.0407	.0401	.0391	.0399	.0405
S.D.	.0190	.0211	.0208	.0177	.0177	.0193

Machinery Sample

	1954	1955	1956	1957	1958	Average
Leverage,						
$ln(1 + h - ih/k)$ ...	−.0506	−.0445	−.0239	−.0250	−.0412	−.0370
S.D.	.1571	.1429	.1361	.1496	.1194	.1410
Stock issue, $ln(1 + q)$ ...	.0154	.0222	.0256	.0242	.0199	.0215
S.D.	.0350	.0420	.0413	.0372	.0295	.0370
Growth, $ln(1 + br + vq)$	.0464	.0458	.0513	.0549	.0431	.0483
S.D.	.0259	.0217	.0229	.0264	.0219	.0238

tion to the problem is to use Eq. (9.13) for the value of v_t. Bias in favor of our theory due to the appearance of P_t on the right side of the equation should not be serious because we multiply v by q and then add it to br. In fact due to an error, the definition employed was $v_t = 1 - W_{t-1}/P_{t-1}$. The accuracy of the variable is reduced, but P_{t-1} and not P_t was employed in obtaining it.

Table 12.5 presents the sample means and standard deviations of $ln(1 + q)$. The five-year average rate of outside equity financing was less than 1 per cent for the food sample and 2.15 per cent for the machinery sample. Manufacturing corporations rely very little on stock issues for money or property to finance their growth. In fact, 33 of the 48 food and 24 of the 48 machinery corporations issued no stock, apart from negligible amounts connected with management stock option plans, over the entire period 1954–58. The variations in outside stock financing among corporations is of course quite large. The smoothed value of the money or property obtained from stock issues was over 15 per cent of the existing common equity in some corporation years.

Summary statistics for the equity accretion rate due to stock financing was not calculated. Table 12.5 presents the means and standard deviations of $ln\,(1 + br + vq)$. Comparison with $ln\,(1 + br)$ reveals that on the average, vq was very small, about .001 for the foods and .003 for the machinery samples. The quantity varies over the five years due to variation in q but more due to v. A corporation with a high q has vq equal to zero if $v = 0$, and for one year it can be seen that vq was negative.

Table 12.6 presents the regression results when $1 + q$ is added to the variables, and vq is added to the growth rate. For the food sample, the outside equity financing rate coefficient is not significant at the 5 per cent level in any year, and it fluctuates widely over the five years. The coefficient has the right sign in every year, and is about equal to or larger than its standard error in all but one year, so that the data appear to provide some support for the hypothesis that the rate of profit required on a share increases with the rate at which the number of shares on the market are being increased. However, the performance of the growth variable is disquieting.

In every year α_2 and to a lesser degree the ratio of α_2 to its standard error is reduced somewhat. The food sample values of vq and q are correlated so that $ln\,(1 + q)$ and the growth variable are correlated. It appears that the addition of vq to the growth variable has simply reduced its accuracy, and the correlation between growth and the outside financing rate has created correlation between the latter and share price.

Among the other variables, the earnings instability and size coefficients were weakened slightly by the introduction of new stock financing, and in some years the leverage coefficient was reduced materially. Only the asset liquidity variable came out unscathed, and this is probably coincidental.

As we have become conditioned to expect, the machinery sam-

TABLE 12.6

REGRESSION STATISTICS FOR THE EKO MODEL
Food Sample

	1954	1955	1956	1957	1958	Average
Const. term, $ln\alpha_0$	2.476	2.403	2.663	2.611	2.755	2.582
S.E.	.158	.136	.185	.130	.144	.151
Dividend, α_1	.803	.883	.892	.764	.672	.803
S.E.	.059	.053	.070	.046	.050	.056
Growth, α_2	11.876	11.515	7.143	8.741	9.248	9.705
S.E.	1.615	1.362	1.875	1.404	1.479	1.547
Earn. inst., $\hat{\alpha}_3$	−5.164	−2.953	−3.117	−7.850	−4.051	−4.627
S.E.	1.897	1.671	2.579	2.031	2.188	2.070
Leverage, $\hat{\alpha}_4$	−.998	−.588	−.466	−.759	−.781	−.712
S.E.	.195	.217	.256	.178	.216	.212
Asset liq., $\hat{\alpha}_5$	.297	.279	.204	.306	.300	.277
S.E.	.164	.156	.206	.138	.149	.163
Size, α_7	.103	.086	.040	.083	.095	.081
S.E.	.037	.031	.040	.027	.033	.034
Stock issue, $\hat{\alpha}_8$	−3.316	−5.221	−2.218	−1.246	−.649	−2.530
S.E.	1.967	1.239	1.816	1.384	1.153	1.512
Coeff. of det., R^2	.924	.947	.886	.938	.919	.923

Machinery Sample

	1954	1955	1956	1957	1958	Average
Const. term, $ln\alpha_0$	2.660	2.543	2.312	2.401	3.012	2.586
S.E.	.195	.182	.156	.173	.178	.177
Dividend, α_1	.876	.853	.850	.860	.836	.855
S.E.	.084	.067	.053	.058	.062	.065
Growth, α_2	4.917	5.617	7.744	3.738	.742	4.552
S.E.	1.227	1.412	1.212	1.216	1.542	1.322
Earn. inst., $\hat{\alpha}_3$	−2.352	−2.858	−.186	−4.566	−.588	−2.110
S.E.	1.685	1.600	1.576	1.941	2.016	1.764
Leverage, $\hat{\alpha}_4$	.277	−.274	−.038	−.142	.322	.029
S.E.	.281	.297	.292	.318	.408	.319
Asset liq., $\hat{\alpha}_5$	−.218	−.169	.069	.029	.646	.051
S.E.	.358	.324	.274	.322	.341	.324
Size, α_7	.064	.111	.135	.116	.062	.098
S.E.	.050	.046	.037	.046	.048	.045
Stock issue, $\hat{\alpha}_8$	.382	−.709	−1.539	−.814	.891	−.358
S.E.	.983	.768	.716	.937	1.103	.901
Coeff. of det., R^2	.830	.872	.920	.892	.879	.879

ples did not perform as well as the food samples. In three of the years, α_8 had the right sign and exceeded its standard error, but in the other two years it did not even have the right sign. The growth coefficient was reduced by varying amounts in every year, and the ratio of α_2 to its standard error was reduced in some years. As far as the other coefficients are concerned there is no material change in their values or significance on the average.

Since outside equity financing is more important in the machinery than the food industry, its poorer performance in the former industry is particularly disappointing. It is evident that further work on the theory and measurement of the variables is required for empirical statements on the influence of outside equity financing on stock prices.

12.6 Conclusions

What conclusions may we draw from the empirical findings presented in the preceding pages? First, in comparing the three models, the food sample results along with the stronger theoretical support for it, argue that the Adlev model is superior to the Simlev model. Theoretical considerations argue for the recognition of outside equity financing, but possibly because of the difficulty of measuring the variable, it cannot be said that the Eko model yields better predictions of the variation in share price with the independent variables than the Adlev model.

Looking only at the food sample results, the Adlev model may fairly be called a resounding success. The dividend, growth, and leverage variables are highly significant and fluctuate in a narrow range over the five years. The other three variables have the right sign and exceed their standard error in every year, and are statistically significant at the 5 per cent level in four years for S, three years for $\check{\sigma}/W$, and two years for π. Also, considering the limitations of least-squares regression analysis and the secondary importance of these variables, the variation in their coefficients among samples is quite modest. The only thing that may be considered a disappointment is the failure of the earnings instability coefficient to come out stronger. Either the variable is not as important as one might imagine or our measurement of it can be improved considerably.

By comparison with the food sample, the machinery sample performance under the Adlev model is at best a modest success. Only the dividend is a "class one" variable, highly significant in every year and stable over the five years. The growth rate coefficient comes up to standard during 1954–56, but it falls sharply in 1957, and in 1958 it is not even statistically significant. The earnings instability and size coefficients have the right sign in every year, but for each variable the coefficients are two or more times their standard errors in only three of the five years. Moreover, α_3 is less than its standard error in two of the years. The coefficients of the remaining two variables, leverage and asset liquidity, have the wrong sign in two of the five years. One cannot even infer with confidence from the data that the variation in share price with each is in the direction predicted by theory. The coefficients certainly do not provide reliable estimates of the parameters.

Before closing this chapter, the results obtained from two other analyses of the data should be reported on briefly. First, the Adlev model was run in each year on the two industries combined in one sample. The coefficients obtained typically fell between the values obtained for the separate samples, and their standard errors were reduced, in many cases quite materially. What conclusions one should draw from these results is difficult to judge. Since our objective was to include all variables that enter into the determination of a share's price, the coefficient estimates for the two samples should not have differed significantly. The failure to obtain this agreement indicates that there is room for improvement in the measurement of the variables and/or the structure and content of the models. It does not seem, however, that combining industries results in better parameter estimates.

The other experiment was somewhat more interesting. It has been acknowledged that in evaluating a share investors may consider information not included in a corporation's past financial statements, particularly in estimating return on investment. In an effort to recognize this information, the shares in the samples were classified in three quality grades, A, B, and C. Security analysis services classify stocks in quality grades, but the basis for this classification is usually objective historical information on the performance of the stock such as past dividend performance, appreciation in the price of the stock, etc.[6] Since such information is already included in our independent variables, these quality grade groupings would be of no help. What we did was classify the corporations in subindustry groups such as material handling equipment, railroad equipment, petro-chemical ma-

---

[6] E.g., see the description of the Value Line ratings in Bernhardt [1959].

chinery, and metalworking machinery. In the food industry, sugar refining, canning, and flour milling were among the subcategories. For the most part the firms in a subcategory were put in the same quality grade. The criterion for the quality grade assigned to a firm was the prospects for future profits and profitable investment judged by the strength of the demand for its products. Accordingly, firms making petro-chemical and material handling equipment were assigned a higher-quality grade than the metalworking and railroad equipment manufacturers. Although past profits were not considered, the reputation of a firm for being vigorous and outstanding resulted in its being but in a different quality grade than the other members of its group.

By the use of dummy variables, the quality grade of a share may be recognized as a variable and the Adlev model was run on the samples with two new variables to recognize the three quality grades.[7] The two new variables had the expected sign and were quite significant in both industries, the significance exceeding the 1 per cent level in a majority of the cases. However, the quality variables were highly correlated with the other variables, particularly growth, earnings instability, and size, and the coefficients of these variables were materially reduced. Since the quality variables significantly reduced the unexplained variation in share price, they clearly contained information not contained in the other variables that investors use in evaluating a share. On the other hand, the high correlation between the quantitative and qualitative variables indicates that they overlap considerably. Consequently, a model that included the quality variables would not provide the best estimates of the parameters of the quantitative variables. Furthermore, it can be argued that these quality variables do not represent really different attributes of a share. Rather, investors use the information they represent to arrive at different estimates of the included quantitative variables than were obtained under the measurement rules employed. The correct course of action would be to adjust our measurement of earnings, rate of return on investment, etc., to take advantage of this information.

[7] To explain the method, assume there is one measurable independent variable, X, and three quality grades. Our regression equation is

$$LnP = a_0 + a_1X + a_2A + a_3C.$$

For firms in quality grade A, $A = 1$ and $C = 0$; for firms in quality grade B, $A = C = 0$, and for firms in C, $A = 0$ and $C = 1$. The regression is then run with the variables A and C taking the values zero or one for each firm. The expectation is that $a_2 > 0$ and $a_3 < 0$, if the order of quality is $A > B > C$.

Chapter 13

VARIATION IN SHARE PRICE WITH THE INDEPENDENT VARIABLES

In the previous chapter our stock price models were examined to establish the sign, statistical significance, and variation among samples in the parameter estimates. Our purpose was to arrive at some judgment on the accuracy of the parameter estimates obtained with each of the models and to find which of the models performed best. However, this type of knowledge, sign, significance, etc., of parameter estimates is not our ultimate objective. The model was created to establish the investment and financing policies that maximize the value of a share. Before undertaking this task it is advisable that we become familiar with the quantitative implications of the model under our numerical values for the parameters. In other words, we will establish and evaluate the quantitative statements on the variation in share price with each independent variable, particularly the investment and financing decision variables, that our empirical results yield. Just looking at statistics of the variables and the coefficient values is not much help, particularly with the relation among the variables logarithmic.

The first thing we will do in this chapter is decide which of the previous chapters' models will be employed and what values will be assigned to its parameters. For reasons to be presented shortly, it is believed that better values can be assigned to the parameters than either the estimates for any one year or an average of the estimates for the five years. Given these parameter values, the variation in share price with each independent variable will be examined. In each case values will be assigned the independent variable in question that cover its range of variation, and a share's price will be computed with fixed values for the other independent variables. The dividend yield and required rate of profit in each case will also be computed, and the economic implications of the results obtained will be dis-

177

cussed. Where there are conflicting theories on the relation between share price and an independent variable, the data will be examined for information on the question.

13.1 The Model and Its Parameters

To establish and evaluate the statements on the variation in share price with the independent variables that result from our theory and data, we must first decide on which of the three models tested in the last chapter will be used. The Eko model is the most general, but the empirical results obtained with it provided no basis for believing that it yielded information on the variation in share price with the rate of outside equity financing. Furthermore, employing the model may result in incorrect statements on the variation in share price with the other independent variables.[1] Between the other two models, the performance of the Adlev model was clearly superior to the Simlev model's for the food samples and no worse at least for the machinery samples. Therefore, the Adlev model will be used.

The five-year average of the food sample estimates of the parameters were:

$$ln\,\hat{\alpha}_0 = 2.521 \qquad \alpha_1 = .803 \qquad \alpha_2 = 10.69 \qquad \hat{\alpha}_3 = -5.08$$
$$\hat{\alpha}_4 = -.844 \qquad \hat{\alpha}_5 = .27 \qquad \alpha_7 = .09$$

The machinery sample averages of α_1 and α_7 were slightly higher, while the values of α_2, α_3, α_4, and α_5 were materially lower. Although there may be some difference of opinion as to what the true values of these parameters are, those who disagree with the food sample estimates, particularly the estimates of α_2 and α_4, certainly would not argue that the true values are lower, i.e., closer to the machinery sample estimates. For instance, the smaller the value of the growth coefficient, α_2, the more the empirical findings conflict with the hypothesis that investors are indifferent to the dividend rate. Also, the larger the amount by which α_4 is below one, the greater the amount by which leverage per se raises share price.

The inescapable conclusion is that the machinery sample parameter estimates should be rejected. The reasons for the values obtained, to be explained shortly, is that problems in the measurement of the variables and the relations among them for machinery corpo-

---

[1] In view of the fact that most corporations engage in no outside equity financing and few place heavy reliance on it, employing a model that does not include outside equity financing may not be too damaging.

rations prevented us from obtaining accurate parameter estimates. It is of course also possible that the structure of firms in the industry and the attitudes of investors toward the firms require a different theory than the one employed.

Should we consider the food sample averages presented above the best estimates of the parameters under our theory? Least-squares regression analysis on sample data provides best estimates of a function's parameters when the sample data satisfies certain conditions. One of these conditions is that the values of the independent variables are free of error. It has been shown that if there are errors in the measurement of the sample values of the independent variable x in the regression $y = \alpha_0 + \alpha_1 x$, the sample estimate of α_1 will have a downward bias. In a multiple regression there will be a general but not necessarily universal tendency for the coefficients of the independent variables to have a downward bias. Obviously the data of investor expectations obtained under our measurement rules are not free of error, and consequently the parameter estimates of the previous chapter are more or less below their true values. Madansky [1959] and others have investigated the problem, but so far methods have not been found for establishing the amount of the bias in a parameter estimate without knowledge of the error in the measurement of the variable.

A second problem posed by the nature of our data is correlation among the independent variables. It has been shown that when the dependent variable is correlated with two or more independent variables that are correlated with each other, the parameter estimate for each independent variable will have a large standard error and its value will fluctuate considerably among samples. Regression equations which include earnings and/or book value per share along with the dividend among the independent variables illustrate these problems with the parameter estimates. Fortunately, earnings and book value do not appear directly among the independent variables in our model, and our parameter estimates do not fluctuate wildly among samples. However, correlation among the independent variables still remains, and the accuracy of the parameter estimates obtained from the samples is open to question.

On the basis of the above considerations we may question whether the food sample averages are the best estimates. In addition, theory and analysis of the data to be reported in the next section argue very strongly that the dividend coefficient $\alpha_1 \sim 1.0$ and not

.803. This analysis also suggests that the growth coefficient $\alpha_2 >$ 10.69. With respect to the other parameter estimates, on the basis of less reliable evidence, largely our knowledge that the errors in the measurement of the independent variables and the intercorrelation among them exist, we believe that the food sample averages of α_3 through α_5 are below their true values, and α_7, the corporate size coefficient, is somewhat greater than its true value.

Estimates of the parameters that are considered superior to the food sample averages are presented below:

$$ln\hat{\alpha}_0 = 2.326 \qquad \alpha_1 = 1.0 \qquad \alpha_2 = 14.0 \qquad \hat{\alpha}_3 = -6.0$$
$$\hat{\alpha}_4 = -1.0 \qquad \hat{\alpha}_5 = .40 \qquad \alpha_7 = .08$$

For all but $ln\hat{\alpha}_0$ the value in each case reflects our judgment supported by the previous observations. The value assigned to $ln\hat{\alpha}_0$ was arrived at to satisfy the condition that given the values of the other coefficients and given the mean values of the independent variables, the stock price equation results in the mean value for share price. Without making this compensating change in $ln\hat{\alpha}_0$, there would be a tendency for the share price predicted for a corporation by the model to be above the actual price. With the change, the sum of the residuals for the sample corporations will be about equal to zero.

In the following sections, devoted to the variation in share price with the independent variables, we will for the most part use the parameter values just stated, but we will also have occasion to use the food sample averages. For identification, the former will be referred to as the *"better values"* and the food sample averages as the *"average values."*

The food sample averages of the sample means for the variables with the dividend mean adjusted slightly[2] are:

$$lnD = .687 \qquad\qquad ln(1 + br) = .039$$
$$ln(1 + \check{\sigma}/W) = .025 \qquad ln(1 + h - ih/\check{k}) = .083$$
$$ln\pi = -.032 \qquad\qquad lnS = 4.47$$

For certain problems to be examined in the pages that follow, the arithmetic is simplified and the analysis is more easily understood without altering the nature of the conclusions by the use of the following values for the independent variables:

[2] The argument by which we arrive at $a_2 = 1$ also suggested that some sample values of the dividend were understated. Therefore, instead of using the actual sample average $lnD = .657$, we take as the average value, $lnD = .687$. This value is used to arrive at $lna_0 = 2.326$.

$D = \$1.00$, or $lnD = 0$ $\qquad\qquad$ $br = .04$, or $ln(1 + br) = .0392$
$ln(1 + \breve{o}/W) = .025$ $\qquad\qquad$ $h = 0$, or $ln(1 + h - ih/k) = 0$
$ln\pi = 0$ $\qquad\qquad\qquad\qquad\quad$ $lnS = 4.47$

The above values for the independent variables will be referred to as the *standard values,* and the samples averages will be referred to as the *average values* of the variables.

13.2 Variation in Price with the Dividend

It will be recalled that in the theoretical development of our stock price models, it was taken for granted that the dividend co-efficient is equal to one. The rationale was that *with everything else the same* a share with a $2.00 dividend is the equivalent of two shares with a $1.00 dividend, and it should sell at twice the price of a share with a $1.00 dividend. In the sample regressions the values of α_1 were

TABLE 13.1

POSSIBLE VARIATION IN PRICE, DIVIDEND YIELD, AND
REQUIRED RATE OF PROFIT WITH THE DIVIDEND*

D	br	LnP	P	D/P	k
$1.00	.04	3.131	$22.89	.044	.084
2.00	.04	3.687	39.92	.050	.090
3.00	.04	4.013	55.29	.054	.094

* The values of lnP, P, D/P, and k are based on the average values of the parameters and the variables presented in Section 13.1.

significant, stable, and close to one, but they were significantly less than one. The average over the five food samples was $\alpha_1 = .803$, and .054 was the average of the standard errors. The consequences of $\alpha_1 = .803$ for share price, dividend yield, and required rate of profit are illustrated in Table 13.1. The values assigned to the dividend of $1.00, $2.00, and $3.00, are approximately the average less one standard deviation, the average, and the average plus one standard deviation.

The values of LnP were obtained with the average values of the parameters and of the variables other than the dividend. To illustrate with the case of $D = \$2.00$,

$$LnP = ln\hat{\alpha}_0 + \alpha_1 lnD + \alpha_2 ln(1 + br) + \hat{\alpha}_3 ln(1 + \breve{o}/W)$$
$$+ \hat{\alpha}_4 ln(1 + h - ih/k) + \hat{\alpha}_5 ln\pi + \alpha_7 lnS$$
$$= 2.521 + (.803)(.692) + (10.69)(.039) - (5.08)(.025)$$
$$- (.844)(.083) + (.27)(-.032) + (.09)(4.47) = 3.687$$

The computation of P and D/P is obvious, and $k = D/P + br$.

Table 13.1 makes clear that with $\alpha_1 = .803$, share price does not vary proportionately with the dividend. That is, with $P = \$39.92$ for $D = \$2.00$, we do not have $\$19.96$ and $\$59.88$, the two other prices. The prices shown, $\$22.82$ and $\$55.29$, indicate quantitatively the departure from proportionately consequent upon $\alpha_1 = .803$. With different values for the other independent variables and their parameters, the values of P would be different, but the relations among the computed and the proportional share prices would be the same. The dividend yield with $\alpha_1 = .803$ rises from .044 to .054, and k rises correspondingly, as the dividend is increased from $\$1.00$ to $\$3.00$.

There are several possible reasons why the data produced $\alpha_1 < 1$. Investors may have a preference for low-priced over high-priced shares because a smaller investment is needed to buy a round lot or because low-priced shares have greater price appreciation potential. The former consideration is not important enough to explain the large variation in dividend yield with the level of the dividend. On the price appreciation potential, the other variables should reflect underlying attributes of a share which give it this attraction. What is more important, few of the food shares are really low priced, say under $\$10.00$, and fewer have the speculative advantages usually associated with low-priced shares.

A reason advanced earlier for $\alpha_1 < 1$ is that investors and corporations identify some dividend figure as being normal. That is, investors do not believe a dividend above the industry average is as likely to experience a discrete increase as a dividend below the average. If this is true, we would obtain $\alpha_1 < 1$.

All of the above reasons for $\alpha_1 < 1$ would justify using the value obtained. The following reason does not. We have assumed that a corporation estimates its normalized current earnings and pays a dividend in relation to this income figure that reflects its retention policy. A corporation is unlikely to pay a higher dividend than this figure, but we can imagine its paying a lower dividend. If earnings drop by a large enough amount to require a cut in the dividend, a corporation may decide it wiser to cut the dividend more than proportionately with the fall in normalized earnings in order to avoid further cuts in the dividend later. In other words, there is an asymmetry in the firm's attitude towards dividend cuts and dividend increases. Periodic small increases in the dividend are good, but one large cut is better than periodic small reductions in the dividend.

If this is true a dividend for which the last change was positive is the normalized current dividend, but one for which the last change was negative is below the normalized current figure. In the latter case, investors expect an abnormal increase in the dividend in the near future.

There will be a general tendency for corporations that have cut their dividend to be paying lower dividends than those which have raised their dividend. Under this chain of reasoning we would expect to obtain $\alpha_1 < 1$ with the current dividend as the dividend variable. In part, to deal with this problem we took at the variable the higher of the current dividend, or 2 per cent of the book value per share. However, inspection of the residuals, the differences between the actual and predicted values of the dependent variable, revealed a marked tendency for corporations with the dividend a small percentage of book value, 2 to 4 per cent, to be selling at prices above those predicted by the model.[3] There was some tendency for shares paying a high dividend in relation to book value to sell at prices below those predicted by the model, but this tendency was considerably weaker. Since shares with a low dividend in relation to book value are largely those paying a low dividend, our measurement of the dividend may be the reason why the data produced $\alpha_1 < 1$.

In running the regression analysis again, I would measure a firm's dividend differently. What I would do for all corporations paying a dividend below some figure, say 5 per cent of book value per share, is take the arithmetic average of the current dividend rate and 5 per cent of book value, and use that rate to compute the normalized current dividend. I believe that the result would be α_1 closer to one and a higher multiple of its standard error. The use of this dividend figure in measuring the rate of growth in the dividend would also, I believe, increase the size and statistical significance of that variable's coefficient. On the above reasoning, $\alpha_1 = 1$ is used in what follows.

One further observation on the dividend may be advisable. It is sometimes found that the correlation between two variables is heteroscedastic, that is, *absolute values* of the residuals are correlated with an independent variable, particularly an important vari-

---

[3] The pricing of a share paying a very low dividend in relation to book value will also be influenced by the possibility of a change in management to one that employs the assets of the firm more effectively.

able such as the dividend. When this is true, deflation by that variable results in a model that yields better predictions of the dependent variable. The use of logarithms of the variables as in our model is another means of avoiding heteroscedasticity, and as noted in Chapter 11, it took care of the problem. There was a slight but by no means significant tendency for the absolute values of the residuals to vary with the size of the dividend.

13.3 Variation in Price with the Growth Rate

The rate of growth in the dividend depends on two variables, r and b, and it is advisable to deal with each in turn. What we will do first is fix b at .5 and vary r in the interval zero to .16. The resultant values of rb center on the food sample mean value, and the

TABLE 13.2

VARIATION IN PRICE, DIVIDEND YIELD, AND REQUIRED RATE OF
PROFIT WITH THE RATE OF RETURN ON INVESTMENT*

r	br	$ln(1 + br)$	lnP	P	D/P	k
.00	.00	.00	2.532	$12.59	.079	.079
.04	.02	.0198	2.810	16.62	.060	.080
.08	.04	.0392	3.082	21.80	.046	.086
.12	.06	.0583	3.349	28.48	.035	.095
.16	.08	.0770	3.612	37.01	.027	.107

* The values of lnP, P, D/P, and k are based on $b = .5$, the standard values of the variables other than br and the better parameter values presented in Section 13.1.

interval between successive values used is about one standard deviation. Table 13.2 presents P, D/P, and k for the different values of br, with standard values for the other independent variables, and the better parameter values. Since the standard value of the dividend is $1.00, $b = .5$ implies that $Y = $2.00.

With the current dividend $1.00 and the rate of growth rising from 0 to 8 per cent, share price rises from $12.59 to $37.21, the dividend yield falls from .079 to .027, and k rises from .079 to .107. It is evident then that P and d are highly responsive to variation in br. The rise in the required rate of profit with br is initially quite small, but it increases quite rapidly as the level of br rises. It is interesting to note the implications of the data for our theorem that k is a function of br. If k did not rise with br but remained at .079, a share with $br = .08$ would sell at an infinite price.

With Y and b smaller, say $Y = $1.50 and $b = .33$ so that $D =$

$1.00 remains, price would increase at a lower rate with r. Reducing b reduces the investment rate at each value for r, and the rate of growth in the dividend is correspondingly reduced. For instance, with $b = .33$ we have $br = .026$ at $r = .08$ and $br = .04$ for $r = .12$. The prices of these two shares are $18.05 and $21.80.

The sharp and uninterrupted rise in P with br that we obtain with b fixed and r increasing does not take place when r is fixed and b is varied. The reason is that as b is increased, the rise in the rate of growth of the dividend is offset more or less by the fall in its current value. To illustrate, assume a corporation with current earnings of $1.67 and a 10 per cent return on investment. Table 13.3 presents the corporation's dividend, P, D/P, and k, under values

TABLE 13.3

VARIATION IN PRICE, DIVIDEND YIELD, AND REQUIRED
RATE OF PROFIT WITH THE RETENTION RATE*

b	br	D	$ln(1 + br)$	lnP	P	D/P	k
.00	.00	$1.67	.0000	3.047	$21.05	.079	.079
.20	.02	1.34	.0198	3.104	22.28	.060	.080
.40	.04	1.00	.0392	3.083	21.82	.046	.086
.60	.06	.67	.0583	2.945	19.00	.035	.095
.80	.08	.33	.0770	2.512	12.33	.027	.107

* Data assume $Y = \$1.67$, $r = .10$, standard values for the variables other than D and br, and the better parameter values presented in Section 13.1.

of b that result in the same values of br as in Table 13.2. Among the values of the retention rate employed, share price is maximized at $b = .20$, i.e., a dividend rate of 80 per cent. The data indicate that share price does not vary materially with retention rate in the interval $0 < b < .5$, and price falls off sharply as b rises above .5. The optimum retention rate and the variability in price with retention will of course vary depending on the rate of return on investment. With $r > .10$, the optimum will fall at a higher value of b, and the point at which the sharp fall off in price begins will also be raised somewhat.

Of particular interest is the reasonableness of the general level of k in Tables 13.2 and 13.3. It is difficult to reach any conclusions on this question, but some comment on the value of k when $br = 0$ may be helpful. It will be recalled that when $h = b = 0$, the rate of profit investors require is

$$k = \alpha_0(1 + \breve{o}/W)^{\alpha_3}\pi^{\alpha_5}S^{-\alpha_7} \qquad (8.13)$$

Under the standard values of the above variables and the better values of the parameters, we obtain $k = .079$. That is, an average food corporation with respect to earnings instability, asset liquidity, and size, and with no debt and all earnings paid in dividends, should sell at a yield of .079. A rate of profit requirement of 7.9 per cent on a share with the properties just described does not seem unreasonable, but it is also true that the independent knowledge we bring to the subject does not set narrow limits on what may be considered reasonable. To get wide agreement one would have to say that under 6 per cent is too low and over 10 per cent is too high for a share with this level of risk and no growth. The accuracy of a figure within these limits is hard to evaluate.

Evaluating the model's statements on the rate of profit required on a share with zero growth and leverage may be aided by setting $\bar{\sigma}/W = 0$ and raising corporate size by two standard deviations. A dividend of one dollar on a share in such a corporation sells at a price of $16.73, or at $D/P = k = .06$. Actually no such share exists, but it may be looked on as being as close as a common stock can come to a good preferred issue. A good preferred usually sells at a lower yield, but it sometimes has speculative features such as convertibility which give it an appreciation value, and it is always senior to a relatively large common equity. In view of this, a rate of return of 6 per cent on a common share in a very strong stable corporation without growth prospects seems reasonable.

13.4 Variation in the Required Rate of Profit with the Growth Rate

The variation in share price with the dividend rate follows from our theorem that the required rate of profit on a share is a function of the rate of growth in its dividend expectation. We saw in Tables 13.2 and 13.3 that our sample parameters result in k increasing with br. However, without further analysis we cannot cite this as evidence in support of the theorem. The form of the functional relation between k and br incorporated in our model makes it impossible for k to remain constant as br varies, but it is not built into the model that k should rise continuously over the entire range of br. *Depending on the value of α_2 which is determined by the data,* k *will fall over some interval of* $\ln(1 + br)$ *before it starts rising.* In fact, the minimum value of k is at br slightly greater than zero. There is nothing in the form of our function that prevented the low point in k from falling somewhere else, say at or about the sample mean value of br, i.e., around $br = .04$. If this had taken place, the data would cast some doubt on the validity of our hypothesis that k is a function of br. It could be argued that k is a constant equal to its value at $br = .04$, but the form of the function used to estimate the relation between the two variables caused k to fall and then rise.

We obtain our low point in k at $br \sim 0$, because the parameter values suggested to us by the data were $ln\hat{z}_0 = 2.325$, $\alpha_1 = 1.0$, and $\alpha_2 = 14.00$. The average values of the food sample parameters differ from these figures, but they produce about the same result, and the machinery sample parameters produce a minimum k at $br < 0$. Therefore, we can say that the data provide support for the proposition that k is a function of br. However, it may be argued that we

TABLE 13.4

POSSIBLE VARIATION IN PRICE, DIVIDEND YIELD, AND
REQUIRED RATE OF PROFIT WITH THE GROWTH RATE*

br	$ln(1 + br)$	lnP	P	D/P	k
.00	.00	2.299	$ 9.97	.100	.100
.02	.0198	2.695	14.81	.068	.088
.03	.0296	2.891	18.02	.056	.086
.04	.0392	3.084	21.85	.046	.086
.06	.0583	3.466	31.99	.031	.091
.08	.0770	3.839	46.48	.021	.101

* The values of *lnP, P, D/P*, and *k* are based on standard values of the variables other than *br*, $ln\hat{z}_0 = 2.092$, $\alpha_2 = 20$, and better values for the other parameters presented in Section 13.1.

admit the existence of error in our measurement of br, and this error results in downward bias in α_2 to an unknown extent. Is it not possible that $\alpha_2 > 14$, and the true value is large enough to make the minimum k fall at about $br = .04$?

Table 13.4 presents the values of P, D/P, and k with $\alpha_2 = 20$ and $ln\hat{z}_0 = 2.092$.[4] The better values are again used for the other coefficients and the standard values are again used for the independent variables. With $\alpha_2 = 20$, k has its minimum in the interval $.03 < br < .04$. At $br = 0$, $k = .10$, as br increases, k falls to a low of about .084 and then rises, reaching .101 at $br = .08$. Over the interval $.02 < br < .06$, the variation in k is very small. Table 13.4 suggests that those who believe $\alpha_2 \sim 20$ is the true value of the pa-

[4] $ln\hat{z}_0 = 2.092$ is used to compensate for the increase in α_2. When the variables have their mean values, the two sets of parameters produce the same price, as can be seen by comparing P for $br = .04$ in Tables 13.2 and 13.4.

rameter would have reason to question the hypothesis that k is a function of br. However, further analysis of the problem reveals that a good deal more is required to reach the conclusion that k is independent of br.

Recall that regardless of what is true with respect to the relation between k and br, the definition $k = D/P + br$ is true. Under our theory

$$D/P = \alpha_0(1 + br)^{-\alpha_2} \tag{13.1}$$

and with $\alpha_0 = .10$ and $\alpha_2 = 20$, k falls until $br \sim .04$ is reached and then k rises with br. The opposing theory that k is independent of br implies that

$$D/P = \alpha_0' - \alpha_2'br \tag{13.2}$$

and that the sample estimate of $\alpha_2' = 1$. We can be most certain that $\alpha_2' < 1$ is what the data will produce. It might then be argued that the reasons advanced for believing α_2 is greater than the sample estimates also apply to α_2'. Let us go along and assume that regardless of the regression estimate the best estimate of $\alpha_2' = 1$. What does this imply with respect to the relation between P and br? The sample mean values of the dividend yield and the growth rate are $D/P = .046$ and $br = .04$. With these values and with $\alpha_2' = 1$, the highest value we can assign to α_0' is .09. What does the result $k = .09$ for all values of br imply over the relevant range $0 < br < .08$? To answer the question, let $b = .5$, $Y = \$2.00$, and r vary from zero to .16. In all cases $D = \$1.00$. At $r = 0$, $br = 0$, $D/P = .09$, and $P = \$11.11$. At $r = .04$, $br = .02$, $D/P = .07$, and $P = \$14.29$. At $r = .08$, $br = .04$, $D/P = .05$, and $P = \$20$. At $r = .12$, $br = .06$, $D/P = .03$, and $P = \$33.33$. Finally, at $r = .16$, $br = .08$, $D/P = .01$, and $P = \$100$. Up to $br = .06$, the assumption that k is independent of br does not yield materially different results than our model. However, beyond $br = .06$, and higher values of br are not unreasonable, the predictions of the two models are materially different, and the linear hypothesis results in extraordinarily, and I believe unreasonably, high share prices. Further, it is first necessary to establish that $\alpha_2' = 1$ and α_0' is not less than .09.

Before leaving the subject, a few observations on the relation between the numerical value of α_2 and our theory may be of interest. We have seen that $\alpha_2 \sim 20$ means that as br rises, k falls for some interval before it begins rising. This is not inconsistent with the theory developed earlier in Part II. The functional relation between k and br established in Chapter 4 allowed k to fall over some interval before it rose as br increased. In Chapter 5 we showed that k may rise or fall depending on the rise in k_t with t, i.e., on the increase in risk with the distance in the future of a payment and on the degree of aversion to risk. Finally, in Chapter 10 we introduced the differential tax treatment of capital gains, portfolio diversification, aggregation over all stockholders, and a number of other factors which might influence stockholder reaction to variation in br. The consequence of these considerations is that the aggregate statistic k appearing in our model may fall over some interval of br before it starts rising. Therefore, improvement in the measurement of br and/or changes in investor preferences resulting in $\alpha_2 = 20$ or even 30 is not inconsistent with our theory. Our model is wrong only if the data indicate there is no basis for believing that k either falls or rises. Our theoretical observations indicate that k may (1) rise, (2) fall, (3) fall and then rise as br increases, and our model fits all three of these situations.

13.5 Variation in Price with Leverage

The variation in share price with leverage is a rather complicated subject, and we might well begin with the statements that can be made without reference to the data. With $\alpha_1 = 1$ and $\hat{z}_4 = -1$, and with no tax on corporate income, price is independent of leverage for a share with $\check{r} = \check{k}$ and $b = 0$. It will be recalled that $\check{r}$ is a corporation's rate of return on investment, and $\check{k}$ is the required rate of profit when $b = h = 0$. We have just seen that $\check{k} = .079$ when the other risk variables have their standard values, and it will be seen later that the food sample average value of $\check{r} = .095$. Therefore, unless $\check{r}$ and $\check{k}$ are very highly correlated among corporations, it is likely that most corporations have $\check{r} > \check{k}$. For these corporations, with $b = 0$ an increase in leverage will raise P, certainly for modest values of h. For corporations with $\check{r} < \check{k}$, an increase in leverage reduces price.

However, $\check{r}$ is the after-tax value of a corporation's rate of return on investment, and we saw on pages 128 to 131 that the corporate income tax increases the attractiveness of leverage. Table 13.5 presents the variation in D, P, D/P, and k under the following conditions. The corporation has a book value per share of $10, and $b = 0$. The corporation's value for $\check{k} = .08$, and the after-tax values of $\check{r}$ and $\check{\eta}$ are the same. The interest rate is $i = .04$, the corporate in-

TABLE 13.5

CORPORATE INCOME TAX INDUCED VARIATION IN PRICE DIVIDEND
YIELD, AND REQUIRED RATE OF PROFIT WITH LEVERAGE*

h	D	$1 + h - ih/k$	k	P
−.60	$ .44	.70	.056	$ 7.86
−.30	.62	.85	.068	9.12
.00	.80	1.00	.080	10.00
.30	.98	1.15	.092	10.65
.60	1.16	1.30	.104	11.15
.90	1.34	1.45	.116	11.55
1.00	1.40	1.50	.120	11.67

* The data are based on Eq. (13.3) with $W = \$10$, $i = .04$, $\check{r} = \check{k} = \check{\eta} = .08$.

come tax rate is .5, and the after-tax rate of interest paid by the corporation is $.5i$. This set of assumptions is designed to indicate the influence of the corporate income tax on the variation in price and the other variables with leverage. The equation that generates the data of Table 13.5 is

$$P = \frac{D}{k} = \frac{W(\check{\eta} + \check{r}h - .5ih)}{\check{k}(1 + h - ih/\check{k})} \tag{13.3}$$

The values of h in Table 13.5 reflect the range in which it varies.

The first point to note is that in the absence of a corporate income tax, the value of D would simply be ten times k for all values of h, and $P = \$10$ would be true for all values of h. The second point is that even with $\check{r} = \check{k}$ a corporation can increase its dividend quite materially by increasing its leverage. This is due to the spread between $\check{r}$ and i. However, the yield required on the share also increases materially and the increase in price with h is comparatively small. For instance, a rise in leverage from zero to .60 raises the dividend by 45 per cent, but the required yield rises by 30 per cent, and share price goes up by little more than 11 per cent. Furthermore, as we increment h by constant amounts, the increase in P falls both absolutely and percentage-wise. Therefore, we may say that a corporation with the properties stated may at the cost associated with the increase in its risk secure a material change in its dividend through leverage, but the change in price is small and smaller as h increases. It would be even smaller and possibly negative in the interval that i may be considered to increase with h.

For a corporation with a rate of return on investment greater than the required rate of profit, the variation in price with leverage is considerably greater. In Table 13.6 we raise $\check{r}$ to .10 and leave everything else unchanged. Values of $\check{r} = .10$ and $\check{k} = .08$ reflect a modest but not small differential between the two quantities. The increase in $\check{r}$ to .10 with $W = \$10$ and $\check{\eta}$ kept at .08 leaves the dividend unchanged at $h = 0$. With $\check{r} = \check{k} = .08$, an increase in h from .30 to .60 raised P by $\$0.50$ or less than 5 per cent. With $\check{r} = .10$, P is raised by $\$1.00$, slightly under 9 per cent. The increase in price with leverage is almost 50 per cent larger, but in absolute amount it is still not very large. A plausible judgment is that very high rates of return on the marginal investment, say two or more times the required rate of profit would be needed to persuade a corporate management

TABLE 13.6

PROFITABILITY OF INVESTMENT INDUCED VARIATION IN PRICE DIVIDEND
YIELD AND REQUIRED RATE OF PROFIT WITH LEVERAGE*

h	D	$1 + h - ih/\check{k}$	k	P
−.60	$ .32	.70	.056	$ 5.71
−.30	.56	.85	.068	8.23
.00	.80	1.00	.080	10.00
.30	1.04	1.15	.092	11.30
.60	1.28	1.30	.104	12.31
.90	1.52	1.45	.116	13.10
1.00	1.60	1.50	.120	13.33

* The data are based on Eq. (13.3) with $W = \$10$, $i = .04$, $\check{k} = \check{\eta} = .08$ and $\check{r} = .10$.

that going beyond a modest amount of leverage justifies the increased risk to the corporation.

The assumption that $b = 0$ is of course most unreal. The food sample average value of $b \sim .40$, and Table 13.7 provides the variation in P, D/P, and k with h for a corporation with $b = .4$. The values assigned to the other variables are $\check{k} = .08$, $\check{\eta} = .08$, $i = .04$, $\check{r} = .10$, and $W = \$16.67$. This value for W keeps $D = .80$ for $h = 0$ with $b = .4$. These values for the variables $\check{k}$, $\check{r}$, and b produce a corporation that has a leverage and growth free risk, a rate of return on investment, and a retention rate that are average. The equation that generates the data of Table 13.7 is

$$P = \frac{(1 - b)W(\check{\eta} + \check{r}h - .5ih)[1 + b(\check{r} + \check{r}h - .5ih)]^{\alpha_2}}{\check{k}(1 + h - ih/\check{k})} \tag{13.4}$$

The value of $\alpha_2 = 14$.

Table 13.7 reveals that a dramatic increase in the variation in

TABLE 13.7

h	D	r	br	$1 + h - ih/k$	P	D/P	k
$-.60$	.32	.052	.0208	.70	\$ 7.62	.0420	.063
$-.30$	.56	.076	.0304	.85	12.53	.0447	.075
.00	.80	.100	.0400	1.00	17.32	.0462	.086
.30	1.04	.124	.0496	1.15	22.26	.0467	.096
.60	1.28	.148	.0592	1.30	27.53	.0465	.106
.90	1.52	.172	.0688	1.45	33.26	.0457	.115
1.00	1.60	.180	.0720	1.50	35.29	.0453	.117

* The data are based on Eq. (13.4) with $\check{\eta} = .08$, $\check{k} = .08$, $\check{r} = .10$, $W = \$16.67$, and $i = .04$.

price with leverage takes place, when the corporation retains some fraction of its income in addition to having a rate of return on investment greater than its leverage and growth free required rate of profit. Price rises from \$17.32 at $h = 0$ to \$27.53 at $h = .6$ to \$33.26 at $h = .9$. The substantial increase in the variation in price with leverage by comparison with Table 13.6 is due to the variation in br with leverage. With $\check{r} > \check{k}$ and with the after tax rate of interest $.5i$, leverage not only raises the current dividend, but it also raises the rate of growth in the dividend. With $b = .4$ and $\check{r} = .10$, $br = .04$ when $h = 0$. By contrast, $br = .069$ for $h = .9$. With respect to the other statistics, the dividend yield rises from .042 to .047 at $h = .3$ and then falls, reaching .045 at $h = 1.0$. The required rate of profit, it is interesting to note, rises continuously from .063 to .117.

The magnitude of the responsiveness of price to leverage and retention combined is further illustrated by multiplying the data of Table 13.6 by 1.667. Both shares now have $W = \$16.67$ and $\check{\eta} = .08$. We find that the share with $h = b = 0$ sells at $P = \$16.67$. Table 13.7 reveals that with $b = .4$ and everything else the same, i.e., $h = 0$, $\check{r} = .10$, and $\check{k} = .08$, and $Y = \$1.33$, the share sells at a slightly higher price, $P = \$17.32$. However, raise h to .6 and the share with $b = 0$ rises to \$20.51, but with $b = .4$ we have a rise in P to \$27.53.

Striking as the variation in price with leverage is, it is difficult to question the results. A more modest variation could be obtained by lowering α_4 or raising α_2. However, if anything, it might be thought that $\alpha_2 = 14$ is on the low side and $\alpha_4 = 1$ is on the high side, and the changes that might be made in them only increase the rise in P with h. Making i a function of h will reduce the variation somewhat. The really critical assumption of course is that $\check{r}$ does not fall as h rises.

It may have been noted that negative values of h reduced share price in all three tables. In Table 13.5, the fall in price takes place because the corporation is lending at a net rate of interest of 2 per cent while individuals can lend directly at 4 per cent. In Table 13.6 price is depressed more as h goes negative because investors require only an 8 per cent yield and the corporation is giving up 10 per cent on each dollar disinvested. Finally in Table 13.7 the fall in price as h falls is proportionately greater because the rate of growth in the dividend is also reduced. It falls from .04 at $h = 0$ to .021 at $h = -.6$. With such a low rate of growth retention has a depressing influence on share price.

13.6   Variation in Price with the Other Risk Variables

The variables of the Adlev model that remain to be considered are the risk variables, leverage-free earnings instability, asset liquidity, and corporate size. Table 13.8 illustrates the variation in

TABLE 13.8

VARIATION IN PRICE, DIVIDEND YIELD, AND REQUIRED RATE OF
PROFIT WITH LEVERAGE-FREE EARNINGS INSTABILITY*

$\check{\sigma}/W$	$ln(1 + \check{\sigma}/W)$	LnP	P	D/P	k
.000	.000	3.232	$25.33	.039	.079
.010	.010	3.172	23.85	.042	.082
.025	.015	3.082	21.80	.045	.085
.041	.040	2.992	19.93	.050	.090
.057	.055	2.902	18.21	.055	.095

* The values of LnP, P, D/P, and k are based on standard values for the variables other than $ln(1 + \check{\sigma}/W)$ and better values for the parameters.

price with earnings instability. Both the average and standard values of that variable, $ln(1 + \check{\sigma}/W) = .025$, and its standard deviation is .015. The data of Table 13.8 are based on standard values for the other variables and better values for the parameters.

Inspection of the data reveals that price and required rate of profit are fairly responsive to variation in leverage-free earnings instability. When $\check{\sigma}/W = .01$ share price is $23.85, and P falls to $19.93 when $\check{\sigma}/W = .041$, and to $18.21 when $\check{\sigma}/W = .057$. The required rate of profit rises from .082 to .090 and to .095. It may be thought that the rate of profit required on an investment varies over a wider range with the uncertainty of the future payments. However, the range of variation in the earnings instability for a large corporation is much narrower than the range of uncertainty for individual assets.

The rate of profit required on individual assets may well vary over a wider range.

Table 13.9 illustrates the variation in P and k with π, the index of the liquidity of a firm's assets. The food sample average value of $ln\pi$ is $-.032$, and the average of its standard deviation is .159. Therefore, $\pi = 1.40$ to $\pi = .60$ pretty well cover the range of variation in the variable. The values of P, D/P, and k are based on standard values for the other variables and better values for the parameters.

Inspection of the data reveals that P falls from $23.45 at $\pi = 1.20$ to $19.90 at $\pi = .80$. Some may consider this responsiveness to the relative importance of inventory versus machinery in a firm's operating assets extraordinarily large. They could argue that .4, the better value for α_5 is too high in view of the fact that the food sample

TABLE 13.9

VARIATION IN PRICE, DIVIDEND YIELD, AND REQUIRED RATE OF
PROFIT WITH ASSET LIQUIDITY*

π	$ln\pi$	LnP	P	D/P	k
1.40	.337	3.217	$24.94	.040	.080
1.20	.182	3.155	23.45	.043	.083
1.00	.000	3.082	21.80	.046	.086
.80	−.229	2.991	19.90	.050	.090
.60	−.511	2.878	17.77	.056	.096

* The values of LnP, P, D/P, and k are based on standard values for the variables other than $ln\pi$ and better values for the parameters.

average was only .27. On the other hand, the rise in k from .083 to .090 does not appear extremely large.

The values of P and k for $\pi = 1.40$ and .80 are of special interest because the former represents a firm with operating assets consisting only of inventory, while the latter represents a firm with only plant and equipment. The spread between the rate of profit required on investment in these two types of assets may be considered larger than the difference between $k = .080$ and $k = .096$. However, there is more spread in risk between an investment in inventory and an investment in a piece of plant equipment than between large going concerns that are collections of these two types of assets.

The last variable in our model is corporate size, and the variation in P and k with size is illustrated in Table 13.10. The average sample value of $lnS = 4.465$, and the average of its standard deviation is .84. The dollar amount in millions of dollars of working

TABLE 13.10

VARIATION IN PRICE, DIVIDEND YIELD, AND REQUIRED
RATE OF PROFIT WITH CORPORATE SIZE*

S (000)	LnS	LnP	P	D/P	k
$ 16,194	2.785	2.953	$19.16	.052	.092
37,520	3.625	3.015	20.38	.049	.089
86,890	4.465	3.082	21.80	.046	.086
201,200	5.305	3.149	23.32	.043	.083
466,000	6.145	3.215	24.94	.040	.080

* The values of LnP, P, D/P, and k are based on standard values for the variables other than lnS and better values for the parameters. Size is measured by total assets net of current liabilities, and the values of S are in thousands of dollars.

capital plus noncurrent assets, our index of size, corresponding to each value of LnS also appears in Table 13.10. The standard values for the other variables and the better variables for the parameters were also used here.

Corporate size per se has a small but not negligible influence on share price. A share in a corporation with assets net of current liabilities of $37,520,000 sells at a price of $20.38 and a $k = .089$. A share in a $201,200,000 corporation sells at a higher price, $23.32, reflecting a lower value of $k = .083$. Size confers benefits apart from the advantages of superior technology, lower interest rates, and greater stability through diversification.

Chapter 14

OPTIMAL INVESTMENT AND FINANCING POLICY

In this chapter we take up the purpose for which our theory has been established—its use by a corporation to find the investment and financing decision that maximizes the value of its stock. Broadly speaking, a corporation might proceed as follows. The independent variables of our stock value equation may be classified as state and decision variables. The decision variables are the corporation's retention and leverage rates, while the state variables include the corporation's size, leverage-free earnings instability, and rate of return on investment. Given numerical values for the parameters and the values for the state variables, a corporation may use the model to find the combination of retention and leverage which maximizes share price.

The task, however, is a little bit more complicated. We will see that in some cases the state variables are functions of the investment rate. It is therefore necessary to establish these functions and numerical values for their parameters. Also, the investment rate must be expressed in terms of the retention and leverage rates. The last two quantities are the sole decision variables, and therefore must be the sole unknowns of the equation. Of course, fixing their values fixes the firm's investment rate.

We will illustrate, as well as describe, the use of the model to find the optimal investment and financing decision. Share price data will be presented for representative combinations of values for the state and the decision variables. In other words, our data will present the optimum leverage and retention rates and the maximized share price for each combination of the state variables, and the data will also show the departure in share price from the maximum at other combinations of leverage and retention.

In Section 14.1 the use of the model to find the optimum reten-

196

tion and leverage rates will be established under the assumption that a corporation's rate of return on investment is a constant. Section 14.2 will have the same purpose as the preceding one, but it will be based on the assumption that a corporation's rate of return on investment is a decreasing function of its investment. In a sense, the data contained in both sections is similar to that presented in the last chapter. However, there we looked at the variation in share price with each independent variable, holding all other variables constant. Here we will examine the variation in share price with leverage and retention under a comparatively large number of combinations of values for the other variables.

After having been so bold as to provide the "simple directions" for using the model to maximize the price of a corporation's stock, it is only fitting that we should take notice of the model's limitations. Section 14.3 will review the observations made earlier with respect to the accuracy of the parameter estimates and the measurement of the variables, emphasizing in the review the problems posed for the present use of the model. Our primary concern, however, will be other problems, such as differences between investor and corporation information on the values of the variables, that are peculiar to the present use of the model.

The determination of the optimal investment by a corporation given its investment opportunities has often been looked at as a problem in the cost of capital. Our solution of the problem, however, does not involve explicit reference to a corporation's cost of capital, and the final section of this chapter examines the relation between our work and the cost-of-capital approach to capital budgeting.

14.1 The Return on Investment a Constant

For a corporation that engages in no outside equity financing, the determination of h, its leverage rate, and b, its retention rate, establishes the corporation's investment. That is, if h' is the change in leverage decided upon at $t = 0$ and h is the new leverage rate, a corporation's investment is exactly equal to $h'W_0 + b(1 + h)Y_0$. Investment is the firm's outlay on nonmonetary assets net of the period's depreciation expense. What we will do is arrive at the values of b and h that maximize P under alternative combinations of values with respect to the corporation's state variables.

With respect to the state variables, all of the risk variables other than the leverage risk variable will be consolidated in one variable.

It will be recalled that the rate of profit investors require on a share when $h = b = 0$ is

$$\check{k} = \alpha_0(1 + \check{\sigma}/W)^{\alpha_3}\pi^{\alpha_5}S^{-\alpha_7} \tag{8.13}$$

We will assume that the values of the variables which determine $\check{k}$ combine with the parameter values to result in $\check{k}$ equal to .08, .10, or .12. These values of $\check{k}$ will be referred to respectively as corporations with low, average, and high risk.

The corporation's return on investment, $\check{r}$, is another state variable, and it is assumed to be independent of the level of the corporation's investment. The values assigned to $\check{r}$ are .05, .10, and .15, referring respectively to a corporation of low, average, and high profitability. The return on the existing capital at $h = 0$, $\check{\eta}$ will be set equal to $\check{k}$, i.e., take on the value assigned to $\check{k}$.[1] Our expression for the price of a share is

$$P = \frac{[(1 - b)Y]^{\alpha_1}(1 + br)^{\alpha_2}}{\check{k}(1 + h - ih/\check{k})^{\alpha_4}} \tag{14.1}$$

In this expression, $\alpha_1 = 1$, $\alpha_2 = 14$, and $\alpha_4 = 1$. The current income is

$$Y = W(\check{\eta} + \check{r}h - .5ih) \tag{14.2}$$

With the corporation subject to a 50 per cent corporate income tax, $\check{r}$ the after-tax rate of return on investment, and i the actual interest paid, the after-tax interest rate is $.5i$. The r appearing in the growth rate is the rate of return on common equity investment and

$$r = \check{r} + \check{r}h - .5ih \tag{14.3}$$

The state variables that remain to be determined are W and i. W is simply a scale variable, and with $\alpha_1 = 1$ it does not matter what

---

[1] Our persistence in keeping $\check{\eta} = \check{k}$ probably calls for an explanation. In Chapter 8 we saw that with $\check{Y}$, $\check{k}$, and $\check{P}$ the earnings, yield, and price on an unlevered share, through leverage on personal account an investor can obtain an expectation of $Y = \check{k}\check{P} + h\check{k}\check{P} - hi\check{P}$. Each possible Y the investor might obtain has a present value of P if it is discounted at a rate $k = \check{k} + h\check{k} - hi$. We therefore concluded that a dividend of Y provided by corporate leverage of h would also be discounted at a rate $k = \check{k} + h\check{k} - hi$. In this expression, $h = L/\check{P}$ and not L/W. The distinction did not matter in Chapter 8 because it was assumed that $W = \check{P}$. However, k is the yield investors require on a share with corporate leverage of $h = L/W$ only if $W = \check{P}$ at $h = 0$. Hence, we must set W and $\check{\eta}$ given $\check{Y}$ so that this condition is satisfied. An alternative means to the same end is to use the actual values of W and $\check{\eta}$ but multiply $h = L/W$ in the income and growth variables by the ratio $\check{P}/W$. The theorems developed since Chapter 8 are not restricted by this consideration. However, in the empirical work represented by Eqs. (12.1) and (12.4) we probably should not have used $h = L/W$ in the leverage risk variable. An estimate of $h = L/\check{P}$ might have yielded better estimates for α_4.

value is assigned to W. Changing W simply changes all results proportionately to the change in W. We will use $W = \$30$. One departure we will make from the assumptions of Chapter 13 is that the interest rate to be employed in determining r is an increasing function of the leverage rate. The function is

$$i = \phi_0(1 + h/\phi_1)^{\phi_1} \tag{14.4}$$

with $\phi_0 = .04$ and $\phi_1 = 3$. Under these values, $i = .04$ at $h = 0$, and it increases with h as illustrated in Figure 14.1.

FIGURE 14.1

<small>VARIATION IN INTEREST RATE WITH LEVERAGE</small>

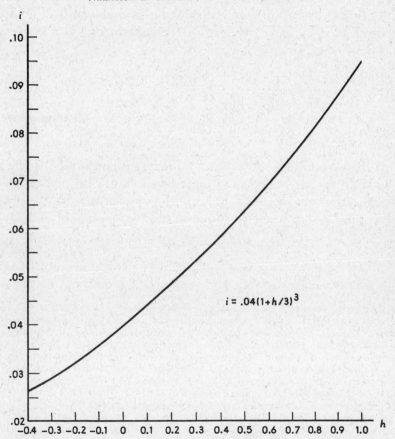

$$i = .04(1+h/3)^3$$

It may appear that $\phi_1 = 3$ results in too rapid an increase in i with h, e.g., at $h = 1$, $i = .095$. While bonds are rarely if ever issued at such high coupon rates of interest, a manufacturing corporation that undertakes this much leverage seldom can issue straight debt instruments. Convertible bonds, bonds with stock warrants, or some such financing is employed, and this type of financing can probably be shown to result in expected yields of 8 per cent or more.

Under our definition of leverage $h < 0$ is possible, and $i < .04$ results. The interpretation is that the rate of interest at which a corporation lends falls as h falls below zero. It might have been more realistic to fix the interest rate at which a corporation lends at .04 or possibly a lower constant for all negative values of h. A final point

TABLE 14.1

VARIATION IN PRICE WITH LEVERAGE AND RETENTION FOR A CORPORATION WITH RETURN ON INVESTMENT CONSTANT AND LOW RISK, $\check{k} = .08$

$h \backslash b$	0	.10	.20	.30	.40	.50	.60
A. Low Profitability, $\check{r} = .05$							
$-.20$	\$30.52 √ ✗	\$29.18✗	\$27.55	\$25.59	\$ 23.28	\$ 20.59	\$ 17.48
0	30.00 √	28.95	27.59✗	25.87✗	23.75✗	21.19✗	18.15✗
.20	29.03 √	28.21	27.08	25.57	23.64	21.24	18.31
.40	27.61 √	26.96	25.98	24.64	22.88	20.65	17.88
.60	25.75 √	25.17	24.29	23.07	21.45	19.38	16.80
.80	23.43 √	22.85	22.00	20.84	19.33	17.42	15.07
B. Average Profitability, $\check{r} = .10$							
$-.20$	26.36	26.64 √	26.57	26.06	25.01	23.32	20.86
0	30.00	31.04	31.67	31.76 √	31.17	29.70	27.13
.20	32.44	34.27	35.69	36.53	36.56 √	35.51	33.06
.40	33.86	36.43	38.63	40.23	40.95 √	40.44	38.27
.60	34.40✗	37.58	40.43	42.71	44.09	44.14 √	42.32
.80	34.15	37.72✗	41.04✗	43.82✗	45.71✗	46.23 √ ✗	44.77✗
1.00	33.15	36.88	40.39	43.42	45.59	46.40 √	45.20
1.20	31.44	35.05	38.48	41.44	43.59	44.45 √	43.39
C. High Profitability, $\check{r} = .15$							
$-.20$	22.19	23.71	24.96	25.82	26.11 √	25.63	24.10
0	30.00	33.26	36.30	38.89	40.69	41.29 √	40.10
.20	35.85	41.14	46.44	51.39	55.50	58.05	58.08 √
.40	40.11	47.53	55.32	63.07	70.09	75.37	77.45 √
.60	43.06	52.50	62.82	73.53	83.82	92.37	97.18 √
.80	44.86	56.08	68.72	82.30	95.89	107.90	115.84 √
1.00	45.65✗	58.26	72.81	88.84	105.39	120.65	131.66 √
1.20	45.50	58.99✗	74.81✗	92.64✗	111.40✗	129.19✗	142.75 √ ✗

with respect to Eq. (14.4) is that ϕ_0 should possibly vary depending on the level of the corporation's leverage-free riskiness, i.e., be a function of $\check{k}$. However, this refinement was not undertaken.

Although the value of i in determining r is given by Eq. (14.4), we hold $i = .04$ for all values of h in the leverage variable, that is, in $1 + h - ih/\check{k}$. The reason is that the rise in i with h should have a depressing effect on the attractiveness of investment, but having i increase with h in the leverage variable offsets the rise in i with h in the rate of return variable. The implication that raising the rate of interest reduces the risk associated with leverage does not seem reasonable.[2]

TABLE 14.2

VARIATION IN PRICE WITH LEVERAGE AND RETENTION FOR A CORPORATION
WITH RETURN ON INVESTMENT CONSTANT AND AVERAGE RISK, $k = .10$

$h\backslash b$	0	.10	.20	.30	.40	.50	.60
			A. Low Profitability, $\check{r} = .05$				
−.20	$31.79 √×	$30.39×	$28.69×	$26.66×	$24.25×	$ 21.45×	$ 18.20×
0	30.00 √	28.95	27.59	25.87	23.75	21.19	18.15
.20	28.16 √	27.38	26.27	24.81	22.94	20.61	17.77
.40	26.21 √	25.60	24.67	23.40	21.73	19.61	16.98
.60	24.10 √	23.56	22.74	21.59	20.08	18.14	15.72
.80	21.79 √	21.25	20.45	19.38	17.97	16.20	14.01
			B. Average Profitability, $\check{r} = .10$				
−.20	28.38	28.69 √	28.61	28.06	26.94	25.12	22.46
0	30.00	31.04	31.67	31.76 √	31.17	29.70	27.13
.20	30.84	32.58	33.94	34.73	34.76 √	33.76	31.43
.40	31.05×	33.41	35.43	36.89	37.56 √	37.09	35.10
.60	30.72	33.55×	36.10×	38.14	39.37	39.42 √	37.79
.80	29.90	33.03	35.93	38.36×	40.02×	40.47 √×	39.19×
1.00	28.61	31.83	34.87	37.48	39.35	40.04 √	39.02
			C. High Profitability, $\check{r} = .15$				
−.20	24.97	26.68	28.09	29.06	29.39 √	28.84	27.12
0	30.00	33.26	36.30	38.89	40.70	41.29 √	40.10
.20	33.52	38.47	43.43	48.06	51.90	54.29	54.32 √
.40	35.89	42.53	49.50	56.43	62.72	67.44	69.30 √
.60	37.34	45.53	54.47	63.77	72.69	80.10	84.27 √
.80	38.00×	47.51	58.22	69.72	81.23	91.41	98.13 √
1.00	37.99	48.48×	60.59	73.93	87.70	100.40	109.57 √
1.20	37.35	48.42	61.43×	76.04×	91.44×	106.05×	117.17× √

With each of the state variables, $\check{r}$ and $\check{k}$, having three possible values, we have what might be called nine different corporations. The three tables in Table 14.1 present share price under various combinations of h and b for corporations with low risk and low, average, and high profitability. In Table 14.2 we have average risk combined successively with low, average, and high profitability, and

---

[2] Modigliani and Miller [1958, p. 273] maintained that the rise in the interest rate with leverage should have no influence on the value of a share. With i an increasing function of h in both the return on investment and the leverage variable, the increase in i has no influence on share price and the optimum leverage rate. This treatment is justified if insolvency does not reduce the value of the equity interest in a corporation. See page 104.

in Table 14.3 high risk is combined with the three levels of profitability. Each of the nine tables show the share prices obtained from all combinations of h and b, with h varying from $-.20$ to $.80$ in intervals of $.20$ and b varying from zero to $.60$ in intervals of $.10$. Certain of the tables also present share prices for higher values of h.

TABLE 14.3

VARIATION IN PRICE WITH LEVERAGE AND RETENTION FOR A CORPORATION WITH RETURN ON INVESTMENT CONSTANT AND HIGH RISK, $k = .12$

$h\backslash b$	0	.10	.20	.30	.40	.50	.60
			A. Low Profitability, $\check{r} = .05$				
$-.20$	\$32.67 $\checkmark\times$	\$31.23$\times$	\$29.48$\times$	\$27.39$\times$	\$24.92$\times$	\$22.04$\times$	\$ 18.71$\times$
0	30.00 $\checkmark$	28.95	27.59	25.87	23.75	21.19	18.15
.20	27.61 $\checkmark$	26.83	25.75	24.31	22.48	20.20	17.42
.40	25.33 $\checkmark$	24.73	23.84	22.61	21.00	18.95	16.41
.60	23.08 $\checkmark$	22.57	21.79	20.68	19.23	17.37	15.06
.80	20.79 $\checkmark$	20.27	19.51	18.48	17.14	15.45	13.37
			B. Average Profitability, $\check{r} = .10$				
$-.20$	29.78	30.10 $\checkmark$	30.02	29.45	28.27	26.36	23.57
0	30.00$\times$	31.04	31.67	31.76 $\checkmark$	31.17	29.70	27.13
.20	29.81	31.49	32.80	33.57	33.60 $\checkmark$	32.64	30.38
.40	29.28	31.50$\times$	33.40	34.79	35.41 $\checkmark$	34.97	33.09
.60	28.44	31.06	33.42$\times$	35.31$\times$	36.45	36.49 $\checkmark$	34.99
.80	27.31	30.17	32.82	35.04	36.55$\times$	36.97 $\checkmark\times$	35.80$\times$
1.00	25.89	28.80	31.55	33.91	35.60	36.24 $\checkmark$	35.30
			C. High Profitability, $\check{r} = .15$				
$-.20$	26.90	28.74	30.26	31.30	31.66 $\checkmark$	31.06	29.21
0	30.00	33.26	36.30	38.89	40.70	41.29 $\checkmark$	40.10
.20	32.02	36.74	41.48	45.90	49.57	51.85	51.88 $\checkmark$
.40	33.23	39.37	45.83	52.25	58.06	62.43	64.16 $\checkmark$
.60	33.80	41.21	49.31	57.72	65.79	72.50	76.28 $\checkmark$
.80	33.83$\times$	42.29	51.82	62.06	72.31	81.37	87.35 $\checkmark$
1.00	33.39	42.61$\times$	53.25	64.99	77.09	88.25	96.31 $\checkmark$
1.20	32.52	42.16	53.49$\times$	66.21$\times$	79.61$\times$	92.33$\times$	102.02 $\checkmark\times$

In order to facilitate inspection of the data in the tables, the optimum retention rate at each leverage rate is checked, and the optimum leverage rate at each retention rate is identified with a cross. Of course if $b = .60$ proves to be the optimum retention rate, the true optimum may be larger, and the same applies to an optimum leverage rate equal to the highest value in the table.

Let us begin with Table 14.2B, which represents a corporation with average risk and profitability, i.e., $\check{r} = \check{k} = .10$. With $h = 0$, price rises from \$30 at $b = 0$ to a maximum of \$31.76 at $b = .30$. The fall in P is to \$29.70 at $b = .50$, and beyond this point P falls off with increasing sharpness. The interesting point to note is that even with

$\check{r} = \check{k}$ and no leverage, P varies with the retention rate. With $\alpha_2 = 14$ and $\check{r} = \check{k}$ at .10, the rate of profit investors require on a share, k, falls over an interval of b before it starts rising, but this is not the reason why P is maximized at $b = .30$. Actually k is minimized at a smaller value of b than the one that maximizes P. Price increases with b as long as $k - br$ falls at a faster rate than the dividend.

Inspection of the data reveals that the optimum retention rate is quite sensitive to the leverage rate. At $h = -.20$, price is maximized at $b = .10$, and at $h = .60$, price is maximized at $b = .50$. The explanation is that raising h raises the return to the stockholders on retention through the leverage on the retention. With negative leverage the rate of return to the common equity on retention is low, and the rate of growth rises very slowly with retention.[3] The small increase in the rate of growth with retention fails to offset the depressing effect on price of the reduction in the current dividend. Conversely, when leverage is high the rate of return on the levered retention is high, and the rise in the rate of growth with retention more than offsets the fall in the current dividend up to high values of b.

The other side of the same coin is seen by examining the variation in P with h for each value of b. At $b = 0$, price rises with leverage up to $h = .40$ and then falls. With $\check{k} = \check{r}$ and $b = 0$, we have price rising with leverage due to the income tax advantage of leverage. However, beyond $h = .40$ the rise in the rate of interest offsets the tax advantage and P falls. At the same time it is clear that at $b = 0$ share price varies over a small range with leverage. Looking to the right of the $b = 0$ column in Table 14.2B we see that the effect of leverage on share price increases with the retention rate. At $b = .50$ price rises from \$25.12 at $h = -.20$ to \$40.47 at $h = .80$. What we can say therefore is that when $\check{r} = \check{k}$ the influence of leverage on P depends largely on the retention rate. At $b = 0$, price is relatively insensitive to leverage. As retention increases, the sensitivity of price rises both by depressing the price at low (negative) leverage rates and raising the price at high leverage rates. Price is sensitive to leverage at high retention rates because the rate of growth in the dividend increases materially with the leverage rate. Finally with respect to Table 14.2B, the optimum combination of h and b is $h = .80$ and $b = .50$.

[3] At $h = -.40$, of every dollar retained \$.40 is invested in monetary assets to earn less than a 4 per cent return.

Moving down to Table 14.2C, we have the variation in P with b and h for a corporation with average risk and high profitability. Comparing P for $h = b = 0$ with the preceding tables reveals that it remains $30. With a zero investment the change in the rate of return on investment does not influence the value of a share. What the rise in $\check{r}$ accomplishes is an increase in the sensitivity of P to both b and h, i.e., retention and leverage have been made more attractive. At $h = 0$ the optimum retention rate has gone up from .30 to .50. Further, at the optimum retention rate, P is now over one-third larger than its value at $b = 0$, and P remains high for all values of b in the interval $.30 < b < .60$.[4] Even at $h = -.20$, price rises materially with retention, reaching a maximum at $b = .40$. At $h = 1.0$ the optimum retention rate is greater than .60.

The optimum values of b and h fall outside our range of values for the variables. They are greater than $h = 1.2$ and $b = .60$. The resultant price may seem abnormally large, but it should be remembered that without the assumption $\check{r}$ is independent of the level of investment, price would not continue rising with b and h at such high values. The only thing limiting the rise in P with h is the rise in the rate of interest, and this is a weak force compared with the spread between $\check{r}$ and $\check{k}$ operating on both the current dividend and the rate of growth in the dividend. Nonetheless, the variation in P with leverage is striking. At $b = .30$, price almost doubles as h goes from zero to 1.2, and at $b = .60$, P almost triples. By contrast in Table 14.2B where $\check{r} = \check{k}$, we see that at $b = .60$, price fails to even double as h goes from zero to 1.0.

Moving back to Table 14.2A we see the variation in price with h and b for a corporation with average risk and low profitability. A rate of return on investment of $\check{r} = .05$ might better be called very low profitability, and Table 14.2A shows the consequences of this depressing state of affairs. Looking to the right and down from $P = $30 at $b = h = 0$, we see that both leverage and retention reduce P. At the highest values, $b = .60$ and $h = .80$, price falls to $14.01, which is less than one half the value at $b = h = 0$. With this unfavorable spread between $\check{r}$ and $\check{k}$, both retention and leverage are undesirable.

It is interesting to note that at $h = -.20$, price is higher than at $h = 0$. It would seem that a corporation with a required rate of profit of $\check{k} = .10$ and a rate of return on investment of $\check{r} = .05$ should

---

[4] Similarly, at $b = 0$ the optimum leverage rate has gone up from .40 to .80, and at the optimum P is now $38.

liquidate as quickly as possible.[5] Putting its capital into monetary assets may be considered the second best course of action on the grounds that a bond without risk paying 4 per cent is a better investment than a nonmonetary asset paying 5 per cent with a risk level of $\check{k} = .10$. However, it is surprising to see $P > \$30$ at $h = -.20$ and $b = 0$. We have this result because the corporation is earning $\check{\eta} = .10$ on $W = \$30$, and on every dollar disinvested it gives up only a 5 per cent return. Of course, with $\check{r}$ equal to .10 or .15, negative leverage depresses price.

Table 14.1 presents the variation in price with leverage and retention for corporations with low risk and the three levels of profitability, while Table 14.3 does the same for high-risk corporations, i.e., $\check{k} = .12$. Tables 14.1 and 14.3 show the same broad qualitative pattern of variation in price with h and b at the three levels of $\check{r}$ as Table 14.2. The optimum values of h and b increase very significantly with $\check{r}$. The optimum b increases with h particularly for average and high $\check{r}$, and the optimum h increases with b for average and high $\check{r}$. These other two tables are of interest largely for the information they provide on the variation in the optimum price as $\check{k}$, the finance-free required rate of profit, is made to vary.

In this connection one point worth noting is the tendency for the optimum leverage rate to fall as $\check{k}$ increases. For instance, in Table 14.1B where $\check{k} = .08$ and $\check{r} = .10$, the optimum leverage rate is $h = .60$ at $b = 0$, while in Table 14.3B where $\check{k} = .12$, the optimum leverage rate is $h = 0$ at $b = 0$. The attractiveness of leverage declines as $\check{k}$ increases, because the leverage risk variable is $1 + h - ih/\check{k}$. The larger the value of $\check{k}$ the greater the amount by which $\check{k}(1 + h - ih/\check{k})$ in Eq. (14.1) increases with h and the sooner an optimum h is reached with $\check{r}$ and b given. However, as b increases, the sensitivity of the optimum leverage rate to $\check{k}$ declines: the spread between the two tables in the optimum h is reduced as b goes up.

The other point revealed by comparing Tables 14.1, 14.2, and 14.3 may be somewhat disturbing: at each value of h, share price is optimized at the same level of b regardless of $\check{k}$. For instance at $\check{r} = .10$ and $h = .20$, price is maximized at $b = .40$ for all three values of $\check{k}$. It is a characteristic of our model that the optimum retention rate is independent of $\check{k}$. Those who question the correctness of this finding, question the correctness of our model.

Doubt arises because a widely accepted proposition in financial

---

[5] The optimum retention rate is negative, and the firm should pay out more in dividents than it earns.

circles is that the fraction of income a corporation retains should be larger the greater the instability of its earnings, i.e., its value of $\check{k}$. There are two possible interpretations of this statement. Under one, the fraction of income a corporation should retain during good years is larger the greater the instability of earnings, because the amount needed to carry it through bad times is correspondingly larger. The structure of our model is in agreement with this interpretation of the proposition. Our income variable is smoothed income. A given fraction of smoothed income is a smaller fraction of actual income at its peak and a larger fraction at its trough, the greater the cyclical instability of income. In this connection, a point to note is that the extra retention due to instability during boom years should be kept in liquid form to be available during bust years. In our model the difference between actual and smoothed income is not recognized, i.e., is not considered available for distribution or investment.

The second interpretation of the proposition is that everything else the same, the reliance by a corporation on retention to finance investment should be larger the more unstable its earnings. It is clear that given the volume of investment, the higher the value of b and the lower the value of h, the more secure the corporation. Hence, to have a given level of security with a given level of investment, the value of b should vary with $\check{\sigma}/W$. However, it is not clear how this policy increases the market value of the corporation, and unless it does we cannot make our optimum b an increasing function of $\check{k}$.

It is perhaps more legitimate to argue that the optimum b should be a decreasing function of $\check{k}$. The more uncertain a dividend expectation, the less an investor might be willing to pay for growth and the lower the optimum rate of growth. However, our growth coefficient and the optimum b are independent of $\check{k}$. In this connection it may have been noted that for any value of b, share price is the same regardless of $\check{k}$ at $h = 0$. For instance, at $h = 0$, $b = .40$, and $\check{r} = .10$, we have $P = \$31.17$ in Tables 14.1B, 2B, and 3B. This does not mean that P is independent of $\check{k}$. P does not vary with $\check{k}$ because $\check{\eta}$ and the current dividend change with $\check{k}$. This is made clearer by recalling that our expression for share price with $h = 0$ is

$$P = \frac{(1 - b)W\check{\eta}(1 + b\check{r})^{\alpha_2}}{\check{k}} \qquad (14.5)$$

Raising $\check{k}$ and leaving everything else unchanged reduces P, but keeping $\check{\eta}$ equal to $\check{k}$ will prevent a change in P. In conclusion, if it is believed that the optimum retention rate should be a function of $\check{k}$, the model's structure must be changed.

14.2 The Model with Return on Investment a Function of the Investment Rate

Given our stock value model and the estimates of its parameters, probably the major objection to the data presented in the preceding section is that they are based on the assumption that a corporation's return on investment is a constant and not a function of its investment. Withdrawing the assumption complicates the use of the model somewhat, and we will deal with the complications as follows:

First, it will be assumed that the corporation's initial position is at $h = 0$. This assumption is made to facilitate the exposition, and it will be withdrawn later. Second, the corporation's return on investment, $\check{r}$, is a decreasing function of investment. The investment will be expressed as the fraction z of its net worth, and the rate of return function to be employed is

$$\check{r} = \rho_0(1 + z)^{\rho_1} \tag{14.6}$$

It should be kept in mind that if a firm undertakes an investment $I_1 = zW_0$ during $t = 1$, $\check{r}$ is the average return on the investment. When $z = 0$, $\check{r} = \rho_0$. The value of ρ_1 is between minus one and zero, so that $\check{r}$ falls continuously as z increases. The determination of the numerical values of ρ_0 and ρ_1 will be discussed later. The lower limit of z may be considered a negative number equal to the fraction the firm's depreciation charge is of its net worth.[6]

Our stock price model remains Eq. (14.1), but now $\check{r}$ in the income and growth rate variables [see Eqs. (14.2) and (14.3)] is given by Eq. (14.6). The final assumption is that earnings respond instantaneously to leverage. That is, adoption of leverage of h at the end of $t = 0$ instantaneously raises the firm's earnings by $W_0h(\check{r} - .5ih)$ and raises the rate of growth to br.[7]

Our task is to specify z in terms of b and h. That is, if a function of b and h is substituted for z in the rate of return equation, that

---

[6] Theoretically we can make the lower limit of z minus one by allowing the firm to sell off its existing assets. The rate of profit given up on an asset sold is the periodic income it provides divided by the sale price of the asset.

[7] What is really assumed is that the lag between a change in h and its effect on earnings do not materially affect the conclusions reached.

equation may be substituted where necessary in the stock value model, and b and h remain the only decision variables.

The task is an easy one if $b = 0$. In this case $z = h$, and

$$Y_0 = W[\check{\eta} + \rho_0(1 + h)^{\rho_1}h - .5ih] \tag{14.7}$$

Looking back at Eq. (14.1) the term in br and $(1 - b)$ disappear. Substituting Eq. (14.7) for Y_0 and Eq. (14.4) for i in Eq. (14.1), we have an expression in which P is simply a function of h.

The task is also not too difficult with $b \neq 0$ and $h = 0$. The firm's investment per share is $b\check{Y}_0$. With the return on existing capital $\dot{\eta} = \check{Y}_0/W_0$, the investment may be expressed as a fraction of the net worth. That is, since $\check{\eta} = \check{Y}/W$, we have $z = b\check{Y}/W = b\check{\eta}$. Hence,

$$r = \check{r} = \rho_0(1 + \check{\eta}b)^{\rho_1} \tag{14.8}$$

Our stock price model with $h = 0$ is

$$P = \frac{(1 - b)\check{Y}[1 + b\rho_0(1 + \check{\eta}b)^{\rho_1}]^{\alpha_2}}{\check{k}} \tag{14.9}$$

The equation may be solved for the annual investment rate b that maximizes P.

Matters are somewhat complicated when both h and b are allowed to vary. To express z in terms of b and h we proceed as follows. Adopting a leverage rate of h results in an investment of hW_0. A retention rate of b results in a current investment of $b\check{Y}_0 = b\check{\eta}W_0$, and leverage of h on the retention of $b\check{Y}_0$ adds $hb\check{\eta}W_0$ to the investment. Therefore, the firm's current investment with $h = 0$ initially is

$$zW_0 = hW_0 + b\check{\eta}W_0 + hb\check{\eta}W_0 \tag{14.10}$$

and

$$z = h + b\check{\eta} + hb\check{\eta} \tag{14.11}$$

We may substitute Eq. (14.11) for z in Eq. (14.6).

Making the indicated substitutions, a corporation's current income is

$$Y = W[\check{\eta} + \rho_0(1 + h + b\check{\eta} + hb\check{\eta})^{\rho_1}h - .5ih] \tag{14.12}$$

and the rate of growth in the dividend is

$$br = b\{[\rho_0(1 + h + b\check{\eta} + hb\check{\eta})^{\rho_1}][1 + h] - .5ih\} \tag{14.13}$$

Substituting Eqs. (14.12) and (14.13) for Y and br in Eq. (14.1), the latter may be used to find the price of a share for any combination of h and b.

FIGURE 14.2

VARIATION IN MARGINAL, AVERAGE, AND TOTAL
RETURN ON INVESTMENT WITH THE INVESTMENT RATE

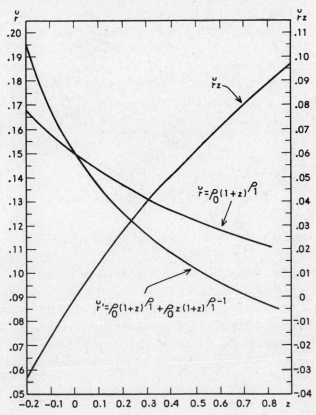

In calculating P for various values of h, b, $\check{k}$, and rate of return on investment, the values .20, .15, and .10 were assigned to ρ_0 in Eq. (14.6) to represent high, average, and low profitability.[8] In all cases, $\rho_1 = -.5$ was used. Figure 14.2 below shows the variation in $\check{r}$ with z under Eq. (14.6) for a corporation with $\rho_0 = .15$ and $\rho_1 = -.5$.

[8] The values assigned to ρ_0 were selected to make low, average, and high profitability roughly comparable with the tables in which $\check{r}$ is a constant. However, $\check{r}$ a constant and $\check{r}$ a decreasing function of z are two radically different conditions, and comparability can only be achieved in the crudest sense so that care must be exercised in any comparisons. In this crude sense the B and C tables are comparable, but most would consider the corporation with $\rho_0 = .10$ more profitable than one with $\check{r} = .05$.

Tables 14.4 to 14.6 present P for various combinations of $\check{k}$, ρ_0, b, and h. In the three tables of Table 14.4 we have $\check{k} = .08$ and $\rho_0 = .10, .15,$ and $.20$. In Tables 14.5 and 14.6 $\check{k}$ is changed to $.10$ and $.12$. In all the tables we of course continue to have $W = \$30$ and $\check{\eta} = \check{k}$. Consequently, we continue to have $P = \$30$ when $h = b = 0$.

TABLE 14.4

VARIATION IN PRICE WITH LEVERAGE AND RETENTION FOR A CORPORATION
WITH RETURN ON INVESTMENT VARIABLE AND LOW RISK, $\check{k} = .08$

$h \backslash b$	0	.10	.20	.30	.40	.50	.60
			A. Low Profitability, $\rho_0 = .10$				
0	$30.00	$31.01	$31.58 √	$31.57	$30.84	$ 29.22	$ 26.52
.10	31.19	32.34	33.03	33.12 √	32.45	30.82	28.04
.20	31.84	33.10	33.88	34.04 √	33.42	31.81	28.99
.30	32.06✕	33.37✕	34.21✕	34.42 √ ✕	33.83✕	32.23✕	29.41✕
.40	31.93	33.26	34.10	34.32 √	33.74	32.16	29.35
.50	31.48	32.78	33.60	33.80 √	33.21	31.63	28.85
.60	30.78	32.00	32.75	32.89 √	32.27	30.69	27.95
			B. Average Profitability, $\rho_0 = .15$				
0	30.00	33.23	36.16	38.55	40.07	40.32 √	38.79
.10	32.89	36.65	40.13	43.02	44.97	45.49 √	43.97
.20	34.95	39.16	43.09	46.43	48.76	49.54 √	48.09
.30	36.35	40.91	45.21	48.91	51.55	52.56 √	51.20
.40	37.21	42.01	46.59	50.55	53.43	54.63 √	53.35
.50	37.61	42.57	47.30	51.43	54.48	55.80 √	54.58
.60	37.62✕	42.63✕	47.43✕	51.63✕	54.73✕	56.11 √ ✕	54.93✕
.70	37.29	42.29	47.03	51.19	54.26	55.61 √	54.43
			C. High Profitability, $\rho_0 = .20$				
0	30.00	35.58	41.34	46.93	51.81	55.24	56.17 √
.10	34.59	41.41	48.54	55.57	61.84	66.42	68.02 √
.20	38.07	45.95	54.30	62.63	70.19	75.90	78.23 √
.30	40.64	49.43	58.82	68.29	77.01	83.77	86.82 √
.40	42.49	52.00	62.25	72.68	82.40	90.08	93.79 √
.50	43.73	53.80	64.72	75.90	86.42	94.85	99.13 √
.60	44.46	54.92	66.31	78.04	89.14	98.13	102.84 √
.70	44.75✕	55.44✕	67.10	79.16	90.61	99.94	104.93 √
.80	44.66	55.41	67.16✕	79.31✕	90.88✕	100.33✕	105.42✕ √

The most striking characteristic of the data is the change in the relation between h and P when $\check{r}$ is made a function of the investment rate. We no longer find P still rising with h as the latter reaches the highest value in our range of observation. For all combinations of the other variables, price is maximized in the range of h shown. For instance, under the most favorable conditions, Table 14.4C, where $\rho_0 = .20$ and $\check{k} = .08$, price is maximized at $h = .70$ or $.80$, depending on the level of b. For lower values of ρ_0, the optimum is at lower values of h, at $h = .60$ for $\rho_0 = .15$ and at $h = .30$ for $\rho_0 = .10$. By comparison with these results with $\check{r}$, a constant equal to .15, price is still rising strongly with h at $h = 1.20$.

A second point to note is that the relative attractiveness of retention by comparison with leverage is increased when $\check{r}$ is a de-

TABLE 14.5

VARIATION IN PRICE WITH LEVERAGE AND RETENTION FOR A CORPORATION
WITH RETURN ON INVESTMENT VARIABLE AND AVERAGE RISK, $k = .10$

$h\backslash b$	0	.10	.20	.30	.40	.50	.60
			A. Low Profitability, $\rho_0 = .10$				
0	$30.00	$31.01	$31.58 √	$31.57	$30.85	$29.22	$26.52
.10	30.38×	31.50	32.18	32.27 √	31.61	30.03	27.33
.20	30.38	31.58×	32.33×	32.49 √ ×	31.90	30.37×	27.68×
.30	30.08	31.32	32.11	32.32 √	31.77	30.28	27.63
.40	29.55	30.79	31.59	31.80 √	31.27	29.81	27.21
.50	28.83	30.03	30.79	30.98 √	30.45	29.02	26.47
.60	27.95	29.07	29.76	29.90 √	29.34	27.92	25.43
			B. Average Profitability, $\rho_0 = .15$				
0	30.00	33.22	36.16	38.55	40.07	40.32 √	38.79
.10	31.73	35.36	38.71	41.52	43.40	43.90 √	42.45
.20	32.82	36.78	40.48	43.63	45.82	46.56 √	45.21
.30	33.43	37.63	41.59	45.01	47.45	48.40 √	47.15
.40	33.64×	38.01×	42.15	45.75	48.38	49.47 √	48.33
.50	33.54	37.98	42.22×	45.92×	48.65×	49.85 √ ×	48.78×
.60	33.18	37.62	41.86	45.58	48.34	49.57 √	48.55
.70	32.59	36.96	41.13	44.78	47.49	48.69 √	47.67
			C. High Profitability, $\rho_0 = .20$				
0	30.00	35.58	41.34	46.93	51.81	55.24	56.17 √
.10	33.07	39.60	46.43	53.15	59.16	63.56	65.10 √
.20	35.27	42.58	50.33	58.06	65.09	70.41	72.58 √
.30	36.77	44.73	53.25	61.84	69.76	75.90	78.68 √
.40	37.73	46.20	55.32	64.61	73.27	80.12	83.45 √
.50	38.25	47.08	56.65	66.47	75.70	83.11	86.89 √
.60	38.41×	47.46×	57.33	67.49	77.12	84.92	89.03 √
.70	38.26	47.41	57.41×	67.75×	77.58×	85.60×	89.91 √ ×
.80	37.85	46.98	56.96	67.30	77.14	85.19	89.54 √

creasing function of the investment rate. The reason for this is that an increase in h depresses $\check{r}$, but the continued investment associated with a given value of b does not depress $\check{r}$, thereby increasing the attractiveness of retention as a method of financing. At the same time it is no longer true that the optimum retention rate is sensitive to the leverage rate. With one exception the optimum retention rate is independent of h for each value of ρ_0. However, with a large enough range of variation in h we would find the optimum b initially increases and ultimately falls as h increases.

It also appears that the optimum leverage rate has become some-what less sensitive to the retention rate. Inspection of the tables reveals that the optimum h still increases as b varies over the range zero to .60, but the rise in h is not as great as it was in Tables 14.1 to 14.3. The reason is that the decline in $\check{r}$ as the investment rate in-

TABLE 14.6

VARIATION IN PRICE WITH LEVERAGE AND RETENTION FOR A CORPORATION
WITH RETURN ON INVESTMENT VARIABLE AND HIGH RISK, $k = .12$

$h\backslash b$	0	.10	.20	.30	.40	.50	.60
			A. Low Profitability, $\rho_0 = .10$				
0	$30.00✕	$31.01✕	$31.58 √	$31.57	$30.84	$29.22	$26.52
.10	29.84	30.95	31.62✕	31.71 √ ✕	31.07✕	29.52✕	26.86✕
.20	29.43	30.60	31.33	31.49 √	30.92	29.44	26.83
.30	28.82	30.01	30.77	30.97 √	30.45	29.02	26.49
.40	28.06	29.24	30.00	30.21 √	29.71	28.33	25.86
.50	27.18	28.31	29.03	29.22 √	28.73	27.38	24.98
.60	26.20	27.25	27.91	28.05 √	27.53	26.20	23.87
			B. Average Profitability, $\rho_0 = .15$				
0	30.00	33.22	36.16	38.55	40.07	40.32 √	38.79
.10	30.96	34.51	37.79	40.53	42.37	42.86 √	41.44
.20	31.44	35.24	38.79	41.81	43.92	44.64 √	43.35
.30	31.55✕	35.53✕	39.28	42.51	44.83	45.73 √	44.57
.40	31.39	35.47	39.35✕	42.72✕	45.18✕	46.22 √ ✕	45.16✕
.50	31.00	35.12	39.04	42.48	45.01	46.13 √	45.15
.60	30.43	34.51	38.42	41.84	44.39	45.53 √	44.60
			C. High Profitability, $\rho_0 = .20$				
0	30.00	35.58	41.34	46.93	51.81	55.24	56.16 √
.10	32.08	38.41	45.04	51.57	57.40	61.67	63.18 √
.20	33.45	40.40	47.76	55.11	61.79	66.85	68.92 √
.30	34.30	41.74	49.69	57.72	65.12	70.87	73.49 √
.40	34.73	42.53	50.94	59.51	67.50	73.83	76.91 √
.50	34.83✕	42.88✕	51.61	60.57	69.00	75.17	79.24 √
.60	34.67	42.85	51.77✕	60.96✕	69.68✕	76.75	80.49 √
.70	34.28	42.49	51.47	60.75	69.59	76.80✕	80.69 √ ✕
.80	33.71	41.84	50.75	59.98	68.77	75.88	79.88 √

creases has such a strong influence in determining the optimum lever-age that the influence of b is reduced.

Beyond the above observations, the variation in price with $\check{r}$, b, h, and $\check{k}$ follows the same broad pattern evidenced earlier. The opti-mum leverage and retention rates increase with the rate of return on investment. The optimum retention rate at each h is independent of $\check{k}$. The optimum leverage rate still is a decreasing function of $\check{k}$, but with $\check{r}$ a decreasing function of the investment rate this is less evident than was the case when $\check{r}$ was dependent of z. Over the values of h and b in our tables, for $\rho_0 = .10$ and $\check{k} = .08$, price is maximized at $b = .30$ and $h = .40$. Changing $\check{k}$ to .10 and .12 reduces the optimum h to .20 and .10 and leaves $b = .30$. For $\rho_0 = .15$ and $\check{k} = .08$, price is maximized at $b = .50$ and $h = .60$. Raising $\check{k}$ to .10 and .12 shifts the maximum price to $h = .50$ and $h = .40$. Finally, at $\rho_0 = .20$ and $\check{k} = .08$ price is maximized at $b = .60$ and $h = .80$.[9] Raising $\check{k}$ to .10 and .12 reduces the optimum h to .70 in both cases.

14.3 Problems in the Use of the Model

Among the problems involved in the use of the model by a corporation to find the investment and financing that maximize the value of its stock, those related to the return on investment function are the most numerous, and it may be advisable to begin with a discussion of them. The first problem we will examine is the derivation by a corporation of its rate of return on investment function. It is evident that $\check{r}zW_0$, the product of $\check{r}$, a corporation's average rate of return on investment, and zW_0, the corporation's investment, is the total periodic income generated by the investment. The total periodic income generated by the investment of zW_0 expressed as a fraction of W_0 is $\check{r}z$. The marginal rate of return on investment when the average rate of return is given by Eq. (14.6) and investment is the fraction z of W_0 is the derivative of $\check{r}z$ with respect to z, or

$$\check{r}' = \frac{d(\check{r}z)}{dz} = \rho_0(1 + z)^{\rho_1} + \rho_0 z \rho_1 (1 + z)^{\rho_1 - 1} \qquad (14.14)$$

The relation among the three curves, $\check{r}$, $\check{r}z$, and $\check{r}'$ is illustrated in Figure 14.2 with $\rho_0 = .15$ and $\rho_1 = -.5$. Both the marginal and the average rates of return on investment fall by decreasing amounts as z increases, but of course $\check{r}'$ falls more rapidly than $\check{r}$. The total return expressed as a fraction of W_0, $\check{r}z$, rises with z, but the increase is by decreasing amounts.

To arrive at the above functions we can visualize a corporation proceeding as follows. (1) Estimate the rate of return on each of its investment opportunities. (2) Rank the investments in a schedule according to their rate of return, and enter in the schedule the rate of return and the cumulative investment. That is, for the jth investment show its rate of return and the total outlay needed to undertake all investments up through the jth. (3) Plot the rate of return against the cumulative investment expressed as a fraction of the cor-

---

[9] Increasing b and/or h will in fact reduce P. The optimum is not merely over the values of b and h in the table.

poration's net worth. This is the corporation's marginal return on investment schedule. (4) Finally, find the values of ρ_0 and ρ_1 that provide the best fit of Eq. (14.14) to the empirical curve. With ρ_0 and ρ_1 established, the average return on investment for any level of investment is readily obtained by means of Eq. (14.6).

Actually the task is not this simple. One complication arises from the lumpiness of investment opportunities. With investment opportunities varying in size, some quite large, it is not possible to have *all* the investments included in a capital budget of *a given size* more profitable than the excluded projects. In moving from a capital budget of z to $z + \Delta z$ the most profitable course of action may be to add a project that costs more than Δz and drop one or more less profitable projects included in the budget of z.[10] What this implies is that for small values of z, $\tilde{r}$ will not be as large as one might imagine, and as z rises, $\tilde{r}'$ and $\tilde{r}$ do not fall as rapidly as would be the case with investment a continuous variable.

There are other problems involved in arriving at a marginal rate of return on investment schedule for a period, including in particular the measurement of rate of return on projects with important qualitative benefits and allowing for the variation in risk among investment opportunities. Many of these problems have been discussed by Dean [1951], Solomon [1956], Lorie and Savage [1955], Terborgh [1949], and others, and they will not be reviewed here.

The second major question with respect to $\tilde{r}$ that we will consider is its value in future periods. Eq. (14.6) provides the relation between $\tilde{r}$ and z at $t = 0$, but our stock price model contains implicit assumptions about the return on investment function in every future period. Specifically, the model finds the optimal current values for b and h under the following assumptions with respect to the return on investment function. Given the current decision with respect to h and b, Eq. (14.6) provides the return on the investment made during the current period. The investor expectation is that h and b will not be changed in the future. For as long as h and b remain unchanged, the investment in each subsequent period will be the fraction $b(1 + h)$ of the period's income or the fraction $\tilde{\eta}b(1 + h)$ of its net worth.[11] With this the investment rate, the re-

---

[10] The project costing Δz was excluded from the budget of z in favor of one or more less profitable projects because its size would have forced the exclusion of some projects that are more profitable.

[11] The investment during the current period will be $\tilde{\eta}b(1 + h) W_0$ plus $h'W_0$.

turn on investment will be unchanged. In other words, the continued investment of $b(1 + h)Y_t$ in each subsequent period will neither move the firm along the function nor shift the function. The firm will realize the same average return on investment as was realized on the investment at $t = 0$.

On the other hand, the model assumes that investment arising through a change in h or b during a subsequent period will move the firm along the return on investment function. That is, an increase in h or b will reduce $\check{r}$ as determined by Eq. (14.6). The rationale for these assumptions with retention alone considered was discussed in pages 93–95. There is an inconsistency in our treatment of the problem, however, in that a given annual investment rate when financed by retention is considered to have no depressing effect on $\check{r}$, while the same investment rate financed by periodic increases in h reduces $\check{r}$. In principle this is wrong and should be corrected if possible. In practice there is a tendency for corporations to use debt to finance extraordinary investment opportunities, the exploitation of which leaves the rate of return on investment lower than it previously was. Further, when and if the next such opportunity will arise is typically unknown. By contrast, the investment opportunities that are created more or less regularly by technological change and other developments over time are financed more commonly by retention.

It probably need not be noted that the function $\check{r}$ of z may shift over time, and the determination of b and h in any period involves the determination of the current values of ρ_0 and ρ_1. This is one reason why we assigned an initial value to h in arriving at the optimal values of h and b. With $\rho_0 = .15$ and $\rho_1 = .5$, a corporation with $h = 0$ has an average and marginal rate of return on investment at $h = 0$ of .15, and we described this corporation as one of average profitability. The corporation could reduce h to $-.40$ by not investing its depreciation allowances and selling off part of its assets. The marginal rate of return at $h = -.40$, that is, the gain by not disinvesting to the point $h = -.40$ is $\check{r}' = .26$. This is reasonable if not low when we consider the losses generally incurred in disposing of used equipment or operating with an inadequate inventory. On the other hand, a corporation at $h = -.40$ would be considered highly profitable if its return on the first dollar invested was $\check{r}' = .26$.

Determining the optimal values of b and h when the corporation's initial position is $h \neq 0$ may appear tedious, but it is really not very difficult. Let h_a be the initial position and h_b the new leverage so that $h' = h_b - h_a$ is the change in leverage. The corporation's investment rate is the change in leverage, plus $b\check{\eta}$ plus $b\check{\eta}$ times the new leverage rate or

$$z = h' + b\check{\eta} + h_b b\check{\eta} \tag{14.15}$$

and this expression is used for z in the return on investment function that determines $\check{r}$. The income variable becomes

$$Y_0 = Y^*_0 + W_0 h'\check{r} - W_0 h'i'_b \tag{14.16}$$

In the above, Y^*_0 is the earnings per share *after interest* on debt with leverage of h_a. To this we add $W_0 h'\check{r}$, the earnings before interest on the leverage of h', and we deduct the increased interest due to the increased leverage. The incremental interest rate, i'_b, may be obtained readily in a number of ways, the choice depending on the circumstances. The growth variable is

$$br = b\{\check{r}(1 + h_b) - i_b h_b\} \tag{14.17}$$

The increased debt in future periods to maintain h_b may be expected to involve an interest rate of i_b. Finally, the leverage variable in the denominator of Eq. (14.1) requires only the substitution of h_b *for* h.

Before leaving the subject of leverage, there is a limitation of the model that should be noted. It is probable that the debt-financing behavior of many corporations can be described as follows. An investment that is attractive or necessary and too large to finance by retention is undertaken by a large increase in h. The corporation, however, does not maintain the higher h but liquidates the debt over a fairly short period of time. Not only does the corporation do this, but investors frequently expect the corporations to do so. Our stock valuation model cannot recognize this expectation.

Probably the haziest problem connected with the use of the model is that of divergence between stockholder information and corporation information. Given the past history of the corporation we represent the stockholder as deciding that the corporation may be characterized by the values h^*, b^*, and $\check{r}^*$ for the variables. The corporation may survey its situation and come up with the conclusion that at h^* and b^*, $\check{r} \neq \check{r}^*$. Further, what knowledge does the investor have of the function $\check{r}$ is of z? Clearly, regardless of how "wrong" the stockholder is, if the corporation wants to maximize P_0 it should use the stockholder's perception of the corporation's return on investment function. Setting b and h on the basis of the corporation's superior knowledge will result in a lower price. It can be argued that since the corporation's information on $\check{r}$ is the best, acting on it will maximize price in the long run. However, consideration of long-run price maximization opens up a Pandora's box, and this is something that we had better not undertake here.

The problems just discussed with respect to stockholder and corporation information on $\check{r}$ apply also to b and h. The value of a share is determined by h^* and b^* and not by what the corporation considers the correct current values of these variables. Further, in estimating the change in price consequent to decisions with respect to h and b, the corporation must estimate what will happen to h^* and b^* as a consequence of the specific actions the corporation will take. In general, we may say that there are three sets of values for $\check{r}$, h, and b: the values produced by our rules of measurement, the values the corporation believes are true, and the values that investors believe are true. The last set of values are what the corporation should use in setting h and b to maximize price.[12]

Finally, the parameter estimates should not pass without notice. Unless they are reasonably stable over time, maximizing a share's price involves forecasting the values the parameters will have in subsequent periods. Further, since a parameter's value varies depending on the industry sample used to obtain it, assigning a firm to the correct industry classification is a problem. What are perhaps more important are the firm effects discussed on page 153. The fact that the residuals for a firm in successive cross sections over time are not randomly distributed with zero mean suggests that the corporation in an industry are not homogeneous. If improvement in the measurement of the variables does not eliminate these firm effects, it may be that the firm effect should be included among the variables. A firm effect variable can be computed from the past values of the residuals obtained without a firm effect variable in the model. The parameters of the model can then be computed with the firm effect among the variables. The result should be better parameter estimates and better explanation of the variation in price among shares.

14.4 The Cost of Capital

In the previous chapters of this book we have used the term *cost of capital* to refer at times to k, the rate of profit that investors re-

---

[12] The values of the variables produced by our measurement rules may be used to estimate the parameters of a stock value model, and then a corporation may use other less objective information to arrive at the values investors assign to its variables.

quire on investment in a corporation's shares. The literature on the investment and financing of corporations, however, has used the term to embrace a good deal more. Writers such as Durand [1952], Solomon [1955], Duesenberry [1958, pp. 87–112], and Modigliani and Miller [1958] look on a firm as making its investment decision in the following way. A minimum rate of return is given. If the rate of return on a project exceeds this minimum, or if the project's cash flows discounted at this rate exceeds its cost, the investment should be undertaken. The figure that a firm is advised to use as its minimum rate of return is its cost of capital, but what is the cost of capital?

The above question has an obvious and simple answer when the future is known with certainty. In this event, the firm can freely lend or borrow at a given rate of interest, and this rate is the firm's cost of capital. The rationale is that any investment with a rate of return in excess of the rate of interest will raise the value of the firm, i.e., the ownership equity. The literature on the investment of the firm has generalized the above treatment of the subject as follows: the cost of capital for a firm is a discount rate with the property that an investment with a rate of profit above (below) this rate will raise (lower) the value of the firm. The next problem has proven to be the difficult one: how do you establish the cost of capital for a firm when the future is uncertain and borrowing is not the only source of funds?

A number of statistics such as the interest rate, the earnings-price ratio, and the return on net worth have been suggested. As mentioned earlier, Durand [1952] has investigated alternative bases for measuring the cost of debt and equity funds. Solomon [1955] arrived at a cost-of-capital function as follows. The cost of funds equal to the depreciation expense is the earnings-price ratio. With earnings retention the cost is an average of the previous figure and the return on investment. Beyond some point given by dividend policy and similar restraints, the cost of retained earnings shoots up, and the cost of new equity financing becomes the relevant source of funds. Duesenberry pieced together a cost-of-capital function in a similar way without always defining the cost of each class of funds in the same way as Solomon.

What is common to all of the above and to most other students of the subject is the acceptance that the cost of capital is not a constant. Rather, it is a function of the level of the firm's investment with the parameters of the function depending on the firm's dividend rate, debt-equity ratio, rate of return on investment, and/or other variables.

By contrast, Modigliani and Miller sought to prove that the problem is not as complicated as the above description suggests. They maintained that a corporation's cost of capital is simply its leverage-free earnings-price ratio, i.e., its earnings plus interest divided by its equity (market value) plus debt.[13] What is most important, the cost of capital is independent of the level of investment: it does not depend on the debt-equity ratio, dividend rate, etc. What appears to have been their grand objective was to show that the neoclassical theory of the investment of the firm remains true under uncertainty. We need only substitute the leverage-free earnings yield for the interest rate and we can proceed as if nothing is changed by the recognition of uncertainty. Of course, the theory and data of the preceding pages do not support their position.

If the cost of capital were a constant and readily observed, capital budgeting would be a comparatively simple task. The decision to accept or reject an investment project would require merely the comparison of its rate of return with the predetermined number. On the other hand, with the cost of capital a function of the level of investment, a corporation cannot look at a project in isolation. The corporation must establish its cost-of-capital function *and* its return on investment function. The return on every investment opportunity must be established and the information put in the form of a function as described at the start of the previous section.

It now becomes evident why the cost of capital as just defined was not employed in our work. The objective in establishing a firm's cost of capital is to find the investment that maximizes the value of the firm. What we did was directly state the value of the firm as a function of its investment. With that function including the return on investment function, the investment and financing of a firm that maximizes its value may be found. There is no need to establish the cost-of-capital function. The opposite is not true.

Let us examine how one would go about obtaining a corporation's cost-of-capital function. Let $P(0)$ be the price of a share with a zero investment by the corporation, and let $z(0)$, $z(1)$, $z(2)$, ... ,

---

[13] They subsequently [1959] qualified this definition as a basis for measurement in the case where the corporation can earn a higher rate of return than its cost of capital. This qualification is not relevant to the present analysis, however.

$z(n)$ refer to successive levels of investment. Find the value of $\check{r}^*(1)$, the average rate of return the investment of $z(1)$ should earn to realize $P^*(1) = P(0)$. This value of $\check{r}(1)$ is the cost of capital at the investment of $z(1)$. With two or more methods of financing and each yielding a different $\check{r}^*(1)$, the figure (and financing) we want is the minimum one. It should be noted that in order to find the $\check{r}^*(1)$ that realizes $P^*(1) = P(0)$, we need a stock value model.

To establish the cost of capital at $z(2)$, we must first find the actual $\check{r}(1)$, i.e., the actual rate of return on the most profitable investment opportunity available. With the true $\check{r}(1)$ we find the $P(1)$ that would prevail under $z(1)$. Next, $\check{r}^*(2)$, the average rate of return the investment of $z(2)$ should earn to realize $P^*(2) = P(1)$ is found in the same way as $\check{r}^*(1)$ was found. The marginal rate of return $\check{r}'^*(2)$ that realizes $\check{r}^*(2)$ is the cost of capital at $z(2)$. For the cost of capital at $z(3)$ we first combine $\check{r}(1)$ and $\check{r}'(2)$ to obtain $\check{r}(2)$, the actual average rate of return at $z(2)$. With it we calculate $P(2)$, the actual price at $z(2)$. We then proceed as before to find the $\check{r}^*(3)$ that realizes $P^*(3) = P(2)$, etc.

What can be seen is that we are simultaneously developing the firm's marginal return on investment function, $\check{r}'(n)$, and its cost-of-capital function, the latter being $\check{r}'^*(n)$, the rate of return on investment that leaves the value of the firm unchanged. Since $\check{r}'(n)$ falls and $\check{r}'^*(n)$ rises as z increases, the investment rate $z(m)$ where $\check{r}'(m) = \check{r}'^*(m)$ maximizes the value of a firm.

Reflection on the above description of how one computes a firm's cost-of-capital function makes evident that it is extremely tedious,[14] as well as unnecessary. However, it is quite likely that corporations find a required rate of profit figure a handy tool in capital budgeting. What they would probably find adequate is a rate of return figure and an interval around it such that a project with a rate of return outside this interval can be immediately accepted or rejected. Decision on the projects inside the interval could be deferred until the capital budget is finalized. At this level of accuracy, a cost-of-capital or required rate of return figure can be obtained. On the assumption that a corporation uses our model to set its capital budget, the marginal rate of return at the optimal investment rate in the prior period can be used as the required rate of profit for the current period. If undertaking all investments with a higher rate of return in

---

[14] The analytic derivation of the function is very difficult, and it will not be attempted here.

the current period does not require a change in h and b, keeping their values unchanged results in the optimum investment and financing. If undertaking all projects with a rate of return in excess of the required rate involves a change in h and/or b, the firm must construct its return on investment function and use the stock value model to compute the optimal values of h and b before finalizing its capital budget for the year.

It may be of some interest to see how the average and marginal rates of return on investment at the optimal values of h and b vary with the state variables $\check{k}$ and ρ_0. Table 14.7 presents the optimal h

TABLE 14.7

AVERAGE AND MARGINAL RATES OF RETURN ON INVESTMENT AT THE
OPTIMAL INVESTMENT RATE FOR CERTAIN VALUES OF REQUIRED
RATE OF PROFIT AND DEGREE OF PROFITABILITY OF INVESTMENT

		Optimal				
$\check{k}$	ρ_0	h	b	z	$\check{r}$	$\check{r}'$
.08	.10	.30	.30	.339	.086	.075
.08	.15	.60	.50	.680	.116	.092
.08	.20	.80	.60	.908	.145	.110
.10	.10	.20	.30	.236	.090	.081
.10	.15	.50	.50	.575	.120	.098
.10	.20	.70	.60	.802	.149	.116
.12	.10	.10	.30	.133	.094	.088
.12	.15	.40	.50	.452	.124	.104
.12	.20	.70	.60	.802	.149	.116

and b and the resultant values of $\check{r}$, $\check{r}'$, and z for the possible combinations of $\check{k} = .08$, .10, and .12 and $\rho_0 = .10$, .15, and .20. The optimal values of h and b for each combination of ρ_0 and $\check{k}$ were obtained from Tables 14.4 to 14.6. Given h and b, the values of z, $\check{r}$, and $\check{r}'$ were computed from Eqs. (14.11), (14.6), and (14.14).

As we would expect, given $\check{k}$ the optimal values of h, b, and z increase with ρ_0. Given ρ_0, the optimal values of h and z fall as $\check{k}$ increases. The optimal b for each ρ_0 is unchanged as $\check{k}$ increases.[15] Since $\check{r}$ is a decreasing function of z, with ρ_0 given raising $\check{k}$ reduces the optimal z and raises $\check{r}$ and $\check{r}'$. Conversely, with $\check{k}$ given, raising ρ_0 raises the optimal z, and the values of $\check{r}$ and $\check{r}'$ at the optimum z are also raised.

What may appear surprising is the variation in the relation be-

[15] As noted earlier, the optimal b is independent of $\check{k}$ for given ρ_0 and h, but it rises as h rises. Hence, as $\check{k}$ goes up and the optimal h falls, the optimal b should fall also. However, the relation is too weak to be evident with b incremented by .1.

tween $\check{k}$ and $\check{r}$, and even more so between $\check{k}$ and $\check{r}'$. At the optimal investment, the marginal rate of return on investment and the cost of capital are equal. Of course, $\check{k}$ is not the marginal cost of capital, but finding $\check{r}' \gtreqless k$ depending on the values of $\check{k}$ and ρ_0 may seem strange. Why should z be carried to the point where $\check{r}' = .088$ when $\check{k} = .12$ and $\rho_0 = .10$ while z is only carried to the point where $\check{r}' = .11$ when $\check{k} = .08$ and $\rho_0 = .20$?

An adequate explanation of the relation among $\check{k}$, $\check{r}$, and $\check{r}'$ at the optimal investment for various combinations of ρ_0 and $\check{k}$ requires an analysis of how k and the cost of capital vary. As stated earlier, the analytic derivation of a corporation's cost of capital is extremely difficult, and the interpretation of the function is even more formidable. This task will not be undertaken here, but the following analysis may clear some of the mystery. Assume a corporation with: (1) no corporate income tax; (2) i a constant; (3) no retention; and (4) $\check{r}$ a decreasing function of z. For such a corporation, it is readily seen that the optimal investment rate, $z = h$, realizes $\check{r}' = \check{k}$, and the Modigliani-Miller theorem holds. That is, investment should be carried to the point where the marginal rate of return on investment is equal to the leverage-free yield at which the share sells.

The introduction of the corporate income tax makes it advantageous to carry investment beyond this point. Assume a corporation with ρ_0 slightly greater than $\check{k}$. With no corporate income tax the optimum z would realize $\check{r}' = \check{k}$. Introducing the tax will raise the optimal z, and we will have $\check{r}' < \check{k}$ at the optimum. Withdrawing the assumption that i is a constant will not make much difference, since the optimum h will be so small that $.5i$ will not be materially different from its value at $h = 0$. Now, assume a corporation with ρ_0 substantially larger than k. This spread combined with the corporate income tax will raise the optimum z materially, but as h increases, the interest rate will rise. Let the spread between ρ_0 and $\check{k}$ be large enough so that the optimal h is greater than the value of h at which the after-tax rate of interest rises to its before-tax value at $h = 0$. It is evident that under this condition, $.5i$ in $\check{\eta} + h(\check{r} - .5i)$ will be greater than the constant i in $\check{k} + h(\check{k} - i)$. The result will be $\check{r}' > \check{k}$ at the optimal investment.

The above is an explanation of the variation in the relation between $\check{r}'$ and $\check{k}$ at the optimal z in Table 13.7. However, it is not the whole story, since we have been assuming that $b = 0$. Bodenhorn [1959, p. 487] has pointed out that with $h = 0$ and k independent of

br, the optimum investment rate involves carrying retention to the point where $\check{r}'$ is less than k. This takes place because the return on investment is a function of the investment *rate*, and additional investment in the current year raises the rate of return on investment in subsequent years. With both leverage and retention used to finance investment and with k a function of br, it is not clear what the relation between $\check{r}'$ and $\check{k}$ will be at the optimal investment for various values of ρ_0 and $\check{k}$.

The above analysis makes clear that we cannot, as in the Modigliani-Miller theory, expect a simple relation between $\check{k}$ and $\check{r}'$ at the optimal investment, and $\check{k}$ can be used as only a *very* rough approximation of a corporation's cost of capital. It is possible that further analysis, particularly on the variation in k and k' with b and h for different values of $\check{k}$ and ρ_0, may allow more accurate estimates of the cost of capital without developing the entire function. At present, the capital budgeting methods described earlier would seem preferable to using $\check{k}$.

Chapter 15

ACTUAL FINANCIAL POLICIES AND STRUCTURE OF CORPORATIONS

The primary objective of this chapter contrasts sharply with that of the previous chapter. There, we sought to describe how our model might be used to find the investment and financing that maximize the value of a share. Here we undertake an analysis of our data for the information it provides on the financial structure of corporations and on the investment and financing policies they actually follow.

In the next section the behavior over time of corporate leverage, retention, and return on investment rates will be examined. The stability of these variables is of interest in its own right, but for us their behavior is of particular interest. In constructing the theory, it was assumed that investors expect each of these three rates to be the same in every future period. Testing these assumptions directly, i.e., finding out what investor expectations are like, is extremely difficult. Our primary source of evidence on the reasonableness of the assumptions, therefore, has been the performance of the model which incorporates them. Additional information, however, is provided by the stability or absence of it in the past values of the variables.

Early in this book it was recognized that in arriving at its investment and financing decisions a corporation might be influenced by other considerations than the price at which its stock sells. Even if this is true, we reassured ourselves, the study would nonetheless be useful, since a corporation is unlikely to be indifferent to the price at which its stock sells. The possible existence of other objectives, however, makes the financial structure and policies of corporations a subject of some importance. Information on the financing policies of corporations is provided by taking the independent variables of our model and certain related variables and examining the correlations

224

among them. A variety of hypotheses with respect to these correlations will be tested in Sections 15.2 to 15.4.

In the last topic of this chapter we go even further afield. Probably the major reason for interest in stock value models has been the desire to find a formula for discovering over- and undervalued shares. Portfolio selection was not our purpose in studying the valuation of common stocks, but our failure to consider the subject might cause some surprise and disappointment. Hence, the problems and possibilities in this use of the model will be surveyed.

15.1 Stability of Leverage, Retention, and Return on Investment Rates

There were two reasons why the development of our stock value model was based on the assumptions that investors expect a corporation's leverage, retention, and return on investment rates to be the same in every future period. First, allowing h, b, and $\check{r}$ to take on different values in each future period would have made the model unmanageably complicated. Some workable compromise between having each variable a constant and allowing it to take on a succession of different values could possibly have been accomplished. Attempting this compromise, however, was discouraged by the other reason for assuming an expectation has the same value for each future period. It was not evident what information might be used to establish expectations for future periods that are different from the current values of the variables.

Notwithstanding the above considerations, we can readily imagine situations in which investors expect h, b, and $\check{r}$ for a share to change, and these expectations should influence the valuation of the share. Consequently, the extent to which our assumptions correctly represent investor behavior is a matter of concern. Although there may be more effective sources of information on the questions, the analysis of our data described below is believed to be of some interest.

For each industry we have observations on a variable over five years for each of the 48 firms. An analysis of variance may be employed to establish the variance in a variable among firms and the variance over the five years within a firm. The variance among firms, the *interfirm* variance, is calculated by averaging the five values for each firm and computing the variance for the 48 firms. The variance among years, the *interyear* variance, is the variance over the five years for each firm averaged over the 48 firms. The ratio of the interfirm to the interyear variance is an index of the extent to which the variation in the variable among firms exceeds the variation within firms.[1] The larger the value of this ratio, the greater the relative stability of the variable over time for a corporation, and the more reasonable is the assumption that the value of the variable is not expected to change.

A corporation's retention rate is $b = 1 - D/\overline{Y}$ with D and $\overline{Y}$ as defined on pages 156–59. The mean and standard deviation of b over the 240 observations are .41 and .171 for the food and .44 and .134 for the machinery industry. The two variances are .029 and .018. An estimate of the food population variance based on the interfirm variance is .093, while it is only .007 on the basis of the interyear variance. For the machinery sample the interfirm variance is .053 and the intrafirm variance is .018. The two F ratios, 12.7 and 6.4, are both highly significant, with the food sample very much the larger of the two.

In interpreting this result it must be remembered that in $b = 1 - D/\overline{Y}$ the value of $\overline{Y}$ for a firm in a year is an exponential average of Y from 1947 through the year. In this average a weight of .3 is given to the current year and a weight of .7 is given to all prior years. This averaging limits the interyear variation in $\overline{Y}$ over time. On the other hand, actual income is known to fluctuate very severely, the averaging process allows considerable room for variation in $\overline{Y}$, and D which also enters into the determination of $b = 1 - D/\overline{Y}$ was obtained without averaging. The most important reason for not discounting these results, however, is that in arriving at the value of past behavior of b for a corporation an investor may be presumed to look at $\overline{Y}_t$ and not Y_t for past values of t.

The data therefore provide strong evidence that the variation in retention rate over time within firms in considerably smaller than its variation among firms. For instance, with the food sample mean, .41, the interfirm standard deviation is .31, while the interyear value is only .084. On the other hand, an interyear standard deviation of .084 is large enough to indicate that retention changes quite materially over time for a substantial minority of firms. Investors are therefore quite likely to forecast changes in b for some corporations, and a model that arrived at and made use of these forecasts would be desirable.

[1] For an explanation of the computations and the rationale of an analysis of variance see Ferber [1949, pp. 279–300].

The data is relevant to the question whether investors can meaningfully differentiate among corporations with respect to their retention rates. Some writers have argued that fluctuations in earnings make this extremely difficult, so difficult that they use the dividend as a surrogate for earnings. What this implies is that investors can do no better than assume all corporations have the same dividend rate. Our data indicate that investors can do considerably better.

A corporation's leverage rate is $h = L/W$ with L and W as defined on pages 161–62. The mean and standard deviations of h over the 240 observations are .242 and .390 for the food, and $-.015$ and .282 for the machinery sample. An estimate of the food population variance based on the interfirm variance is .721, and on the basis of the interyear variance it is .029. For the machinery sample the two figures are .366 and .019. The two F ratios are 25.1 and 19.4, and both are highly significant.

The very small interyear variation in h, by comparison with the interfirm variance, cannot be attributed to averaging, since h is the actual value in each period. However, h is a stock and not a flow variable, and its value is an average of the prior period stock and the current period's flow. Consequently, what may appear to be small year-to-year changes in h for a corporation may represent a large fraction of the investment in each period. The critical question is whether or not the year-to-year changes in h largely offset each other over a period of years, so that the changes in h do not represent an important source of funds on balance. More information on this question was reported in Gordon [1960a]. The data analyzed there indicated that a large fraction of corporations changed their leverage rate little if at all over an eight-year period, but a significant minority increased or reduced their leverage rates substantially over the period. Further, no single reason stood out to provide an explanation of their behavior.

Our definition of a corporation's rate of return on investment, $\check{r} = \check{\overline{Y}}/W$, was obtained as follows. First $r = \overline{Y}/W$ was obtained with $\overline{Y}$ smoothed trend adjusted current earnings and W the end of year net worth per share. Then $\check{r}$ was obtained by solving the equation

$$r = \check{r} + h(\check{r} - i) \tag{15.1}$$

with r and h for the corporation known and $i = .04$. The average and standard deviation of $\check{r}$ over the 240 observations are .095 and .045 for the food corporations and .115 and .063 for the machinery corporations. The two variances are .002 and .004. The estimates of the population variances based on the interfirm variances are .008 and .013. The interyear variances yield population estimates of .000 and .002. The two F ratios are 173.0 and 7.4. Both are significant, but the tremendous value for the food sample is striking.

Clearly the averaging process by which $\check{r}$ is calculated for a firm had some influence on the results. But once again it should be noted that in estimating a corporation's rate of return during a year investors are more reasonably presumed to average earnings in some way than to just look at the current value. Therefore, the year-to-year changes in our variable may be used to represent the year-to-year changes in the rate of return investors assign to a corporation. If the year-to-year departures in actual income from a trend value are small and have zero mean, the food sample statistics result. If the fluctuations in actual income are large, and if the resultant movement in $\overline{Y}$ is different from that of $W + L$, the data will be closer to the machinery sample results.

It is most interesting to note that for each of the variables b, h, and $\check{r}$, our food sample F ratio was larger than the machinery sample statistic. In other words, the variation over time within a corporation for a variable was smaller in relation to the variable's variation among corporations for the food than for the machinery sample. This result can be interpreted to mean that our assumptions were better suited to the food than the machinery sample. To a greater degree the assumptions that investors expect b, h, and $\check{r}$ to be the same in every future period were correct for the food sample, and the model performed better in explaining the prices of shares in that industry.

15.2   Correlation among the State Variables

The independent variables of our model and certain related variables provide information on the financial structure, financing policies, and investment policies of a corporation. In this and the next two sections the correlations among these variables will be examined to establish the generalizations that can be made on the interrelations among them. The variables are:

$s = lnS$ = corporate size index.
$u = ln(1 + \check{\sigma}/W)$ = earnings instability index.
$\check{r}$ = rate of return on investment.
b = retention rate.

h = leverage rate.
q = outside equity financing rate.
h' = change in leverage rate.
z = investment rate.

The measurement of all the variables but h' and z has been defined earlier, and for each the value for a corporation is a simple average of the values for the years 1954 to 1958.

The change in leverage, h', is h for 1958 minus h for 1954 divided by four, that is, the average annual change in h over the four years covered by the period from the end of 1954 to the end of 1958.[2] The investment rate for a year is the end of year minus the start of year operating assets divided by the end of year common equity. Operating assets include all assets but monetary assets (cash, government bonds, receivables, and abnormal inventory). The average of z over the four years 1955 through 1958 is our variable.

Our data consists of two samples, one food and one machinery, and each sample contains 48 observations on each variable. Table 15.1 presents the mean and standard deviation of each variable and the simple or zero order correlations among them. The eight variables may be classified as state and decision variables, the former being corporate size, earnings instability, and rate of return on investment. The state variables may be presumed to have some influence on the decision variables, while the reverse is not true. Therefore, we will consider the relations among the state variables first.

The correlation between size and earnings instability in both samples is negative. The food correlation between size and earnings instability, cor. $su = -.104$, and the machinery cor. $su = -.429$. Only the latter is statistically significant at the 5 per cent level.[3] Crum [1934] and others have found the stability of earnings tends to increase with the size of the corporation, and our data agree with this proposition.

The correlation between size and rate of return on investment is very small: cor. $s\check{r} = .028$ for the food and $-.120$ for the machinery sample. Both variables are correlated somewhat with earnings instability. Allowing for the correlation that s and $\check{r}$ have with u we have cor. $s\check{r} : u$ of .065 and .060 for the two samples. These two figures

[2] To have h' comparable with the other statistics, the change from 1953 to 1958 should have been used. Doing so, however, was not convenient.

[3] With a sample size of 48, a zero order correlation is significantly different from zero at the 5 per cent level if its absolute value is .288 or higher.

do not differ materially from zero, and the data therefore suggest that there is little if any tendency for the profitability of corporations to increase with their size.

The correlation between rate of return and earnings instability is very strong in both samples. The food cor. $\check{r}u = .320$, and the machinery cor. $\check{r}u = .396$. Allowing for the fact that both $\check{r}$ and u are

TABLE 15.1

MEAN STANDARD DEVIATION, AND CORRELATION AMONG CORPORATE STATE AND DECISION VARIABLES IN FOOD AND MACHINERY SAMPLES*

	s	u	ř	b	h	q	h'	z
	Size	Earnings Insta- bility	Rate of Return	Reten- tion Rate	Lever- age Rate	New Equity Financ- ing	Change in Le- verage	Invest- ment Rate
Food Sample								
Mean	4.461	.025	.095	.410	.242	.009	−.016	.065
Std. dev. . .	.832	.014	.041	.135	.376	.017	.063	.070
Correlations:								
s		−.104	.028	−.078	.162	.213	−.004	.163
u			.320	.054	−.414	.071	−.188	−.105
ř				−.348	−.530	.083	−.161	−.108
b					.276	−.025	.029	.308
h						.301	−.200	.424
q							−.453	.413
h'								.363
z								
Machinery Sample								
Mean	3.861	.040	.115	.444	−.015	.022	.001	.084
Std. dev. . .	.772	.020	.051	.102	.268	.037	.043	.073
Correlations:								
s		−.429	−.120	.093	.584	.341	.015	.453
u			.396	.098	−.487	−.268	.023	−.287
ř				−.312	−.528	−.196	.199	.002
b					−.098	−.131	−.086	.036
h						.641	−.110	.630
q							−.008	.679
h'								.481
z								

* There are 48 observations for each variable, obtained by averaging the five values for 1954–58 for each firm. The mean is the average over the 48 values, and the standard deviation is over the 48 firm averages.

inversely correlated with s in the machinery sample, cor. $\check{r}u : s = .38$. The data indicates that the variation in rate of return among corporations increases with the instability of their earnings. A widely accepted proposition is that the rate of return corporations require increases with the instability of their earnings, and it appears that on the average they succeed in obtaining the higher rate of return.

15.3 Correlation between the Decision and the State Variables

Our purpose in this section is to examine the influence of the three state variables on four of the decision variables—retention, leverage, change in leverage, and outside equity financing. The correlation between each of the decision variables and each of the state variables will be examined. The objective will be to establish the influence of the state variables on the decision variables.

The correlations between retention and size are −.078 and .093 for the food and machinery samples. Recognizing the correlation b and s have with the other state variables does not alter the cor. bs materially. Contrary to what one might expect, there is no tendency for large corporations to retain smaller fractions of their income than small corporations. This conclusion may hold, however, only in the size range of our sample which does not include any really small corporations.

The simple correlations between retention and earnings instability are .054 and −.098 for the food and machinery samples. However, both b and u are correlated with size, and particularly with rate of return. Cor. bu net of the correlation due to their associations with $\check{r}$ and s is cor. $bu : \check{r}s = .180$ for the food sample and .059 for the machinery sample. The data indicate there is some tendency, not a strong one, for corporate retention rates to increase with the instability of the firm's earnings. A stronger association is probably what one would have expected.

Retention and earnings instability are also correlated with other decision variables, e.g., leverage, but there was no adjustment made for the correlation of b and u with h. The partial correlation, cor. $bu : \check{r}s$ was obtained on the grounds that u, $\check{r}$, and s may all influence b, and the partial correlation is needed to obtain the net influence of u on b. On the other hand, it is not considered reasonable to believe that h influences b, and it therefore would not be correct to get cor. $bu : h$.

The really surprising result is produced by return on investment. Cor. $b\check{r} = -.348$ for the food and −.312 for the machinery sample. Cor. $b\check{r} : us$ is not materially different, −.38 and −.30 for the two samples. In both industries there is a statistically significant tendency for the retention rate to fall as the corporation's rate of return increases. We must conclude that either $\check{r}$ is a poor measure of rate of return on investment or that corporations are not primarily influenced by the price of their stock in setting their dividend rates. It should be noted, however, that the negative cor. $b\check{r}$ does not imply that for a corporation of a given size the funds retained fall as $\check{r}$ increases. Increasing $\check{r}$ raises the funds from operations, and the absolute amount retained may remain unchanged or rise even though the fraction retained may fall.

Turning to leverage, we find that cor. $hs = .162$ and $.584$ for the food and machinery samples. Very little of this correlation is due to the correlation that h and s have with $\check{r}$ and u. The data confirm the proposition that reliance on debt financing increases with corporate size, with the association very strong in the machinery industry.

Another expected result is inverse correlation between leverage and earnings instability. Cor. $hu = -.414$ for the food and $-.487$ for the machinery sample. However, in both industries, the latter in particular, a considerable part of the gross relation between the variables is due to their opposite relation with $\check{r}$ and s. For instance, cor. $h\check{r}$ is negative, while cor. $u\check{r}$ is positive. The result is that cor. $hu : \check{r}s$ is only $-.14$ for the machinery sample. The food cor. $hu : \check{r}s = -.29$. In both industries the reliance on leverage increases with the stability of the firm's earnings, but the relation is not as strong as one might expect in the machinery industry.

Our second unexpected result is inverse correlation between leverage and rate of return on investment. The food cor. $h\check{r} = -.530$, while the machinery figure is $-.528$. It might be imagined that a good part of this gross association is due to the fact that cor. hu is negative and cor. $\check{r}u$ is positive. However, the food cor. $h\check{r} : us = -.47$ and the machinery figure is $-.51$. It does not appear that profitable corporations undertake leverage in order to take advantage of their investment opportunities. On the contrary, it seems that unprofitable corporations turn to leverage in order to show respectable profits, to obtain otherwise unavailable funds, or for some other reason. The other possible explanation of our findings is that correlation does not exist between $\check{r}$ and $\check{\eta}$, a corporation's return on its existing net worth. This is most disquieting since our empirical work was based on the assumption that η is an approximation of r.

The correlation between outside equity financing and size is positive. The food cor. $qs = .213$, and the machinery figure is $.341$. Netting out the influence of $\check{r}$ and u brings the two figures together.

Cor. $qs : \check{r}u = .27$ for both samples. One would expect the reliance on outside equity financing to increase with the size of the corporation, and this is what we get.

The correlation between outside equity financing and earnings instability is somewhat confusing. Cor. $qu = .071$ and $-.268$. Taking account of $\check{r}$ and s does not turn the food correlation negative. It remains unchanged while the machinery cor. $qu : \check{r}s$ becomes $-.09$. There does not appear to be any tendency for corporations with unstable earnings to prefer or avoid outside equity financing.

The relation between outside equity financing and rate of return does not follow the pattern laid down by retention and leverage. The food cor. $q\check{r} = .083$, and the machinery value is $-.196$. The partial cor. $q\check{r} : us$ are $.05$ and $-.12$. The best we can say, however, is that there is no strong correlation positive or negative between rate of return and outside equity financing.

The final financing variable is h', the change in leverage. Cor. $h's = .004$ and $.015$ for the two samples, and recognition of u and $\check{r}$ does not make the correlations materially different from zero in the two samples. Turning to earning instability, cor. $h'u$ is $-.188$ and $.023$. The partial correlations, $h'u : \check{r}s$, are $-.15$ and $-.05$. There is a slight tendency for corporations with unstable earnings to reduce their leverage. One might expect that in a relatively prosperous period there would be a strong tendency for risky corporations to reduce their leverage, but the years 1954 to 1958 were far from being all boom years for these two industries.

The correlation between rate of return and change in leverage is mixed. The simple correlations are $-.161$ and $.199$. The partial cor. $h'\check{r} : us = -.11$ for the food and $.21$ for the machinery sample. We therefore cannot even say whether the association between change in leverage and rate of return is positive or negative.

To summarize the above results, with one striking exception, the data tend to agree with the propositions on corporate financial policy that have become generally accepted. The striking exception is return on investment. We would expect retention, leverage, and stock issue by corporations to vary with their profitability. Instead there was strong inverse correlation between profitability and both retention and leverage. With respect to the other two financing variables, stock issue and change in leverage, the data showed neither strong positive or negative correlation. It is possible that the influence of other objectives subordinates the maximization of stock value in corporate financing policy. Alternatively, our assumption that return on investment is satisfactorily estimated by return on existing assets does a poor job.

15.4 Correlation among the Decision Variables

In this section we will examine first the correlation between the investment rate and the other variables and second, the correlations among the decision variables. A vast array of partial correlation coefficients can be computed, but we will try to confine ourselves to those for which an economic rationale exists.

In both industries the investment rate is correlated with size. Cor. zs is .163 and .453 for the food and machinery samples. Cor. $zs : u\check{r}$ is .16 and .38 in the two samples. The data indicate, therefore, that there was tendency, strong in the machinery sample, for large corporations to invest at a higher rate than small corporations.

The investment rate is inversely correlated with earnings instability. Cor. zu is $-.105$ and $-.287$ in the two samples, and after allowing for size and rate of return, we have cor. $zu : s\check{r} = -.06$ and $-.15$ in the food and machinery samples. There is a weak tendency, therefore, for the investment rate to decline as earnings instability rises.

The correlation between investment rate and rate of return is not materially different from zero. Cor. $z\check{r}$ is $-.108$ and .002 in the food and machinery samples, and the partial correlations are $-.09$ and .12. To repeat our earlier conclusion, if corporations set their investment rates with the objective of maximizing the prices of their shares cor. $z\check{r}$ should be positive. The absence of positive correlation suggests that other conflicting objectives also influence managements, or our measurement of $\check{r}$ is poor. That is, $\check{\eta}$ is not a good approximation of $\check{r}$ for a corporation, and there is no correlation between return on stock and investment rate. However, the present results are not as disquieting as the strong inverse correlation with retention and leverage.

As we would expect, the investment rate is correlated with the financing variables. In the food sample the correlation varies from .308 for retention to .424 for leverage. In the machinery sample, cor. zb is only .036, but the other correlations are very strong. Cor. $zh' = .481$, and the correlations with leverage and new equity financing are over .60. Holding the state variables constant, the partial correlations between investment rate and each financing variable are higher in some cases and lower in others than the simple correlations. The changes are commonly not very large.

The correlation between the investment rate and a financing variable indicates the extent to which a corporation with a high investment rate turns to this method of financing and those with low investment rates give up this source of funds. The food sample cor. $zb = .308$ indicates there is some tendency to rely on retention to finance increased investment, but the machinery cor. $zb = .036$ indicates that in this industry other forms of financing are undertaken to vary the investment rate. Cor. zh of .424 and .630 in the two industries indicates that corporations with high investment rates have high leverage rates. Cor. zq of .413 and .679 and cor. zh' of .363 and .481 indicate that high investment rates are also financed quite commonly by undertaking outside equity financing and raising the leverage rate.

It is interesting to note the extent to which different forms of financing substitute or complement each other. Since all types of financing will vary more or less with the investment rate, what we will do is examine the partial correlations among the financing variables with the investment rate held constant. Correlation between retention and leverage also exists because both have a strong inverse correlation with rate of return. Holding both $\check{r}$ and z constant, we have cor. $bh : \check{r}z$ $-.01$ and $-.10$. Therefore, leverage and retention rates are practically independent of each other apart from the association created by investment rate and rate of return.

There is negative correlation between retention and outside equity financing, but the inverse relation is not a strong one. In the food sample, cor. $bq : z = -.17$. In the machinery sample, it is $-.21$, but also allowing for $\check{r}$ results in $bq : z\check{r} = -.32$. With respect to change in leverage, once again the variation with retention is inverse, but the relation is very weak. Cor. $bh' : z$ is $-.09$ and $-.12$ for the two samples.

The conclusion to be drawn with respect to retention and other forms of financing is quite clear. With investment held constant, there will be some tendency for retention and other forms of financing to be inversely related.[4] The weak negative correlation that exists between retention and each of the other sources of funds indicates quite clearly that retention neither substitutes for or comple-

[4] If investment and all other forms of financing are held constant, the correlation between retention and each alternative form of financing will be strongly negative.

ments other sources of funds. Retention rates are set independently of the other methods of financing employed.

Apart from its relation with retention, the story on leverage is quite different. Holding rate of return as well as the investment rate constant, the correlation between leverage and outside equity financing is positive. Cor. $hq : z\tilde{r} = .27$ in both samples. Corporations that *have* high leverage rates rely more heavily on new equity financing than those with low leverage rates. Also, there is a very strong tendency for corporations with high leverage rates to reduce them, and vice versa. Cor. $hh' : z$ is $-.42$ and $-.61$ in the two samples, and also holding rate of return constant results in $hh' : z\tilde{r}$ of $-.58$ and $-.64$. Therefore, corporations with high leverage rates reduce them, relying heavily on new stock financing to do so. We can probably also conclude that corporations with low leverage rates tend to allow them to rise. As we would expect, there is very strong inverse correlation between new equity financing and change in leverage. Cor. $qh' : z$ is $-.71$ and $-.52$. The picture that emerges is that the reduction in leverage by corporations with high leverage rates is accomplished largely by means of outside equity financing. Conversely, corporation's with low leverage rates allow them to rise and engage very little in outside equity financing.

15.5 The Discovery of Over- and Undervalued Shares

It would appear that our model can be used in the following way for the purpose of discovering over- and undervalued shares. First, take a sample of corporations and obtain values for the model's parameters as was done in Chapter 12. Second, compute the price predicted by the model for these and any other similar shares of interest. Similar shares might be those belonging to firms in the same industry. Third, compare the actual and predicted price for each share, and select all shares for which the two differ by at least some margin, say one standard deviation. If $ln\hat{P}$ and lnP are the predicted and actual prices respectively, and Δ is the minimum difference, then $ln\hat{P} - lnP > \Delta$ results in a buy recommendation, and vice versa.

A number of conditions must be satisfied for the recommendations produced by the model to be correct, i.e., for a share with $ln\hat{P} - lnP$ to rise in price, and vice versa. First, there must be a structure in the market's valuation of a share, and our model must accurately represent this structure. Second, the values we use for the variables in arriving at $\hat{P}$ must be the correct values, i.e., the values the market uses. Third, given a change in information, i.e., a change in the values of the variables that determine a share's price, the market reacts to this information with a lag that varies in some random manner among shares. To elaborate on the last point, the stock market may be looked on as being a giant computer that generates the price of each share under a program that operates on certain information. However, in updating the price of every share on the basis of new information, the computer may fall behind with some shares, or an imperfection in the program will result in the generation of the wrong price for a relatively *short* period of time. Our model simulates the stock market without suffering the same limitations, and thereby allows discovery of the shares for which the market has not generated the up-to-date and/or correct prices.

Under what conditions will our model fail to produce correct buy and sell recommendations? First, our model may not faithfully represent the "program" under which the stock market generates the price of each share. In this event, an overpriced share may simply be priced above our prediction because we have failed to consider an attribute of the share that the market considers. This is no idle speculation. We mentioned earlier that an examination of the residuals, $ln\hat{P} - lnP$, for a corporation over successive cross-section samples, revealed the presence of firm effects. That is, instead of their average being zero, there was a strong tendency for a firm's residual to remain positive (or negative) over a number of years. One way of putting this result is that instead of $|ln\hat{P} - lnP| > \Delta$ being a temporary aberration in the market's operation, it is a chronic defect. However, given our criterion for successful performance by the model, it is no consolation to conclude that we are right and everyone else is wrong.

The problem of firm effects in the use of the model can probably be handled satisfactorily. As noted earlier, the residuals for a firm over the prior years can be averaged in some way and the average can be introduced as an additional variable. Presumably, the residuals after including firm effect as an additional variable would have zero mean, and the residual in any year for a share would be a more effective basis for buy and sell advices.

Possibly a more serious problem is the accuracy of the variable values used to obtain $\hat{P}$. If we use an incorrect value for one or more of the independent variables, we get an advice that reflects our error and not the market's error. Of course, in using the model, we are not restricted to the measurement rules employed to obtain the parameter estimates. In other words, our measurement rules may be considered adequate for obtaining parameter estimates, while the analyst is free to arrive at $\hat{P}$ using whatever value for each independent variable he considers best.[5] It can be argued that if an analyst looks at dividends, earnings, financial position, etc., in arriving at the price at which a share should sell, whatever errors he makes in assigning values to their values will show up regardless of the method of valuation he uses. Therefore, problems of measuring the variables are not peculiar to our model.

There is an obvious empirical test of the model's usefulness if the above is the only problem. Take a population of shares and estimate our model's parameters by means of a sample from that population. Use the model to select buy and sell recommendations among the shares in the population. Finally, frame a set of rules whereby an individual with a given sum of money decides how much to buy and sell of each share. Insofar as possible, use the same set of rules with another scheme for portfolio selection over the same population. The other scheme may also be a scientific formula, it may be a random process, or it may rely on mystical signs. The position of the investor at the end of some time period under the two methods of portfolio selection could be compared to decide between them.

One element in the comparison would be the cost of using the system. Clearly, the cost of operating our system of portfolio selection is very high, and it could be justified only for a stock market advisory service or a large mutual fund. In this connection, it should be noted that our system particularly with the modification suggested below is very similar to that employed by the Value Line Investment Survey as described by Bernhard [1959].

The previous few observations suggest that after eliminating firm effects, averaging out the losses on incorrect advices due to error in measurement of the variables, and deducting the cost of operating the system, the gain on its use may not be very impressive. It may be that the stock market does a good job in keeping small the difference between the current price and what it should be on the basis of existing information. Looking at what security analysts do supports this hypothesis. They actually devote very little effort to discover which shares are over- or undervalued on the basis of existing in-

---

[5] It would not be necessary to recompute the valuation parameters whenever new information made a new computation of $\hat{P}$ desirable.

formation. What they are concerned with primarily is the prediction of information, i.e., of variable values that will determine a share's price next month or next year. It is small consolation to say that though the stock market went down, our buy recommendation went down less on the average. It is even less consolation to say a buy recommendation went down, but this was due not to a failure in the performance of our model but to a decline in earnings. Our model predicts share price on the basis of current earnings, etc., and does not forecast future earnings.

Consequently, what security analysts want most is a formula for predicting the general movements in the stock market, and most research on the stock market has been of the times series variety. Such a formula has been as difficult to find as the golden fleece. The next best thing is to pick up information on a company such as development of new products, merger talks, changes in back-order book, or other information that provides a clue as to the comparative level of earnings and dividends in the next period. An increase in one or both of these variables is likely to raise a share's price regardless of whether the share is over- or underpriced currently.

The Value Line Survey arrives at buy and sell recommendations by obtaining the above type information on a company, converting it into predictions of future dividends, earnings, etc., and generating the price of the share through a stock value model. In other words, the Value Line Survey combines the work of the security analyst with the scientific interpretation of his findings. The same can of course also be done with the present model, and quite naturally I think that it can be done better with the present model. However, it is clear that the critical element in the success of the buy and sell recommendations is the discovery and interpretation of the events that will raise or lower a corporation's dividend, earnings, etc.

BIBLIOGRAPHY

ALEXANDER, SIDNEY S. "Income Measurement in a Dynamic Economy," in *Five Monographs on Business Income*. New York: Study Group on Business Income of the American Institute of Accountants, July 1, 1950.

ANDREWS, P. W. S. "A Further Inquiry into the Effects of Rates of Interest," *Oxford Economic Papers,* 3 (February, 1940), pp. 32–73.

ARROW, KENNETH J. "Alternative Approaches to the Theory of Choice in Risk-Taking Situations," *Econometrica,* 29 (October, 1951), pp. 404–37.

BAKER, M. R., and others. *Tested Approaches to Capital Equipment Replacement.* New York: American Management Association, Special Report No. 1, 1954.

BENISHAY, HASKELL. *Determinants of Variability in Earnings Price Ratio of Corporate Equity.* Ph.D. thesis, University of Chicago, School of Business Administration, 1960.

BERNHARD, ARNOLD. *The Evaluation of Common Stocks.* New York: Simon & Schuster, 1959.

BIERMAN, HAROLD, JR., and SMIDT, SEYMOUR. *The Capital Budgeting Decision.* New York: Macmillan Co., 1960.

BODENHORN, DIRAN. "On the Problem of Capital Budgeting," *The Journal of Finance,* XIV (December, 1959), pp. 473–92.

BROWN, ROBERT G. *Statistical Forecasting for Inventory Control.* New York: McGraw-Hill Book Co., Inc., 1959.

BUTTERS, J. KEITH, and LINTNER, JOHN. *Effect of Federal Taxes on Growing Enterprises.* Cambridge, Mass.: Graduate School of Business Administration, Harvard University, 1945.

CHENERY, HOLLIS B. "Overcapacity and the Acceleration Principle," *Econometrica,* 20 (January, 1952), pp. 1–28.

CLARK, J. M. "Business Acceleration and the Law of Demand," *Journal of Political Economy,* 25 (March, 1917), pp. 217–35.

CRUM, W. L. *The Effect of Size on Corporate Earnings and Condition: An Analysis of 1931 Income Tax Statistics.* Cambridge, Mass.: Harvard University Division of Business Research Studies No. 8, 1934.

CYERT, R. M., and MARCH, J. G. "Introduction to a Behavioral Theory of Organizational Objectives," in *Modern Organization Theory,* M. Haire, ed. New York: John Wiley & Sons, 1959.

DEAN, JOEL. "Measuring the Productivity of Capital," *Harvard Business Review,* 32 (January–February, 1954), pp. 120–30.

———. *Capital Budgeting.* New York: Columbia University Press, 1951.

——— and SMITH, WINFIELD. "Has MAPI a Place in a Comprehensive

System of Capital Control? *Journal of Business* (October, 1955). Reprinted in *Management of Corporate Capital,* ed. Ezra Solomon. Glencoe, Ill.: Free Press, 1959.

DUESENBERRY, J. S. *Business Cycles and Economic Growth.* New York: McGraw-Hill Book Co., Inc., 1958.

DURAND, DAVID. "The Cost of Capital, Corporation Finance and the Theory of Investment: Comment," *American Economic Review,* XLIX (September, 1959), pp. 639–55. Reprinted in *The Management of Corporate Capital,* ed. Ezra Solomon, as "The Cost of Capital in an Imperfect Market: A Reply to Modigliani and Miller." Glencoe, Ill.: Free Press, 1959.

———. *Bank Stock Prices and the Bank Capital Problem.* New York: Occasional Paper 54, National Bureau of Economic Research, 1957a.

———. "Growth Stocks and the Petersburg Paradox," *Journal of Finance,* 12 (September, 1957b), pp. 348–63.

———. "Costs of Debt and Equity Funds for Business: Trends and Problems of Measurement," Conference on Research in Business Finance, pp. 215–47. New York: National Bureau of Economic Research, 1952.

——— and MAY, ALAN M. "The Ex-Dividend Behavior of American Telephone and Telegraph Stock," *The Journal of Finance,* XV, 1 (March, 1960), pp. 19–31.

ECKAUS, R. S. "The Acceleration Principle Reconsidered," *The Quarterly Journal of Economics,* 67 (May, 1953), pp. 209–30.

EISNER, ROBERT. "A Distributed Lag Investment Function," *Econometrica* (January, 1960).

———. "Expectations, Plans and Capital Expenditures, A Synthesis of Ex Post and Ex Ante Data," *Expectations, Uncertainty and Business Behavior,* M. J. Bowman, ed., pp. 165–88. New York, 1958.

———. "Determinants of Capital Expenditures: An Interview Study," *Studies in Business Expectations and Planning,* No. 2. Urbana, Ill.: University of Illinois, 1956.

FERBER, ROBERT. *Statistical Techniques in Market Research.* New York: McGraw-Hill Book Co., Inc., 1949.

FRIEDMAN, MILTON, and SAVAGE, L. J. "The Utility Analysis of Choices Involving Risk," *Journal of Political Economy,* 56 (1948), pp. 279–304. Reprinted with a correction in *Readings in Price Theory,* G. J. Stigler and K. E. Boulding, eds. Homewood, Ill.: Richard D. Irwin, Inc., 1952.

GORDON, M. J. "The Savings Investment and Valuation of a Corporation," *Review of Economics and Statistics* (February, 1962).

———. "Security and a Financial Theory of Investment, *Quarterly Journal of Economics,* 74 (August, 1960a), pp. 472–92.

———. "The Optimum Dividend Rate," published in *Management*

Sciences: Models and Techniques, Proceedings of the 6th International Meeting, Institute of Management Sciences. London: Pergamon Press, 1960b.

————. "Dividends Earnings and Stock Prices," *Review of Economics and Statistics,* 41 (May, 1959), pp. 99–105.

————. "The Payoff Period and the Rate of Profit," *Journal of Business* (October, 1955). Reprinted in *Management of Corporate Capital,* Ezra Solomon, ed. Glencoe, Ill.: Free Press, 1959.

———— and GANGOLLI, RAMESH. "A Model for Investigating Choice among and Play on Lottery Type Alternatives," mimeographed, M.I.T. (1961).

———— and SHAPIRO, ELI. "Capital Equipment Analysis: The Required Rate of Profit," *Management Science,* 3 (October, 1956), pp. 102–110. Reprinted in *Management of Corporate Capital.* Glencoe, Ill.: Free Press, 1959.

GRAHAM, B., and DODD, D. L. in collaboration with Charles Tatham, Jr. *Security Analysis: Principles and Technique.* New York: McGraw-Hill Book Co., Inc., 1951.

GUTHMAN, H. G., and DOUGALL, H. E. *Corporate Financial Policy,* 2d. ed. New York: Prentice-Hall, 1948.

HABERSTROH, CHADWICK J. Control as an Organizational Process," *Management Science,* 6 (January, 1960), pp. 165–71.

HART, A. G. "Anticipations, Uncertainty and Dynamic Planning," *Studies in Business Administration,* XI, 1 (Chicago, 1940).

HELLER, WALTER. "The Anatomy of Investment Decisions," *Harvard Business Review,* 29 (March, 1951), pp. 95–103.

HICKS, J. R. *A Contribution to the Theory of the Trade Cycle.* Oxford: Clarendon Press, 1950.

HIRSHLEIFER, J. "On the Theory of Optimal Investment Decision," *Journal of Political Economy,* 66 (August, 1958), pp. 329–52.

HOEL, PAUL G. *Introduction to Mathematical Statistics.* New York: John Wiley & Sons, Inc., 1947.

HUNT, P.; WILLIAMS, C. M.; and DONALDSON, G. *Basic Business Finance.* Homewood, Ill.: Richard D. Irwin, Inc., 1958.

KALECKI, M. *Theory of Economic Dynamics.* London: Allen & Unwin, 1954.

————. "A Comment on the Principle of Increasing Risk: A Reply," *Economica,* 5 (November, 1938), pp. 459–60.

————. "The Principle of Increasing Risk," *Economica,* 4 (November, 1937), pp. 440–47.

KAYSEN, CARL. "A Dynamic Aspect of the Monopoly Problem," *Review of Economics and Statistics,* XXXI (May, 1949), pp. 109–13.

KLEIN, L. R. *Economic Fluctuations in the U.S., 1929–1941,* Cowles Commission Monograph 11. New York: John Wiley & Sons, Inc., 1950.

KLEIN, L. R., and GOLDBERGER, S. A. *An Econometric Model of the U.S., 1929–1952.* Amsterdam, No. Holland, 1952.

KNIGHT, FRANK. *Risk, Uncertainty and Profit.* Boston: Houghton-Mifflin Co., 1921.

KUH, EDWIN. "Capital Stock Growth: A Micro-Econometric Approach," Cambridge, Mass.: Massachusetts Institute of Technology, 1961.

————. "Capital Theory and Capital Budgeting," *Metroeconomica,* XII (August–December, 1960), pp. 64–80.

————. "The Validity of Cross-Sectionally Estimated Behavior Equations in Time Series Applications," *Econometrica,* XXVII, 2 (April, 1959).

LINTNER, J. "Distribution of Incomes of Corporations among Dividends, Retained Earnings and Taxes," *American Economic Review,* 46 (May, 1956), pp. 97–113.

LORIE, J., and SAVAGE, L. J. "Three Problems in Capital Rationing," *Journal of Business,* 32 (October, 1955). Reprinted in *Management of Corporate Capital,* Ezra Solomon, ed. Glencoe, Ill.: Free Press, 1959.

LUTZ, FREDERICK and VERA. *The Theory of Investment of the Firm.* Princeton, N.J.: Princeton University Press, 1951.

MADANSKY, A. "The Fitting of Straight Lines When Both Variables Are Subject to Error," *Journal of the American Statistical Association,* LIV, 285 (March, 1959), pp. 173–205.

MANNE, A. S. "Some Notes on the Acceleration Principle," *Review of Economics and Statistics,* 27 (May, 1945), pp. 93–99.

MARKOWITZ, HARRY M. *Portfolio Selection,* Monograph 16, Cowles Foundation for Research in Economics at Yale University. New York: John Wiley & Sons, Inc., 1959.

————. *Portfolio Selection,* pp. 77–91. Chicago: Cowles Commission for Research in Economics, 1952. Reprinted from *Journal of Finance,* VII, 1 (March, 1952).

McHUGH, LOUGHLIN F. "Financing Small Business in the Postwar Period," *Survey of Current Business,* 31 (November, 1951), pp. 17–23.

MEADER, J. W. "Conclusion—Failure for J.W.M.," *The Annalist, Magazine of Finance, Commerce & Economics* (June 27, 1940) (published 1913–1940).

————. "A Formula for Determining Basic Values Underlying Common Stock Prices," *The Annalist, Magazine of Finance, Commerce & Economics* (November 29, 1935).

MERWIN, CHARLES L. *Financing Small Corporations in Five Manufacturing Industries, 1926–36.* New York: National Bureau of Economic Research, Financial Research Program, III, Studies in Business Financing No. 2, 1942.

MEYER, J. R. and KUH, EDWIN. *The Investment Decision: An Empirical Study.* Cambridge, Mass.: Harvard University Press, 1957.

MODIGLIANI, FRANCO, and MILLER, MERTON. "The Cost of Capital, Corporation Finance and Theory of Investment: Reply," *American Economic Review,* XLIX (September, 1959) , pp. 655–69.

———— and ————. "The Cost of Capital, Corporation Finance and Theory of Investment," *American Economic Review,* XLVIII (June, 1958) , pp. 261–97.

NATIONAL ASSOCIATION OF ACCOUNTANTS. *Return on Capital as a Guide to Managerial Decisions,* Research Report 35. New York: December, 1959.

NEISSER, HANS. "Critical Notes on the Acceleration Principle," *Quarterly Journal of Economics,* 68 (May, 1954) , pp. 253–74.

POLAK, J. J. and TINBERGEN, J. *The Dynamics of Business Cycles. A Study in Economic Fluctuations.* Chicago: University of Chicago Press, 1950.

SIMON, HERBERT. *Models of Man.* New York: John Wiley & Sons, Inc., 1957.

SOLOMON, EZRA, ed. *The Management of Corporate Capital.* Glencoe, Ill.: Free Press, 1959.

————. "The Arithmetic of Capital Budgeting Decisions," *Journal of Business,* 29 (April, 1956) , pp. 124–29. Reprinted in *The Management of Corporate Capital,* ed. Ezra Solomon.

————. "Measuring a Company's Cost of Capital," *Journal of Business,* 28 (October, 1955) . Reprinted in *The Management of Corporate Capital,* ed. Ezra Solomon.

SOULE, R. P. "Trends in the Cost of Capital," *Harvard Business Review* (March–April, 1953) , pp. 33–47.

TERBORGH, G. W. *Dynamic Equipment Policy.* New York: McGraw-Hill Book Co., Inc., 1949.

TINBERGEN, J. *Statistical Testing of Business Cycle Theories.* Vol. I: *A Method and Its Application to Investment Activity;* Vol. II: *Business Cycles in the U.S., 1919–1932.* Geneva, Switzerland: League of Nations, 1939.

————. "Statistical Evidence on the Acceleration Principle," *Economica,* N.S. 5 (May, 1938) , pp. 164–76.

TODHUNTER, R. *The Institute of Actuaries' Text Book on Compound Interest and Annuities Certain.* 4th ed., revised by R. C. Simmonds and T. P. Thompson. Cambridge, Mass., 1937.

USHER, DAN. *The Debt Equity Ratio.* Ph.D. thesis, University of Chicago School of Business Administration, 1960.

WATSON, J. H., III. "Controlling Capital Expenditures," *Studies in Business Policy,* No. 62, National Industrial Conference Board (April, 1953) .

WILLIAMS, J. B. *The Theory of Investment Value.* Cambridge, Mass.: Harvard University Press, 1938.

WINTERS, PETER R. "Forecasting Sales by Exponentially Weighted Moving Averages," *Management Science,* 6 (April, 1960) , pp. 324–42.

Appendix A
SAMPLE FIRMS

Tables A.1 and A.2 below list the firms in the food and machinery samples. The description of how the firms were selected and how the values of the variables were obtained requires elaboration on only two points beyond that contained in pp. 149–50 and Chapter 12.

First, each sample initially comprised all firms included in certain industry sub-groups of the Value Line Investment Survey early in 1959. The food sample subgroups were corn refining and food processing, milling and baking, sugar and confectionery, dairy, and soap and vegetable oil. The machinery sample subgroups were machinery and machine tool. After firms that did not meet the requirements stated in the text were deleted, firms were added to have both samples adequate in size and equal in number. For the food sample, the additional firms were arbitrarily selected from the tobacco industry, and for the machinery sample the firms were arbitrarily selected from the railroad equipment industry. In addition, the United Shoe Machinery Company was included.

The other point not covered earlier is the treatment of corporations with fiscal years different from the calendar year. For corporations with fiscal years ending between September 30 and April 1 of the following year, fiscal year earnings were used—that is, assumed to be equal to earnings for the calendar year. For corporations with fiscal years falling between April 1 and September 30, quarterly or semiannual earnings data were used to estimate calendar year earnings. For book value per share, the same rules were used. Calendar year dividends were available and used unless the last quarterly dividend was declared a few days after the end of the year.

TABLE A.1

List of Food Sample Firms

Allied Mills, Inc.	American Tobacco Co.
American Bakeries Co.	Archer-Daniels-Midland Co.
American Chicle Co.	Bayuk Cigars, Inc.
American Crystal Sugar Co.	Beatrice Foods Co.
American Sugar Refining Co.	Beech-nut Life Savers, Inc.

247

Borden Co.
California Packing Corp.
Carnation Co.
Colgate-Palmolive Co.
Consolidated Cigar Corp.
Continental Baking Co.
Corn Products Co.
Cuban American Sugar Co.
General Baking Co.
General Foods Corp.
General Mills, Inc.
Glidden Co.
Great Western Sugar Co.
H. J. Heinz Co.
Hershey Chocolate Corp.
Holly Sugar Corp.
Libby, McNeil & Libby
Liggett & Myers Tobacco Co.
P. Lorillard Co.

National Biscuit Co.
National Dairy Products Corp.
National Sugar Refining Co.
Penick and Ford, Ltd., Inc.
Pet Milk Co.
Pillsbury Co.
Procter and Gamble Co.
Quaker Oats Co.
Ralston Purina Co.
South Puerto Rico Sugar Co.
Spencer Kellogg & Sons, Inc.
A. E. Staley Mfg. Co.
Standard Brands, Inc.
Stokeley–Van Camp, Inc.
Sunshine Biscuits, Inc.
United Biscuit Co. of America
United Fruit Co.
U.S. Tobacco Co.
Wm. Wrigley, Jr., Co.

TABLE A.2

LIST OF MACHINERY SAMPLE FIRMS

Alco Products, Inc.
American Brake Shoe Co.
American Chain & Cable, Inc.
American Machine & Foundry Co.
American Steel Foundries
Babcock & Wilcox Co.
Baldwin-Lima-Hamilton Corp.
The Black & Decker Mfg. Co.
Blaw-Knox Co.
E. W. Bliss Co.
Brown & Sharpe Mfg. Co.
Bucyrus-Erie Co.
Carborundum Co.
Caterpillar Tractor Co.
Chain Belt Co.
Chicago Pneumatic Tool Co.
Cincinnati Milling Machine Co.
Clark Equipment Co.
Combustion Engineering, Inc.
Continental Motors Corp.
Cooper-Bessemer Corp.
Dresser Industries, Inc.
Ex-Cell-O Corp.
Food Machinery & Chemicals Corp.

Foster Wheeler Corp.
Gardner Denver Co.
General Railway Signal Co.
Ingersoll Rand Co.
Link-Belt Co.
Mergenthaler Linotype Co.
Mesta Machine Co.
Monarch Machine Tool Co.
L. E. Myers Co.
National Acme Co.
N.Y. Air Brake Co.
Pittsburgh Forgings Co.
Reed Roller Bit Co.
Rockwell Mfg. Co.
Simonds Saw and Steel Co.
L. S. Starret Co.
Stone & Webster Engineering Corp.
Torrington Co.
United Engineering Co.
United Shoe Machinery Corp.
United States Industries, Inc.
Westinghouse Air Brake Co.
Worthington Corp.
Yale and Towne Mfg. Co.

Appendix B
GUIDE TO THE NOTATION

In order to avoid the use of an excessive number of symbols, superscripts, and subscripts, the text employs a flexible notation the general nature of which is described below.

The subscript, t, denotes the end of the period t for a stock variable and the period t for a flow variable. For instance, P_o is the price at the present time, that is, when the share is being looked at, and Y_o is the income in the period just ended. For brevity, current values of the variables are written without time subscripts, that is $Y = Y_o$ and $P = P_o$.

When the text indicates that t refers to a date or period in the future, the value of the variable is its expected value. Y_t is the expected value of income per share in period t. On occasion it is necessary to distinguish between a possible value of a variable and its expected value. In that discussion, Y_t is a random variable with a known frequency distribution, and $\bar{Y}_t$ is the expected value of the variable.

When the text refers to a period in the past, a distinction is sometimes drawn between the realized value for a past period and a normal or average value for the period. In those cases, Y_t refers to the actual value realized during t, and $\bar{Y}_t$ denotes the normal or average value for the period. When the distinction between the two quantities is not at issue, Y_t and in particular, $Y_o = Y$ refers to the average or normal value for the period.

Rate variables, such as retention rate, which are expected to have the same value in each future period are generally used without time subscript and they refer to the value currently expected to prevail. Finally, in Chapter 2, the notation employed follows Lutz and Lutz [1951] for the most part, and the definitions below do not apply to that chapter.

Definitions of the commonly used terms appear below.

AR accounts receivable.
α_j the coefficients of the stock value model. See pp. 155 and 170.
$\hat{\alpha}_j$ $\hat{\alpha}_0 = 1/\alpha_0$ and $\hat{\alpha}_j = -\alpha_j, j = 1 \rightarrow 8.$

b fraction of income a corporation is expected to retain.

C_t depreciation expense during t.

CE common equity. Sum of corporate net worth accounts including contingency reserves.

CG cash and government bonds.

d dividend yield or current dividend divided by current price.

D_t dividend on share during t.

h leverage rate or debt equity ratio $h = L/W$.

i rate of interest.

I_t investment net of depreciation expense during t.

ID intermediate term debt.

INV inventory. $\overline{INV}$ = normal inventory. $\widehat{INV}$ = excess of actual over normal inventory.

k rate of return investors require on a share, i.e., the discount rate that equates the dividend expectation a share provides with its price.

$\check{k}$ the value k would have if the corporation's leverage and retention rates were both equal to zero.

k_t as of time zero the rate at which the payment expected for t is discounted. k is an average of the k_t.

K a corporation's operating assets per share. $K = W + L$. Operating assets are inventory, plant and equipment, and other operating assets.

L net debt per share. See p. 80.

L' net debt per share with the elements of L weighted according to their maturity.

LD long-term debt.

LR liability reserves.

λ factor by which a variable is multiplied to obtain its value net of the corporate income tax. $1 - \lambda$ is the corporate income tax rate.

λ_1 factor by which a dividend is multiplied to obtain its value net of the personal income tax. $1 - \lambda_1$ is the personal income tax rate.

λ_2 factor by which a capital gain is multiplied to obtain its value net of the capital gain tax. $1 - \lambda_2$ is the capital gain tax rate.

n_t number of shares issued by a corporation during t.

N_t number of shares outstanding at the end of t.

η a corporation's rate of return on its existing common equity. $\eta = Y_0/W_0$. $\check{\eta}$ is the value η would have in the absence of leverage.

OOA other operating assets. Nonmonetary assets other than inventory, plant, and equipment.

P_t price at which a share is selling at end of t.

PE plant and equipment.

PS preferred stock.

π operating asset liquidity index. See pp. 74–75.

q funds a corporation raises during t through outside equity financing expressed as a fraction of its net worth per share. $q_t = Q_t/W_{t-1}$.

Q_t funds raised during t through the sale of additional common stock.

r a corporation's rate of return on common equity investment. If I_t is the investment or capital budget during t and $I_t h$ is the portion of the outlay financed by borrowing, $I_t(1-h)$ is the common equity investment. r is the discount rate that equates $I_t(1-h)$ with the payment expectation net of interest created by the investment of I_t.

$\hat{r}$ a corporation's rate of return on investment. The discount rate that equates the payment expectation created by I_t with I_t.

R_t the receipt or payment expected in t net of operating expenses in t but before deducting interest and depreciation. For $R_{t,w,\tau}$ see p. 86.

ρ_0 the value of $\hat{r}$ when the corporation's investment rate, $z = 0$.

ρ_1 a parameter of the function $\hat{r}$ is of z.

S index of a corporation's size.

σ standard deviation of a probability distribution.

σ/W index of the variability in a corporation's past earnings expressed as a fraction of its net worth. $\breve{\sigma}/W$ is the value σ/W would have in the absence of leverage. See p. 159.

u a general index of the uncertainty of an expectation.

U a general index of the uncertainty of an expectation.

v the fraction of the funds invested by new stockholders which accrues to the equity of the existing stockholders. See p. 120.

V_o the value placed on a share at the end of $t = 0$ by an investor when a distinction exists between this value and the market price of the share.

W_t a corporation's net worth or common equity per share at the end of t.

y earnings yield or Y_0/P_0.

Y_t earnings per share during t. $\breve{Y}_t = Y_t$ in absence of leverage.

$\bar{Y}_t$ normal or expected value of Y_t. Empirically it is a trend adjusted exponential average of the past Y_t.

z investment of a firm during t expressed as a fraction of its net worth. $z = I_t/W_{t-1}$.

INDEX

253

*This book has been set on the Linotype in 11
point Baskerville, leaded 2 points, and 10 point
Baskerville, leaded 1 point. Chapter numbers
and titles are in 18 point Spartan Medium. The
size of the type page is 27 by 45 picas.*